CW00801379

INTRODUCTION TO ANTIPHILOSOPHY

INTRODUCTION TO ANTIPHILOSOPHY

BORIS GROYS

Translated by
David Fernbach

VERSO
London • New York

This English-language edition first published by Verso 2012

© Verso 2012

Translation © David Fernbach 2012

Translation of Chapter 9 © Maria Carlson

First published as *Einführung in die Anti-Philosophie*

© Carl Hanser Verlag 2009

Chapter 9 was first published in English in *Nietzsche and
Soviet Culture: Ally and Adversary*, Bernice Glatzer Rosenthal, ed.;
Chapter 10 was first published in English as 'A Genealogy of
Participatory Art', in B. Groys et al., *The Art of Participation
from 1950 to Now*, London: Thames and Hudson, 2008

© Cambridge University Press 1994

1 3 5 7 9 10 8 6 4 2

Verso

UK: 6 Meard Street, London W1F 0EG

US: 20 Jay Street, Suite 1010, Brooklyn, NY 11201

www.versobooks.com

Verso is the imprint of New Left Books

ISBN-13: 978-1-84467-756-6

British Library Cataloguing in Publication Data
A catalogue record for this book is available from the British Library

Library of Congress Cataloging-in-Publication Data
A catalog record for this book is available from the Library of Congress

Typeset by Hewer Text UK Ltd, Edinburgh
Printed in the US by Maple Vail

CONTENTS

PREFACE TO THE ENGLISH-LANGUAGE EDITION: Antiphilosophy, or Philosophical Readymades

This short preface to *Introduction to Antiphilosophy* serves the goal of defining more precisely my use of the term 'antiphilosophy'. This term had already been used by Lacan, and more recently has been taken up by Alain Badiou. However, I did not have psychoanalysis in mind as I decided to use the word 'antiphilosophy' in the title of this book. Unfortunately, at that time I was unaware of the book by Badiou, *Wittgenstein's Antiphilosophy*. The texts that are collected in this book were written at different times, for different purposes, in different languages, and initially they were not intended to be read together. However, as I prepared the book for publication in 2008, I realized that all these texts commented on authors who, in similar ways, brought philosophical practice as such into question.

Their discursive strategies – being, of course, very heterogeneous – reminded me namely of certain artistic practices that, since the appearance of the book by Hans Richter, *Dada: Art and Anti-Art* (1964), have often been characterized as 'anti-art'. The most famous example of

these practices is the readymades of Duchamp. The
Duchampian use of readymades was celebrated by some,
but deplored by others as the end of art. Indeed, if art
is understood as the production and display of things
that are different from all the other, ordinary things –
namely 'artworks' – then the readymades mark the end
of art because they demonstrate that any ordinary object
can be exhibited as a work of art. In the light of this
discovery, the whole business of art production, distribution and consumption began to be seen as an
unnecessary and futile activity that could have only one
purpose: profit-making by pretending that 'aesthetic
experience' can be delivered only by exceptional objects,
namely artworks, produced by artists of genius. This
insight produced the radical critique of art as an institution. It seemed that, after the emergence of the practice
of the readymade, art institutions lost their legitimation
and became obsolete. In fact, however, the practice of
artistic readymades functioned after Duchamp as a
continuation of the art tradition – not as its repudiation.
I will return later to this point, but now I would like to
draw some parallels between 'anti-art' and what I call,
by analogy, 'antiphilosophy'.

The authors I treat in this book can be understood
as readymade philosophers, by analogy with the readymade artists. In an extremely simplified way, philosophy
can be characterized as production, distribution and
consumption of the discourses that generate an effect
of universal self-evidence, or a 'truth effect'.
Philosophical texts are supposed to emanate, irradiate
truth as self-evidence – to shine by their own light. Of
course, in any particular case one can always assert
that this light is a false, treacherous light – and, accordingly, that this or that philosopher is in fact a sophist.
But the ethical dimension of philosophical discourse
does not affect its basic characteristic: the truth of

philosophical texts is, unlike the truth of scientific texts, not dependent on any empirical verification. The self-evidence of traditional philosophical discourse is supposed to be its inner quality – independent of any external factors. In this sense, traditional philosophy functions, indeed, similarly to traditional art: the ability of an individual artwork to generate, emanate, irradiate the 'aesthetic experience' is generally also regarded as an effect of its own, inner structure – independent of its relation to the external world.

Now, the discourses that are able to generate an effect of self-evidence are not rare. But, as a rule, these discourses rely on the common cultural experience that unites the speaker or writer with his or her audience. Thus, one can say that the majority of self-evident discourses remain situated inside the contexts of limited cultural identities and life horizons. However, philosophy pretends to produce the universally self-evident discourses that transcend the limits of any particular cultural identity. The truly philosophical discourse has to be not only self-evident, but also universally self-evident. The possibility of producing such a universal meta-discourse seems to require a philosopher to take a meta-position in relationship to his or her own cultural identity and life situation. This requirement was very powerfully formulated by Husserl. According to Husserl, to become a philosopher, a subject has to overcome – by an act of phenomenological reduction – his or her ordinary, 'natural' attitude that is dominated by the will to self-preservation, and to take another, phenomenological, truly philosophical attitude beyond an interest in one's own survival in the world. We have here a secular form of *metanoia* – the radical 'change of mind' through which a subject rejects everything that connected this subject to the 'old', ordinary, limited life perspective, and opens itself up to a new, universal, infinite perspective of philosophical evidence. It is this experience of personal self-evidence that the philosopher mediates through his or her discourse. According to the philosophical tradition, philosophical discourses are self-evident because they have their origin in the evidence that was experienced by their authors – after they had been through the act of philosophical *metanoia*.

Now, it is obvious that such an heroic act of self-reduction can be accomplished only by exceptional, superior personalities – so-called 'great men'. The reason for this is simple: philosophical *metanoia* follows no explicit rules and has no explicit models. Here we find a further analogy between philosophy and art. Artistic genius creates without and beyond rules. That is why the artworks that are created by an artistic genius shine by their own light. Philosophical discourses also irradiate evidence because they are produced in a way that (unlike scientific theories) cannot be formalized and reproduced. The rest of mankind is reduced here to the role of consumers of philosophical texts written by great philosophers.

Of course, this exceptionalism of philosophy and philosophers was often criticized during the period of modernity. Philosophical *metanoia* and the meta-position were proclaimed to be illusionary – or even consciously deceptive. The philosophical pretension was described as laughable. Today, we tend to believe that an individual cannot suspend at will his or her cultural identity and life horizon, that all the 'subjective' forms of self-evidence remain specific to particular cultural perspectives, and that no universal self-evidences are possible. This scepticism towards traditional philosophical claims leads to two different theoretical options. One of them results in a cultural relativism that is based on the belief in the impossibility of escaping from one's cultural identity – the impossibility of changing one's mind, of *metanoia*. Here, the possibility of subjective evidence is not negated, but any particular evidence is supposed to be determined by

specific cultural and social conditions. This means that all
the self-evident discourses are believed to be particular,
relative and uncertain. Thus, the subject is required to
remain cautious towards his or her own self-evidences –
and tolerant towards the self-evidences of others.

The second option results in antiphilosophy – in other
words, a readymade philosophy that ascribes universal
philosophical value to certain already-existing ordinary
practices, in the same way in which practices of the
artistic readymade ascribe artistic value to ordinary
objects. To achieve this goal, the antiphilosopher looks
for ordinary experiences and practices that can be interpreted as being universal – as transcending one's own
cultural identity. Thus, one can show that the modern
economy transcends any cultural borders (Marx), that
the rites of giving and returning the gift are similar for
different cultures (Mauss), that will to live (or to die)
moves everybody in the same manner (Nietzsche), that
angst (Kierkegaard) or boredom (Heidegger) are able to
relieve a subject from any cultural determinations, that
we all share tears and laughter (Bataille, Bakhtin) and
that we all are united by the electronic media (McLuhan).
In all these cases, a thoroughly ordinary practice substitutes for traditionally 'exclusive' philosophical practices
like logic, mathematics and, 'thinking' in general – and
opens the subject up to a possibility of universal self-
evidences (of angst, boredom, desire, excess, and so on)
without an obligation to listen to the teachings of exceptional personalities qua philosophers. As in the case of
readymade art, readymade (anti)philosophy dispenses
with the heroic philosophical act and substitutes it by
ascribing philosophical dignity to the practices of ordinary life. And, most importantly: antiphilosophy
dissociates the production of evidence from the production of philosophical discourses. Accordingly, the
production of evidence can use any experience, practice,

object or attitude – including philosophical attitudes and philosophical discourses. The experience of self-evidence (of truth) is here produced in the same way in which the 'aesthetic experience' is produced in the case of artistic readymades: it can be attached to any possible object.

This analogy between artistic and philosophical ready-mades becomes especially clear in the case of Kierkegaard. As I have tried to show in my chapter on Kierkegaard, he uses the figure of Christ as a proto-readymade. In other words, he asserts that the figure of Christ cannot be visually recognized as a divine figure – or, rather, as a figure of the divine – because the figure of Christ is a thoroughly ordinary figure that does not manifest any visual traits that are culturally codified as signs of the divine – such as wings, proliferation of arms and legs, and so on. Moreover, the figure of Christ cannot be 'remembered' by an act of philosophical anamnesis transcending any cultural conventions – as was recommended by Plato. Christ as son of God can be identified neither by an operation of verification, nor by the traditionally understood experience of self-evidence. If the figure of Christ becomes situated in the cultural context of his time, then, according to Kierkegaard, there is nothing in this figure that would differentiate it from the ordinary figure of the wandering preacher that was typical of the time. The figure of Christ acquires its power of self-evidence only if it is placed in a different context – in the context of impersonations of the divine. Then it becomes clear that this figure is indeed exceptional, precisely because of its ordinary character – and announces in this way a new era in the development of religious consciousness. Here the analogy to Duchamp's 'Fountain' becomes obvious: the 'Fountain' looks like a completely ordinary urinal in the context of a public toilet – but it begins to look exceptional if it is located within the context of art history.

The experience of self-evidence emerges here not at

the origin of the object or the production of the text, but as an effect of their contextualization. Any object or text can be put in the limited context of the cultural field in which it was 'originally' produced and situated. But it can also be taken out of this limited context, and placed in the universal context of philosophical or artistic comparison, where other criteria of evidence are at work. A traditional philosopher is like a traditional artist: an artisan producing texts. An antiphilosopher is like a contemporary art curator: he contextualizes objects and texts instead of producing them. Production of philosophy can be interpreted as an extraordinary, mysterious, 'poetic' process that is accessible only to a chosen few. Antiphilosophy does not abolish philosophical *metanoia*, but rather democratizes it. Evidence becomes an effect not of production but of post-production. It irradiates no longer through the work, but emerges as an effect of different contextualizations of this work.

The democratization of *metanoia* produced in some minds a certain kind of nostalgia towards the good old days in which great philosophers and artists lived, created and were recognized and admired by their communities. Thus, one often tends to think that antiphilosophy is only a temporary illness of philosophy that will be overcome by the future return of great, robust, vital philosophical production. However, it seems to me that this hope is doomed to remain forever futile, because antiphilosophy is the final, absolute stage of philosophy. Indeed, one can speak here about absolute philosophy in the same sense in which Kierkegaard spoke about absolute religion. Kierkegaard believed that Christianity is an absolute religion because, as has already been noted, Christianity is not based on any act of recognition or comparison, verification or evidence – and, therefore, cannot be relativized by such an act.

Absolute (anti)philosophy is also independent of any empirically identifiable difference between ordinary and philosophical text, or between ordinary and philosophical practices (such as logic or mathematics).

On the contrary, traditional philosophy is heavily dependent on the culturally codified ability of its readers to differentiate between philosophical and non-philosophical texts – disregarding any experience of evidence. Indeed, philosophical texts are not always written by great philosophers who are able to produce an effect of evidence through their discourses. As in any other cultural field, the majority of philosophical texts are of average quality, but they are still easily recognizable by readers as philosophical texts on the mere grounds of their external appearance. Thus, the suspicion emerges that all philosophical discourses, including the discourses of the great philosophers, are purely conventional texts that do not need any *metanoia* or experience of evidence and truth in order to be successfully produced and consumed. The conventional character of the standard philosophical discourses – which undermined their claims of self-evidence – was from the beginning the main target of antiphilosophical critique. Antiphilosophy does not produce any conventionally identifiable philosophical texts, but instructs us how to change our mind in such a way that certain practices, discourses and experiences would become universally evident. Or, in other words, antiphilosophy produces not the universally self-evident texts and objects, but universal evidence as such. That is why antiphilosophy – like anti-art – not only does not destroy philosophy as an institution but, rather, offers the only possible path for its survival.

PROLOGUE

Philosophy is generally understood as a search for truth. This gives rise to two reasons why it is seldom practised in our day. Firstly, studying the history of philosophy generally leads to the conclusion that the truth is unreachable, so it is not very sensible to set out in search of it. Secondly, we have the feeling that, if there were such a thing as truth, finding it would only take us half-way. It would be far more difficult to sell the truth that had been discovered, in order to live by it in more or less secure conditions – a task that experience shows cannot be ignored. The market for truth today seems to be more than saturated. The potential consumer of truth is faced with the same superfluity as the consumer in other sectors of the market. We are besieged on all sides by advertisements for truth. Truths are to be found every-where and in all media, whether scientific truths, religious truths, political truths or truths for practical life. The person seeking truth thus sees little prospect in sharing the treasure they might find with other people – and, in due course, gives up the quest. As far as truth is concerned, people today are accordingly equipped simultaneously with two basic convictions: that there is no truth, and that there is too much truth. These two convictions seem to contradict one another, but they both lead to the same conclusion: the search for truth is not good business.

Now this scene, which we can describe as the scene of the quest for truth today, was also the original scene of philosophy. We can observe it in miniature in the Greek *agora*, when that first prototypical truth-consumer, Socrates, began to examine the offers of truth on the market at that time. It was the sophists who maintained that they had found truths; they offered these truths for sale. Socrates, however, as is well known, did not define himself as a sophist, but rather as a philosopher – as someone who loved truth (wisdom, knowledge, *sophia*), but did not possess it; or, to put it another way, someone who has no truth for sale, but would be glad to acquire truth if he could be convinced that this really was truth and not simply an appearance of truth. The change from the position of the sophist to that of the philosopher is the change from the production of truth to the consumption of truth. The philosopher is not a producer of truth. Nor is he a seeker for truth in the sense that there are seekers for treasure or raw materials. The philosopher is a simple man in the street, who has wandered into the global supermarket of truths, and is now seeking to find his bearings there – or at least an exit sign.

It is often lamented that philosophy has not developed in the course of its history, that it has not brought any results or shown any progress. It would indeed be quite amazing if philosophy did develop historically, for if the situation of the truth-producer changes with time, the situation of the truth-consumer always remains the same. It is only the supply of truth that changes, not the helplessness of the consumer faced with this offer. Every 'authentic' philosophy is nothing other than the articulation of this helplessness in language. Why then does this helplessness have to be articulated and formulated at all? Why can it not just remain silent?

In fact, Socrates offers the image, already familiar to us, of an ill-favoured and chronically discontented consumer, constantly in a bad mood and eager for dispute. Every time Socrates hears the fine words of the sophists, he destroys the good mood by finding some kind of logical defect and unsatisfactoriness in their words, which would otherwise not interest anyone, let alone disturb them. We ourselves often meet such people in everyday life – in business, in hotels and restaurants. They are always discontented, they love to quarrel with the staff, and they really get on the nerves of other consumers. Faced with these quarrelsome and nerve-racking figures, it is not surprising that people yearn for the good old days when this kind of person could be quickly pacified with the help of a cup of hemlock.

On top of all this, critical argument in Socrates' case seems to be extremely ambivalent. When we listen to Socrates, it is not completely clear whether he presents himself as a critical consumer who criticizes the offers of truth that were present in his day and age, but does not give up hope that he might at some point come up against genuine truth, or whether he fundamentally rejects treating truth as a commodity and taking it to market. There are many indications that the latter assumption is more plausible. Socrates was the actual inventor of market criticism. The mere fact that a particular offer of truth functions as a commodity in the context of a market economy is basically sufficient for Socrates to reject this offer. Bringing to light all the other insufficiencies and contradictions that Socrates goes on to discover in each particular offer of truth may be instructive and exciting,

but it is superfluous for the general gesture of basic rejection. Establishing the commercialization of a doctrine of
truth, understanding the commodity formation of the
corresponding truth, discovering the economic interests
hidden behind the formulation and distribution of this
doctrine – these are sufficient to reject its claim to truth.
From Socrates, via Marx, to the critical theory of
Frankfurt provenance, it is held that any truth that
appears as a commodity is no truth. And this means in
particular that there is not a truth in general, since under
the conditions of the market economy no doctrine of
truth can escape commodity status. There certainly
remains the often-postulated 'weak messianic hope' for
the advent of a truth beyond truth – an absolutely other
truth, which would not even appear as truth, as doctrine,
book, theory or method, not even consciously or uncon-
sciously, and which would therefore fundamentally
escape commercialization. But clearly this hope is only
postulated in order to be repeatedly disappointed.

Such a hope, moreover, can already be diagnosed in
Plato. In his allegory of the cave, Plato describes the
figure of a truth-seeker who succeeds in seeing the truth,
and returns to the human world in order to report his
discovery. In this allegory, therefore, what we have is
not a philosopher, as is often maintained (for the philosopher is denied the contemplation of truth), but rather
a sophist, who actually has seen the truth. Yet precisely
because he has seen it, he is so blinded and overpowered by the truth that he peddles those fine-sounding,
smooth and well-considered words that are typical of
the sophist. This sophist is an untalented, clumsy sophist; but he is this precisely because he is a true sophist.
And so men, who expect a certain cleverness in the
practice of this profession, actually kill him. This clumsy
sophist is the prototype not only for the figure of the
son of God – who ended up on the cross precisely

because he was the son of God – but also for all romantic artists, poets and revolutionaries who seek to be
seen as true artists, poets and revolutionaries precisely
because they cannot paint or write properly, or make
successful revolutions. Since then, however, we have
known that calculated failure can also be a commodity,
and indeed is so. And in order not to leave the critical
diagnosis incomplete, this diagnosis itself does not
escape the commodity form.

Philosophical criticism, therefore, has led to a situation in which every truth is identified as a commodity,
and accordingly also discredited. This result, however,
allows a different suspicion to emerge: Is it not philosophy itself that transforms every truth into a commodity?
And indeed, the philosophical attitude is a passive,
contemplative, critical attitude, and thus in the last analysis a consuming one. In the light of this attitude,
everything present appears as a commodity on offer,
whose suitability has to be checked so that it might
possibly be bought. Let us assume that a person no
longer spends time going through this procedure of
checking, but rather simply takes what comes into their
hands by chance: acquaintances, lovers, books, conver-
sations, theories, religions, authorities and truths. In this
case, truth loses its commodity form, as it is no longer
checked out but rather practised – just as you practise
breathing by taking in the air that surrounds you. In
certain circumstances, the air that you breathe may
actually be deadly; but not breathing is of course also
deadly. In both cases, therefore, it is impossible to
develop a distanced, contemplative, critical, consuming
behaviour towards breathing – you carry on breathing
even while you are buying a new air conditioner.

This understanding led to a new branch of philosophy, which can be described as antiphilosophy, by
analogy with anti-art. This turn, which began with

Marx and Kierkegaard, does not operate with criticism, but rather with command. The command is issued to change the world, instead of explaining it; or to become an animal, instead of continuing to think; or to transform one's own body into a body without organs, and think rhizomically instead of logically. All these commands are issued in order to abolish philosophy as ultimate source of the consuming, critical attitude, and in this way to liberate truth from its commodity character. For following a command, or refusing to do so, is something quite other than accepting or rejecting a doctrine of truth as the result of a critical investigation. The basic assumption of command-issuing (anti-)philosophy, in other words, is that truth only shows itself if the command is followed: the world must first be changed, then it will show its true nature; the leap into faith must be made, then the truth of religion manifests itself. Or again, to return to Plato, you first have to emerge from the cave, and then you see the truth. What is involved here is a choice before choosing: a decision in the dark that precedes any possible criticism, since the object of this criticism only shows itself as a result of deciding to follow the command. A decision to refuse the command, on the other hand, leaves you for all time in the dark – you cannot even be critical, since you do not know what you really should criticize. In this way, the decision between fulfilling the command and refusing it is characterized both by its inescapability and by its urgency, which leave no time to cultivate a calm, critical and consuming attitude. In other words, what is involved is not a purely philosophical decision, but rather a life decision, which cannot be postponed because life is too brief.

This antiphilosophical turn within philosophy itself has not remained without consequences. Anyone who teaches philosophy today, or writes about it, knows that we live in an age in which any critical attitude, whether in the realm of politics, art or nutrition, simply irritates the public, and is rejected almost in a reflex action. The reason for this, of course, does not lie in the fact that in recent times the 'affirmative' attitude to the world, inner agreement with the 'general condition of blindness' – *allgemeiner Verblendungszusammenhang*, in Adorno's term – or acceptance of the prevailing conditions, have suddenly acquired unchallenged hegemony in public consciousness. Today's readers do not believe what is stated either in texts or in any other media, and do not even think of believing in it – and, for this very reason, they also have no occasion to criticize such statements. Instead they either do what they are told, or simply do not do it. Texts today are not analyzed, but perceived as instructions for action that can be used differently in practice if one decides to do so. Texts that contain explicit instructions are particularly popular: books with culinary recipes, gardening and decorating tips; books on good marketing strategies; advice on combating the American empire with the help of the 'multitude', on establishing contemporary images of a left- or right-wing activist – and so on. But other books, too, which do not offer such clear instructions, are increasingly read as indicating a certain behaviour. Their readers, who follow the corresponding instructions, feel personally affected by any criticism of these books, and reject any critical attitude towards them. And they also reject any criticism of texts that they do not themselves follow – precisely on grounds of decency and tolerance: so as not to upset unnecessarily the people who do follow those texts. In both cases, the public feel that any criticism of a text is unfair, since it misses the point. This point, in other words, is not the text itself, but rather what individuals have made and make of it in their own lives. Just as different people draw different conclusions from the Koran, and thus make any criticism of it unnecessary and actually impossible. Or as artists often reply, if a theory is criticized in their presence: You may be right, it is a stupid theory, but I made good use of it – and for this reason I believe in it and would rather not listen to any more of your criticism. If the text as such is no longer seen as the place where truth appears and offers itself to the critical reader, but simply as a sum of instructions for a reader who is summoned to act rather than to think, then the only thing that is relevant is the manner in which the reader translates these instructions in his everyday conduct. But this cannot be criticized, as it is now life itself that starts to function as the supreme judge.

The reader of the essays collected in this book will notice how their heroes are all modern command-giving authors; they are all of them antiphilosophers. But the essays themselves do not offer any instructions – and can only be disappointing in the context of the post-antiphilosophy that is prevalent today. At the same time, however, they do not make any return to the tradition of philosophical criticism. Their author's attitude in this case is rather a benevolently descriptive one. This attitude has its roots in the phenomenology of Husserl, who relatively early on raised the question of how one might react to the new command-giving tone in philosophy without this leading to repetition of the old mistakes of critical philosophy. Husserl therefore offered the following command: Before even starting to think, the phenomenological reduction has to be carried out. This phenomenological reduction consists in the subject's taking a mental distance from his own life interests – even the interest in his own survival – and in this way opening up a perspective in considering the world that is no longer confined by the needs of his empirical ego. By way of this broad phenomenological perspective one obtains the ability to do justice to all commands, by starting to experiment freely both in obeying them and refusing them. At the same time, the subject of the phenomenological reduction finds himself no longer required to transform the commands he receives into his conduct of life, or, conversely, to oppose them, since the phenomenological ego thinks as if it were not living. In this way one acquires for one's phenomenological ego a realm of 'as if' – an imaginary perspective of limitless life, in which all decisions of life lose their urgency, so that the opposition between carrying out and rejecting a command dissolves in the infinite play of life possibilities.

SØREN KIERKEGAARD

Writing an introduction to the thought of Kierkegaard presents difficulties of a quite particular kind. The underlying reason for these difficulties is in no way that Kierkegaard's philosophy is particularly complicated or obscure, nor again the fact that its understanding would require a special, professional philosophical training. On the contrary, Kierkegaard always insists on the private, dilettantish and unpretentious character of his philosophizing. Kierkegaard writes for everyone – and perhaps least of all for a readership of learned specialists. Rather, these difficulties result from the fact that Kierkegaard's philosophy itself has the character of an introduction.

Kierkegaard's philosophizing has an introductory, tentative and preparatory character because Kierkegaard rejects the right of any philosophical text, even his own, to assert its validity as a bearer of truth. His celebrated formulation that 'subjectivity, inwardness, is the truth'[1]

---

1. This is the title of Chapter 2 of Kierkegaard's 'Concluding Unscientific Postscript' to *Philosophical Fragments*.

means that truth cannot be 'expressed', still less printed as a philosophical text. Limits are thereby drawn to philosophical discourse; it can no longer be the bearer of truth or embody truth in itself. A text only becomes true by the agreement of truth-giving subjectivity. The conditions, the procedure and the manner of this agreement, for their part, can only be described in a text in an introductory and provisional fashion – and Kierkegaard's texts precisely attempt such an introductory description.

The act of agreement, however, is for Kierkegaard something autonomous and free, and cannot be derived simply from descriptions. A philosophical text is first and foremost a thing, an object among many other objects, which, by virtue of its objectivity, remains separated from the subjectivity of the reader – and likewise from the subjectivity of its author – by an unbridgeable gulf. The reader has to leap over this gulf in order to identify himself with the text, but no one and nothing can force him to make such a leap. This leap is accomplished, in the final analysis, by the free will of the reader, of which only a living, existing, finite subjectivity – in other words, one that actually exists outside of the text – is capable, and not the abstract, purely methodologically equipped subjectivity that is described within the philosophical text. Philosophy always depicts the living, existing subject as the sum of texts, systems and methods that are external to it. A philosophical text can never radiate that spontaneous, immediately convincing, overwhelming force of truth, which so many philosophers have dreamed of, and which would supposedly compel the reader by the mere act of reading. In order to leap to an identification with the text, the reader must make a corresponding decision, which presupposes a certain overcoming of self. The act of reading is separated from the act of agreement by a time, no matter how brief, of indecision and delay. It is this time in which subjectivity shows itself as existing, as foreign to the text, as autonomously deciding, and hence as not describable and controllable by philosophy. This figure of the existential leap, which takes place in the internal timeframe of subjectivity, is central for Kierkegaard. It is worthwhile therefore to consider this figure more closely.

The principal question here is why Kierkegaard should have any need of this figure of the existential leap. Previous philosophy managed perfectly well without it. For Kierkegaard, the introduction of the existential leap means equally the leap out of the whole millennial tradition of Western philosophy. This is indeed why the tone of his writings is often so tense and unquiet.

The basic figure of the European philosophical tradition was, right from the start, trust in immediate self-evidence, including the self-evidence of the true philosophical word. Since Socrates, philosophy had distrusted all myths, tales, authorities, handed-down opinions and revelations; but this meant that the true philosopher was all the more ready to believe unconditionally what presented itself to him as completely self-evident. Thus Plato trusted in the Ideas that presented themselves self-evidently to his inner soul, after he had rejected all opinions about the things of the outer world as not self-evident. Descartes, who at the start of the modern age renewed the tradition of philosophical scepticism with a previously unknown radicalism by also subjecting to radical doubt all sensory data that had their origin in the outside world, once again trusted the inner self-evidence of the *cogito ergo sum*. This trust in self-evidence, or, to put it another way, in reason, was celebrated by the philosophical tradition as the highest freedom. By following his own reason – trusting what was self-evident – man freed himself from the external power of authority, tradition and social institutions, and obtained a true inner sovereignty.

It was precisely this foundational philosophical belief that Kierkegaard subjected to a new and more radical doubt. For liberation from external constraints and necessities only served, in the philosophical tradition, the inner logic of submitting oneself unconditionally to inner necessity, inner self-evidence, one's own reason, which was misinterpreted as the authentic expression of one's subjectivity. In truth, what the individual subjected himself to in this case was a logical constraint that remained external, since one trusted the self-evidence of rational demonstration that was erected into a system of 'objective' logical conclusions. True freedom now meant liberation not only from external constraints, but also from the internal logical constraints of reason. Self-evidence had therefore to lose its millennial magic. We had to learn to mistrust even what presented itself to us as completely self-evident. It was no longer possible, however, to adduce any logical reason for such mistrust, for if we were to do so, we would thereby confess trust in the self-evident power of this reason we adduced, and be thereby delivered again to the force of logical self-evidence. We therefore have to learn to mistrust without rational grounds, to reserve the right of free decision and delay the act of our assent in case we are unconditionally infatuated with the logical self-evidence of the idea. This is where the necessity of the existential leap arises, presenting itself as an effect of this delay and postponement, which Kierkegaard wants to teach us because it frees us from the inner bondage of the rule of self-evidence. The existential leap, in other words, becomes necessary when immediate self-evidence loses its power; but despite this, adopting a position towards actuality remains unavoidable.

It is certainly no accident that this Kierkegaardian

project should have arisen in a particular historical era. At this time, Hegelian philosophy exerted an almost unlimited intellectual domination. And Hegelian philosophy was nothing more than a tremendously efficient machine for exchanging external constraints for internal logical constraints. The reader of Hegelian philosophy was supposed to understand as completely self-evident that everything that constrained him from outside was an objectified form of internal, logical, rational necessity, which he must not contradict if he was to be a good philosopher. The Hegelian philosophical narrative strides from one supersession to the next – from one conclusive self-evidence to the next – until the final self-evidence presents itself, concluding the whole narrative, and with it the whole of human history that is grasped by this narrative. For the person who still has to carry on living in *posthistoire* after all this conclusive self-evidence, the whole of external reality presents itself as the image of logically self-evident internal necessity. This can be seen as the final victory of philosophy. But it can also be seen as a parody of philosophy, which finally betrays its original striving for sovereignty.

Philosophy was indeed predisposed from its very origin to a betrayal of this kind, precisely because it was ready at any time to abandon its doubt in favour of self-evident insight. Free and sovereign subjectivity, however, is constituted by way of doubt. Once doubt is abandoned, subjectivity is lost – even if the basis for this abandonment is an internal and subjective one. Cartesian doubt, therefore, is still insufficient. This doubt may well have constituted the subjectivity of the modern age, by liberating it from external constraints on thought. But, at the same time, Descartes weakened this subjectivity and condemned it to failure by introducing doubt as finite, provisional and methodological, so that this doubt would supposedly lead to self-evidence by virtue of its own logic. The Hegelian system was only the most radical consequence of this self-denying strategy of modern subjectivity. Kierkegaard was thus faced with the task, as soon as he sought to escape the external constraints of his existence following their internalization in the Hegelian system, of discovering a new and unlimited doubt, which would remain immune to any self-evidence, whether logical or otherwise, and could found a new, unlimited and unchallengeable subjectivity. Cartesian doubt was an introduction to unlimited self-evidence. Kierkegaard, on the other hand, sought to write a self-evident introduction to unlimited doubt.

Self-evidence of any kind has its effect not only by way of fascination, but also by sobering, rationalizing and trivializing. Philosophical understanding is at bottom this fascination by sobering. The work of philosophical *Aufklärung* consisted, as is well known, in reducing everything wonderful, deep and extraordinary to the commonplace and obvious. Once this reduction was effected, explanation was understood as completed – and any further enquiry was called off. What was commonplace and trivial, what was already explained and understood, was thereby accepted without any further doubt, as it had shown itself to be self-evident. It was precisely in this place, however, that Kierkegaard established his radicalized doubt. For the commonplace can conceal the extraordinary behind it, in just the same way as the extraordinary conceals the commonplace. This suspicion opens the way to an infinite and absolute doubt, which no longer knows any limits. And Kierkegaard's writings deal in virtuoso style with the possibilities of this radicalized doubt. Whenever he speaks of something that arises in any sphere of life and lays claim to extraordinary validity, Kierkegaard proceeds like a typical *Aufklärer*, drawing this claim into doubt and mocking it. But whenever something commonplace and obvious is involved,

Kierkegaard maintains that behind this the radical Other is concealed, and he demands a leap of faith behind the surface of things. In this way, the author's subjectivity becomes infinite, since it moves in constant and unsurpassable doubt.

Of course, the mere assertion that something Other lies hidden behind the self-evident and commonplace does not provide sufficient foundation for such an infinite doubt. It has to be shown, on top of this, how and why the self-evident can conceal the Other behind it. In the articulation of this new kind of suspicion, the concept of the new plays a decisive role for Kierkegaard. In his *Philosophical Fragments*, published under the pseudonym 'Johannes Climacus', Kierkegaard shows how, ever since Socrates, self-evidence has been understood as the effect of recollection, for the soul can only identify as self-evident what it has already seen before. This was the reason that Socrates' method consisted not in teaching people something new, but simply in returning them to themselves, so that they could discover the truth within themselves, as already present in their souls. Thus, Socrates negates his status as a teacher, his concern being to find the truth in his disciples. Socrates thereby made himself virtually nonexistent; he dissolved his living existence in the self-evidence to which he led his students. The time of his own life, for Socrates, was simply the transition to eternity, and thus had no autonomous existential value.

According to Plato, Socrates' disciple, the soul recognizes the eternal Ideas as self-evident, because it has already seen these Ideas before it was born into the world. Self-evidence thus always follows from a return to the origin, to the past, to recollection. For Hegel, too, the figure of recollection plays a key role: understanding the rationality of external reality arises by comparison with the historical forms that the absolute spirit has gathered in the course of its history. The internal spaces of the soul are thus equipped with images that the soul has already received before birth as the legacy of the beyond or the collective history of humanity. The effect of self-evidence arises if the experiences that the soul has in reality correspond to these images. The essential claim of the Hegelian system is that in it the collection – the museum or archive of all images that the individual soul needs in order to experience the world as self-evident – is exhaustively present. Even if one were to deny this claim and say that the Hegelian system needs further supplement, one would remain caught up within this system, for the theoretical victory of this system would only be historically postponed, as it is for example in Marxism.

In this way, traditional philosophical understanding excludes from self-evidence the radically new. And the new, for Kierkegaard, is simply that which has no models, and cannot be identified on the basis of a comparison with the past. But if self-evidence, reason and logic do not allow the new, then they thereby devalue individual existence. If truth is self-evidence and self-evidence is recollection, this means that the individual lives in vain: nothing new can happen in his life that is really important. What Kierkegaard introduces against this is the decisive historical example of Christianity.

Christianity is the event in time. And it is an event that cannot be identified by recollection. God has shown himself in a human form that was commonplace in its time: the human form of a wandering preacher. This form, moreover, could be easily identified. Christ's contemporaries thus had no recognizable ground for acknowledging Christ as God, for the divine did not show itself in the external appearance of Christ in a way that could be identified as self-evident from outside. There was no external distinction between a man and a god who becomes man: if there had been such a distinction, which could be established as self-evident, Christianity would have been simply a philosophical matter.

The absolute newness of Christianity, therefore, consists in the absolute commonplaceness of the figure of Christ. Kierkegaard defined the radically new in such a way that it does not display any external characteristics of its particularity, and is thus not outwardly different from the commonplace. If such characteristics were present, the new could be 'cognized' or 'recognized' as such, which would mean that it was not really new. The radically new is the internal, concealed distinction in the externally identical – or, if you like, in the absolutely commonplace.

The commonplace can be defined as an unnecessary, superfluous multiplication of particular images and forms beyond their immediate self-evidence. For example, what Nietzsche would call 'the type of the wandering preacher' was always already familiar. Too many wandering preachers therefore were commonplace and superfluous: it was already enough that the corresponding type was present in the gallery of human types superseded in spiritual history. The existence of any one individual wandering preacher – at the time of Christ or today – had to be a lost existence, being completely commonplace. This existence, however, regains its significance if it can be said that only *this* wandering preacher among all others who seem similarly commonplace is the true God. And this, moreover, makes all such seemingly commonplace wandering preachers equally interesting, since they all then acquire under this new assumption an infinite importance, or at least personal chance.

For Kierkegaard, therefore, the radically new is a decision, not founded on any additional evidence, in favour of the individual who is thereby selected from the mass of the identical, the commonplace, the indistinguishable. What is involved here is an absolute, infinite, concealed distinction, which can no longer be recognized as it does not display any outward sign, corresponding only to a choice that cannot be founded on reason. This, moreover, opens up the possibility of taking a particular figure, one that in terms of spiritual history is already superseded, into the archive of the spirit for a second time. If this figure has already been accepted into the archive, it can be accepted a second time, since something Other is possibly concealed behind it.

Kierkegaard discovered the commonplace, the serial, that which reproduces itself as concealing, which escapes the philosophical discourse of the self-evident, since what is involved here is a seemingly senseless multiplication of the already historically familiar. If, however, the suspicion arises that this commonplace, reproductive multiplication conceals behind it a radical distinction precisely by way of its commonplaceness and seeming identity, then the commonplace becomes interesting as the medium of the radically new. Kierkegaard reacts first and foremost in his discourse to the commonplaceness of modernity, which became obvious to all as a result of the new supremacy of industrial production precisely in the nineteenth century. A commonplace, superfluous, serial-type modern existence acquires, by the new Kierkegaardian suspicion, new justification as the site of an invisible, non-self-evident difference, and of a new doubt that cannot be ended by any self-evidence. The time of this doubt, moreover, is no longer an historical time, since it no longer displays any form of historical–dialectical reflection. The potentially unlimited multiplication of the commonplace beyond any historical dialectic corresponds to the unlimited doubt of a subjectivity that has also become unlimited. This doubt can only be interrupted by a leap, a decision, though even this does not finally abolish it: self-evidence may be definitive, but decisions can be revised. The existential leap does not put an end to doubt, but only manifests it.

This suspicion of the difference concealed in the commonplace opens up the possibility of a strategy that more than compensates for the celebrated 'loss of aura' that Walter Benjamin diagnosed in his time as the result of technical reproducibility. It is no accident that Arthur Danto should begin his discussion of the readymade procedure, in which the artist declares an object from a mass-produced series to be an individual artwork, with a reference to Kierkegaard.[2] The decision to select precisely this object as an artwork is unfoundable in just the same way as that of selecting a man as God, if a visible distinction from other objects or people is missing. Instead of reacting with resignation to the appearance of the commonplace, like Hegel, or contempt, as Nietzsche did later, Kierkegaard attempted to find the theoretical means for valorizing the commonplace as a legitimate object of philosophical reflection.

It is precisely the question of the relationship to the commonplaceness of modern life that already stands at the centre of Kierkegaard's first major text, *Either/Or*. Here an opposition is constructed between two radically incompatible positions: an aesthetic and an ethical one. The aesthete seeks to escape the commonplaceness of his existence. He constantly changes cultural masks and identities. He transforms his life into a theatre, in which he himself assumes all the roles that the history of superseded literary and visual forms of culture puts at his disposal. Kierkegaard describes the figure of the aesthete with obvious sympathy. The desire to escape the monotony of life in a small provincial city, as Copenhagen

2. Arthur C. Danto, *Die Verklärung des Gewöhnlichen. Eine Philosophie der Kunst*, Frankfurt 1984, pp. 17ff.

undoubtedly was at that time, is certainly more than understandable. And the only space into which it is possible to escape is that of one's own imagination, populated as it is with forms from history, literature and art, which at all events seem to be more fascinating than the average Copenhagen citizen.

Kierkegaard, however, discovered a deep despair as the true inner constitution of the aesthete, which he described both in 'Diapsalmata' and then in still more lurid colours in the fragment 'The Unhappiest One'. The potentially infinite number of attitudes, roles and identities that the aesthete can assume clearly overspills the limited time that the aesthete, like anyone else, has available for his life. The aesthete discovers his own existence in the world as limitation, lack and defeat. This gives rise to despair with oneself, with one's own finitude, which is experienced as the basic mood of the aesthetic. If Kierkegaard describes this self-indebted despair of the aesthete with a certain trace of *schadenfreude*, he nonetheless values the aesthete's attitude as the first and indispensable step towards self-discovery – even if initially in a negative form. If the aesthete discovers himself as his own limit and despairs at himself, this discovery opens up at the same time the possibility of a later positive valuation. A still more radical despair, in other words, leads to the ethical attitude – in other words, to the decision to accept one's own existence in its full commonplaceness.

Kierkegaard seems to be following here the trusted Hegelian dialectical method: radicalized negation collapses into positivity. The very direction of the theoretical thrust seems to be the same. Kierkegaard argues against the romantic 'beautiful soul' that loses itself in fictional infinities, and calls on it finally to acknowledge and accept reality. The difference with Hegel seems at first to be minimal.

This difference, however, subsequently proves to be

decisive. Kierkegaard's ethicist does not choose his own existence either from better understanding or conviction, from inner necessity or newly won self-evidence. The act of choice does not of itself abolish the inner despair. He rather chooses himself as a new mask among many others. The infinite distance between his inwardness and his external, commonplace, ethical existence remains unbridgeable: it is not brought to a synthesis by any inward self-evidence. One can rather maintain that the ethicist, by his choice, puts himself at a still greater distance from himself than the aesthete ever does.

This contention forces us to inquire more closely into the constitution of the existential choice – the choice of oneself. This choice does not in any case mean a change in the condition in which the chooser always already finds himself: if this were the change involved, the choice would always still be aesthetic. Rather, the existential choice means renouncing the quest for alteration. A choice of this kind obviously does not lead out of the inwardness of despair, but rather radicalizes this despair, in as much as one becomes capable of considering and choosing oneself as a kind of museum-piece worthy of preservation.

In this way, the average existence of a married, domesticated citizen, behaving in a programmatically commonplace way, as Kierkegaard describes his ethicist B., is endowed with an infinite dignity and an infinite value of the radically new, by the assertion that behind the mask of this commonplace existence lies concealed the deepest possible despair at the whole of world history, which deserves to be accepted into world history. In other words, Kierkegaard is little concerned at bottom with external reality – unlike Hegel – and least of all when he chooses this reality as a sign of his radical desperation. For Kierkegaard, all that matters is creating the possibility for himself, and also for his contemporaries, to discover a new entry into the world history of the spirit, after Hegel has fastened on its door the sign: 'Closed forever.' Kierkegaard was naturally aware that ethicist B. had scarcely any chance of finding a place in the internal spaces of the spirit, for in comparison with all Platos, Ciceros and Cleopatras, he was obviously nothing special. What had to be chosen for this contemporary, therefore, was what lay concealed within him. And if outwardly he was not distinguished by anything in particular, he had therefore to have everything hidden in himself.

The choice of oneself, for Kierkegaard, was thus completed by an internal distance that made an identification with oneself impossible: the choice of oneself in no way meant an acceptance of oneself or an approval of oneself. It is particularly instructive in this connection that, in the chapter of *Either/Or* devoted to the ethical attitude, the situation of the ethicist B., who makes and describes the choice of himself, is described as the opposite of the situation in which Kierkegaard found himself at the time that he drafted this text. Kierkegaard finished his manuscript in Berlin, directly after he had broken off his engagement with Regina Olsen without giving any plausible reason. The decision that Kierkegaard had made here certainly seemed to have the form of an arbitrary and unfounded choice, but at the same time it represented the opposite of the existential choice as this is described in the papers of the ethicist B. What was at issue here was in no way simply a self-ironizing on the part of the author, which remained accessible only to him. The break with Regina Olsen raised a great sensation precisely in the social circles of the small town of Copenhagen, in which Kierkegaard must have assumed the readers of his text to live. The book was thus deliberately addressed to readers who knew only too well that the figure of the ethicist, who chose himself by marrying and completely inserting himself into family life, in no way corresponded to the real figure of Kierkegaard, so that this choice of oneself could not be misunderstood as a reconciliation of Kierkegaard with the role socially prescribed for him. Kierkegaard's public conduct corresponded instead to the figure of the aesthete, who is described in *Either/Or* as a conscienceless seducer who plays with the feelings of the naive young girl. This is how Kierkegaard presented himself to Regina Olsen during the parting scene, if we can trust the indications about this that are to be found in his letters.[3]

The real reasons for Kierkegaard's decision to break off his engagement with Regina Olsen have been the object of much puzzling. But whatever the case may have been, this decision seems to have been conceived as an additional help for the reader, so that he can better understand the basic line of thought of *Either/Or*. The visible discrepancy between Kierkegaard's theoretical decision in favour of the ethical choice and his decision at the same time in his own life shows that the two decisions were played out at quite different levels, which are separated from one another by an unbridgeable gulf.

This means that the reproaches that have since been raised time and again against Kierkegaard are somewhat shortsighted. The choice of one's own existence and the existential leap have frequently been interpreted as figures of reconciliation with a bad reality, which it would be better instead to change. Several examples of such judgements can be given. For Adorno, 'Inwardness presents itself as the restriction of human existence to a private sphere free from the power of reification . . . By denying the social question, Kierkegaard

---

3. Letter to Emil Boesen of 1 January 1842, in Kierkegaard, *Briefe*, Düsseldorf 1955, p. 82.

falls to the mercy of his own historical situation, that of the *rentier* in the first half of the century.'[4] And Sartre introduces the concept of *mauvaise foi* to warn against the choice of an existing bad reality.[5] From what we have said above, however, it follows that Kierkegaard, in the very act of choosing his own reality, actually takes the greatest possible inner distance from it, most radically despairs of it, and proclaims his non-agreement with it most consistently. If Kierkegaard did actually sacrifice his relationship with Regina Olsen to the better understanding of his book, the conclusion must be drawn from reading some of his critics that this sacrifice was in vain.

The difficulties that confront the reader of Kierkegaard result, among other things, from the fact that, in his quest for a possible way to go beyond the Hegelian dialectical closure of the world history of the spirit, Kierkegaard made no compromises. It would have been far easier for him, for example, to thematize his own Danish identity, which found no particular consideration in the Hegelian system, with a view to smuggling this particular identity into the internal museum of world history *post factum*, in a way that is still successfully practised today. But Kierkegaard did not choose this, as so many others have done. He took the Danish life of his time in its radical commonplaceness and normality – intending, as we have said, to sacralize precisely this post-historical commonplaceness. The question remains, however, of what the power was with which Kierkegaard believed he could carry through this sacralization.

The ability to speak performatively is attributed by a particular office or institution. A king can pronounce a

4. Theodor Adorno, *Kierkegaard: Construction of the Aesthetic*, Minneapolis 1989, pp. 47–8.

5. Jean-Paul Sartre, *Being and Nothingness*, London 1969, pp. 47ff.

law, or a government make an appointment.[6] In Hegel, the absolute spirit rules in complicity with the power of the actual: what is institutionalized by it is only what has always already prevailed in fact. But the individual is not an institution. The words of the individual can describe reality; they cannot create it. And the finite, individual spirit does not have the power to make its pronouncements prevail. Kierkegaard thus found himself in a situation that was certainly not novel for Protestant theology, but had never before been reflected on and described with such radicalism. In order for the inner spaces of the spirit to be opened up again to post-historical actuality, the individual had to conceive of himself as an institution that could speak performatively. But finite subjectivity is then faced with the paradox of self-institutionalization, or, one might say, of self-authorization. The possibility of the choice of oneself must be grounded in the capability of making such a choice. But this capability is paradoxical. Kierkegaard does not attempt to resolve this paradox, so as to ground the possibility of choice in terms of rational understanding. Instead he intends to show that any seemingly rational understanding has the same paradoxical composition internally as the existential choice. In his later writings, Kierkegaard practised with growing radicalism this strategy of disclosure of a concealed paradox behind the smooth surface of a rational demonstration.

This helps to explain the acerbic, sometimes deliberately insulting tone that Kierkegaard gradually adopted. He sought to provoke the invisible opponent – the rationally thinking philosopher or theologian – to bring him onto the stage in order to extract from him the confession that his philosophy or theology could never

---

6. J. L. Austin, *How to Do Things With Words*, Oxford 1962.

in fact be justified with self-evidence. Kierkegaard made fun of Hegel, who had journeyed to China and India in the guise of the spirit in order to convince himself and others that he had neglected nothing essential in his considerations – but had forgotten to ask himself in what way he could take on the infinite wisdom of the world spirit during his own finite human life. No less ironically did Kierkegaard react to the contention that Christianity had been universally established in his time: if a modern Christian were transported to the time in which Christ lived, he would have the same inner diffi-culties in acknowledging Christ as God as did the people of that time. Which meant in turn that the modern Christian was in no better a situation in relation to his belief than were the first Christians.

Hegel could not maintain that he had learned the truth in such a definitive way that it would be sufficient for subsequent generations to recollect his philosophy in order to make contact with the truth, any more than the apostles could recognize God in Christ in such an evident way that it was enough simply to repeat later on their act of faith in order to affirm themselves as Christians. If, in his *Philosophical Fragments*, Kierkegaard had shown that the moment of subjective decision, as already explained, cannot be replaced by a figure of recollection of the original, so he sought in his subsequent 'Concluding Unscientific Postscript' to demonstrate that even the recollecting return to philosophical or religious history is not in a position to dispense with individual choice. For subjectivity as such there is no history, no progress, no accumulation of knowledge. Subjectivity lives in its own unhistoric time of unending doubt. If subjectivity emerges from this inner time by the act of choice or the existential leap, this is its free decision, which no evidence, no logic and no tradition can compel. The inner time is never the time of recollection – it is the time of the project, a time which is oriented to the future and capable of adopting the radically new, the eventful, the unforeseen.

This discovery of an inner time of absolute openness to the future by way of a radical doubt of everything in the past – a time that escapes the history of reason and in which subjectivity can freely decide over itself – made a deep impression on many thinkers after Kierkegaard. In Heidegger's *Being and Time*, in particular, the reader can readily recognize the basic concepts that Kierkegaard deployed for describing the situation in which a subjectivity placed in the world finds itself: care, anxiety, decision, being-unto-death. Many other of Heidegger's analyses, for example the 'discovery of the ego in absent-mindedness and boredom',[7] show their similarity with Kierkegaard's analyses – in this case, with his analyses in *The Concept of Dread*. Heidegger, moreover, interprets the inward time of subjectivity as a time of decision, as a time of being-unto-death, as a finite time of individual existence, a time which, in contrast with the supposedly infinite – and hence deceptive – time of universality, of the anonymous 'one', is a true and particular time that reveals the true ontological condition of the individual. For Kierkegaard the inner time of subjectivity is likewise a time of individual decision; but as such – as existential condition for the possibility of a decision – it is simultaneously the time of infinite indecision that transcends the finitude of historical supersessions. The decision or choice that Kierkegaard speaks of is precisely the choice between what you might call the individual and the non-individual interpretations of one's own existence. For Kierkegaard, however, this choice remains open; the author Kierkegaard constantly swings between corresponding alternatives,

---

7. Martin Heidegger, *An Introduction to Metaphysics*, Bloomington 1995, pp. 135ff.

delays decision or makes it paradoxical and impossible. In this way Kierkegaard continually renews the time of his inner existence. For Heidegger, on the other hand, the choice of finite existence-unto-death presents itself unambiguously as the only correct choice, which one can seek to escape only 'improperly'. Dread-unto-death, however, forces the individual, even without his will, to this correct choice, even if this individual subjectively overlooks the possibility of his death. Heidegger thereby essentially agrees with Kierkegaard's ethicist B. in his analysis of his own existence within commonplace modernity, thus resolving the tension of *Either/Or* by a definite, even if tense insight, so that the time of subjectivity again becomes finite.

With Kierkegaard, on the other hand, the ethical choice does not put an end to the infinite time of the aesthetic attitude. Rather, this time becomes, one might say, still more infinite, since the repertoire of playing with the masks of reality is extended by a further mask: the mask of commonplaceness. It is particularly striking in this connection that Kierkegaard no longer speaks, in his analyses, of the leap or the choice that he offered after *Either/Or*, about the choice of oneself – or, if he does so, he speaks of the self as the person who chooses another. The Christian, therefore, is the person who chooses Christ as God, in which connection this choice is just as paradoxical as the choice of oneself. The distinction, however, is that the choice of oneself as a Christian could only appear commonplace in the context of nineteenth-century Copenhagen society. But since Kierkegaard insists that the decision for Christianity remained, even in the nineteenth century, just as exotic as was the choice of the first Christians, he concedes that subjectivity can also make unusual, non-commonplace, non-individual decisions in favour of particular historical forms – yet only on the basis of what these may conceal. This strategy is reminiscent of Nietzsche's later readiness to find the ancient Greeks interesting again precisely because the cheerful aspect they historically express was deceptive, and concealed behind it a tragedy.

For Kierkegaard, this gives rise to the possibility of duplicating the ethical–aesthetic play and adopting the same cultural forms, historically always already believed and valued, ever anew in the inner spaces of subjectivity. The perspective is thus opened of a potentially unending recycling process, which however escapes the disconnectedness of the aesthetic attitude. It is true that recurrence is always made anew to the same historical figures. Yet these are afforded each time a radically new significance, by the question being asked what they conceal behind them. In this connection, however, the question arises as to the extent to which this inner secret can still always be subsumed under the generally acknowledged ethical categories. For everything that is concealed appears criminal. The fear of self-evidence can be interpreted as a sign of bad conscience. If the philosopher as *Aufklärer* is the prototype of the modern detective, the person who conceals something from him is obviously a criminal.

With the lack of terror at the consequences of his own thought that is so typical of him, Kierkegaard also follows this path of reflection to its conclusion. It led him to what is perhaps his most radical book: *Fear and Trembling*. Kierkegaard describes the biblical character of Abraham as one who from an outside perspective has the profile of a criminal, an ordinary murderer, who is prepared to kill his own son for a reason that is incomprehensible. Kierkegaard emphasizes here that this criminal act cannot be understood in the traditional sense as a tragic sacrifice, since there is no obvious necessity that might justify such a sacrifice in an understandable way. Kierkegaard contrasts Abraham with Agamemnon, who sacrificed his daughter Iphigenia in order to be able to win the war with Troy, and shows how Abraham did not act as a tragic hero who sacrifices his private feelings to his duty towards the generality. Abraham rather follows his innermost voice, which he certainly recognizes as the voice of God, but from which he cannot learn any reasons for the sacrifice demanded of him.

Once again, as in the cases of the ethicist B. and the first Christians, we are confronted with a choice that cannot appeal to any recollection and be justified on that basis, since there is no visible difference between a crime committed from a dreadful individual mood and an act of piety. Abraham's act is not conventionally tragic; it has in its outward appearance the banality of evil. As always with Kierkegaard, therefore, what is involved here is once again something commonplace that conceals the decisive difference behind it. But in *Fear and Trembling* this already familiar figure of an act beyond any rational calculation acquires a new dimension, as in this case the act breaks with all customary ethical conventions. Abraham prepares to kill a child without explaining his action to other people, without being able to give any understandable reason for the decisive difference between ordinary infanticide and sacred sacrifice. This impossibility of communication with others is not simply a refusal on Abraham's part to talk about his decision. It is rather that an action of this kind cannot be communicated, since speech works only with visible differences, by articulating them. The invisible difference is at the same time inarticulable. The ethicist B. always sought to explain himself, and therefore to remain within society. Abraham steps outside of society by his silence, for social life is life in communication. Abraham's act is therefore a non-communicative one. It was not by chance that Kierkegaard published *Fear and Trembling* under the pseudonym 'Johannes de Silentio'.

In *Fear and Trembling*, therefore, Kierkegaard does not hesitate to approve of a crime, by opening up the possibility of recognizing in the criminal a dimension of the sacred: a theme that would later assume a central role for Bataille and others. An interpretation of crime as renunciation of society, of language and evidence, as *acte gratuit*, which displays the ambivalence of the criminal and the sacred, is used here in order to lend the outwardly banal criminal acts and wars of modernity a deeper and hidden dimension. Precisely at this point, however, Kierkegaard's most radical book offers an indication as to how its author's reconciliation with reality was to be effected. For Kierkegaard clearly identifies himself inwardly far more with Abraham than with the ethicist B. from *Either/Or*. It goes without saying that Kierkegaard sees himself as a citizen of Copenhagen who essentially leads the same commonplace lifestyle as his contemporaries. And it is for this reason that he wants to obtain both for himself and for other people a place in the world history of the spirit, in order to escape the feeling of having lived in vain. But ethicist B. conceals behind the surface of normality an infinite distance from himself, and is in this sense the furthest removed from a reconciliation with reality, with this inner distance remaining invisible from outside and impossible to disclose. Abraham, on the other hand, creates a visible distance between himself and all others precisely by the obvious inexplicability of his act. It is especially by his inwardly enforced silence that he excludes himself explicitly from the society of others. Abraham thus manifests in a way that others can also experience the inner distance that separates him from himself and from others. The parallels with Kierkegaard's situation are apparent. By his inexplicable breach with

Regina Olsen, Kierkegaard 'outed' himself, as one might say today. The interpretation this suggests cannot be overlooked: Kierkegaard sacrificed Regina just as Abraham intended to sacrifice his son. By this sacrifice, which remains inexplicable, Kierkegaard found himself in a permanent state of social isolation that he never attempted to overcome – neither by a new marriage, nor by acquiring a firm social position. He rather followed his course ever further outside of society, by practising an ascetic and isolated lifestyle that was incomprehensible to others, and continuing to write incomprehensible books. Kierkegaard demonstrated and thematized increasingly openly for the rest of his life the inner distance that divided him from himself and from others. And yet this path did not lead to a complete objectification of this inner distance.

If Kierkegaard speaks of three attitudes to life that he also understands as stages of life – the aesthetic, the ethical and the religious – the religious attitude is nothing more than a new interpretation of the aesthetic attitude, just as the ethical attitude represents a new interpretation of social normality. The paradox of the religious man plays the role of an inner justification of the extraordinary, a role that the aesthetic attitude alone cannot fulfil. Just as the commonplace acquires a hidden dimension by way of the ethical, so that it can no longer appear in a one-dimensional form, so the aesthetic likewise acquires in the religious man a deeper and hidden significance. The striving for the extraordinary, the flight from the commonplaceness of actuality, is accordingly dictated only externally by the quest for diversion, gratification and forbidden joys. Inwardly, the same quest for the extraordinary can follow from an authentic – and hence inexplicable – religious impulse. As in the case of the ethical, however, this difference between the aesthetic and the religious remains hidden. If Regina

Olsen later said that Kierkegaard had sacrificed her to God,[8] this interpretation, which is often suggested in *Fear and Trembling* and other later writings by Kierkegaard, is never directly expressed. The 'aesthetic' explanation that Kierkegaard gave in his farewell to Regina was certainly indirectly recanted. But the ambivalence and undecidability remain. This tension lasted to the end of both of their lives.

It is hard today to avoid the impression that this famous breach of promise on the part of Kierkegaard was simply a literary artifice that allowed him to embark on writing. A reflective intellectual from the middle class, a naive young girl who loves him, his egocentric betrayal that he later bitterly regretted, form a constellation that marks the whole of nineteenth-century literature, and could be described without exaggeration as the myth of the nineteenth century. Repeating this myth gave the writer a welcome opportunity, without having to exert himself in the search for a new subject and thereby divert his own and the reader's attention from the essential, to turn precisely to this essential: the inner philosophical reflections of the hero on his passions, duties and guilt. We know that this procedure was used extensively by Dostoyevsky, who took the subjects of trivial literature in order to bring his heroes rapidly into a situation without a way out, in which they could then calmly philosophize about their situation for a further 300 pages. Nor is Kierkegaard that dissimilar from Dostoyevsky in the character of his philosophizing: the same valorizing of commonplaceness by an internal tension pervades it, the same quasi-crime lends the hero a spiritual depth.

This parallel already shows how deeply Kierkegaard's writing is anchored in the literary imagination of his

---

8. Regina Olsen, letter to Henrik Lund of 10 September 1856, in Kierkegaard, *Briefe*, p. 278.

century. The essential difference, however, lies in the fact that Kierkegaard not only takes up the common subject of the trivial literature of his time, but even stages it himself. This artifice was certainly possible only in the context of a small town such as Copenhagen was at that time, and of a petty literature such as was Denmark's. Since the readers of Kierkegaard's writings were familiar with his life story and could thus relate his writing to this subject, Kierkegaard was able to spare himself the unwelcome trouble of unnecessarily repeating this subject in his writings. He thus became the hero of his novel, instead of being its author.

This strategy also explains why Kierkegaard needed so many pseudonyms; most of his books were published under them, and he also constantly played first with distancing himself from his books and then making himself known again as their real author. Instead of inventing a hero and himself functioning as the author, Kierkegaard invented the authors who describe him as their hero. All these pseudonymous authors treated his life story from different perspectives and gave this subject different interpretations. In this way Kierkegaard built a stage for himself out of diverse interpretations and descriptions of situations, in order to appear on this stage – which is densely populated by invented authors, heroes invented by these invented authors, historical characters invented in turn by these invented heroes, and so on – as impenetrable existential hero. In this connection, he reserves himself the right of final assent to all these interpretations and descriptions – and in fact never redeems this right.

Kierkegaard never directly confides in his authors and their readers, from his own position as hero, whether they are right or not in their interpretations of his inner reasons. In this way Kierkegaard reverses the customary relationship between the omniscient author and his transparent heroes. If Mikhail Bakhtin maintained that Dostoyevsky in his novels sought a balance between the positions of the author and the hero,[9] Kierkegaard stages the triumph of the hero over the author: the hero dies without the several pseudonymous authors being able to maintain that they guessed his inner motivations. The approval of the hero thereby remains a blind spot in the whole literary staging of subjectivity. The action of the play remains unconcluded.

If Kierkegaard's hero persists in unsurpassable doubt as to whether or not the commonplace reality with which he is confronted has a higher, divine meaning, he equally uses this doubt to make himself impenetrable to an external spectator. Kierkegaard's hero cannot be judged or condemned, since his motives remain undefinable. We have no criteria, as spectators of his deeds and hearers of his words, by which we could judge whether he is led by lower, aesthetic motives or higher, sacred ones. Neither the hero himself nor anyone else can settle this question by conclusive evidence. But so that this uncertainty could arise, the whole immense literary work that Kierkegaard completed is used to put himself into this situation of undecidability.

This fact, moreover, forces us to a certain caution in evaluating later philosophical discourse that appeals directly or indirectly to Kierkegaard. With the later Heidegger, after his celebrated turn, a still more significant shift in the reception of the Kierkegaardian legacy was announced. The infinite doubt that with Kierkegaard found its place in the subjectivity of the individual, received with Heidegger, after he had finally grasped the individual *Dasein* as finite, an ontological anchorage: being is hidden behind the visible surface of the existent. And it is where the existent shows itself most explicitly

---

9. Mikhail Bakhtin, *Problems of Dostoyevsky's Poetics*, Minneapolis 1984.

that being is hidden most radically. This profile of the *Sein* hidden behind the existent unambiguously refers to Kierkegaard's analysis. It is simply that for Kierkegaard this figure is part of the whole self-staging of subjectivity. The hero who does not know whether he remains on the aesthetic surface of things or follows the summoning voice of God is a particular literary figure that Kierkegaard describes in various pseudonymous texts, often under disparate and mutually contradictory assumptions. This hero is very peculiar and idiosyncratic – even if he depicts and reflects his own life history as a trivial subject.

It would be over-hasty to generalize the description of this hero simply as 'human being', as Heidegger does in his later writing when he describes the human being as he who is claimed by self-concealing being.[10] By means of this kind of generalization, the initiative passes in fact from the individual to being as such, to whose call man can do no more than react. The infinite doubt as to the accessibility of being that constitutes the subjectivity of the individual becomes with Heidegger the ontological characteristic of being as such, with which the finite human consciousness is compulsorily confronted: the only thing that remains for this consciousness is to react insightfully to the onto-logical concealment of being. In Heidegger's work, the radicalized subjectivity of the Kierkegaardian hero receives an unexpected democratization. What for Kierkegaard is freely chosen and carefully staged is for Heidegger onto-logically anchored and compulsive.

Several of the most interesting intellectual approaches

---

10. '[O]nly what already is can really be accomplished. But what "is" above all is being. Thinking accomplishes the relation of being to the essence of the human being. It does not make or cause the relation . . . Thinking, in contrast, lets itself be claimed by being so that it can say the truth of being.' Martin Heidegger, 'Letter on "Humanism"', in *Pathmarks*, Cambridge 1998, p. 239.

and theories of a later time can be read as the direct
continuation of this strategy of Heidegger's. When
Derrida, for example, seeks to show in his book
Counterfeit Money that it is impossible, under the conditions of literary convention, which are also the conditions
of writing in general, to establish whether a coin that is
described in a text (in this particular case a tale by
Baudelaire) is genuine or false, Derrida evidently has
recourse to Kierkegaard's figure of the impossibility of
making an unambiguous, self-evident and rational decision about the internal composition of the Other.[11] But,
as with Heidegger, what is at issue for Derrida is not a
decision of subjectivity to put itself in a situation in
which such an impossibility prevails; rather, this impossibility is described as the underlying condition of
literature and writing as such, which constrains the individual and which he can do no more than insightfully
reflect. Baudrillard also thematizes time and again the
impossibility of guessing the meaning or reality behind
the surface of things, explicitly emphasizing that this
impossibility is the consequence of a strategy of the
world, or, as he puts it, of the object itself, which subjectivity can do no more than comprehend.[12]

Under the shock of the Kierkegaardian analyses of
rational self-evidence, therefore, philosophical discourses
have arisen that deploy the existential paradox itself for
the purpose of system-building. Here it is not man that is
the site of doubt; rather, Being doubts itself, language
doubts itself, or writing doubts itself. And all of these
doubt man, who consequently is endowed with an unconscious that is produced by this doubt: man can no longer

---

11. Jacques Derrida, *Counterfeit Money*, Chicago 1992, p. 150.

12. 'On the horizon of simulation, not only has the world disappeared
but the very question of its existence can no longer be posed. But this is
perhaps a ruse of the world itself.' Jean Baudrillard, *The Perfect Crime*,
London 1996, p. 5.

see through himself, but everyone else sees through him
all the more easily. Subjectivity seems therefore to be
shattered, since it is robbed of its constitutive principle
– namely, doubt. All it may do now is simply annex the
objective doubt about systems to itself, for this systemic
doubt is conceived as infinite (as the infinite work of
différance, infinite sign-play, infinite desire, and so on),
in the face of which the subjectivity of the individual
remains finite.

The really paradoxical situation thus arises in present-
day philosophical discourse in which subjectivity is
indeed confronted with a description of the situation
that essentially stems from Kierkegaard, and yet this
situation is presented in Hegelian fashion: as a system-
determining necessity that the individual can only
accept. The whole difference consists simply in the fact
that subjectivity was previously supposed to cleave to
the infinite inner self-evidence of the system – to the
Absolute Spirit – whereas it now has to accept the no
less infinite and absolute inner doubt of the system about
itself. Kierkegaard's philosophical writings, therefore,
are read today with mixed feelings. On the one hand his
analyses seem highly contemporary. On the other hand,
however, the reader who has internalized the linguistic
customs of today finds the language of subject-philosophy that Kierkegaard uses antiquated, and almost
automatically tries to translate it into the language of
poststructuralist discourse, particularly since such a
translation suggests itself and is already frequently practised. In this perspective, Kierkegaard acquires a
particular historical place as someone who, provision-
ally still in the language of subject-philosophy, attempted
a transition from the construction of self-evidence to its
deconstruction.

This leads, however, to the overlooking of something
that was of decisive importance for Kierkegaard: his

struggle against the historicizing of the individual – his attempt to open up for subjectivity an escape from its historical fate. For Kierkegaard, his own thought and his own doubt were not universalizable, and could not be objectivized in the form of a system. Even his own name reads, in the list of his writings, as one more pseudonym in a whole series. Kierkegaard stages the secret of his own subjectivity above all, however, in the way that he creates the ambivalence between his role as author and as hero in his own text. This new kind of literary construction certainly seduces us into interpreting it as a radically new description of the world. But such an interpretation forgets that Kierkegaard's literary construction functions independently of the particular description of the world that its hero is confronted with. The finite subjectivity of the individual finds itself in the same situation, whether it accepts Hegel's infinite constructions or their no less infinite deconstructions.

It is true that Kierkegaard himself, in the final years of his life, acknowledged an 'actual' position in the 'actual' world, insofar as he embarked on an open dispute with official Danish Christianity, and that this struggle directly or indirectly dominates his last writings. In this way Kierkegaard seems to have abandoned the theatre of subjectivity and put himself in the actuality of faith. But Kierkegaard did not in any way 'go further' here. He himself ironizes about such an interpretation in one of his letters: '[E]verything modern certainly goes further ... People "go further" than faith – rising to a system! They "go further" than the individual – rising to the community! They "go further" than subjectivity – rising to objectivity! And so on and so forth.'[13] If Kierkegaard signed his most important

---

13. Letter to Rasmus Nielsen of 4 August 1849, in Kierkegaard, *Briefe*, p. 218.

philosophical texts, *Philosophical Fragments* and 'Concluding Unscientific Postscript', with the pseudonym Johannes Climacus, he signed *The Sickness Unto Death: A Christian Psychological Exposition for Edification and Awakening* with the pseudonym Anti-Climacus, which the reader can interpret either as an ascending or a descending movement. But Kierkegaard commented further in the same letter: 'Climacus = Anti-Climacus, I see this as a happy epigram.' Here again, an identity arises that conceals the difference between highest and lowest, and makes it unknowable. Kierkegaard's writing thus remains an introduction into the infinity of subjective doubt, which was practised to the end by its author as provisional, never as descriptive and conclusive.

LEO SHESTOV

The name Leo Shestov (1866–1939) says relatively little to the Western reader today. Even in the most active period of his life, between the two world wars, he was scarcely familiar to the wider public. And yet Shestov was highly esteemed in certain narrower intellectual circles, and his thinking exerted a significant if hidden influence on some of the best representatives of the cultural scene of that time. After emigrating from Russia in 1920, Shestov lived in Paris, where he wrote a great deal in the French philosophical press and for publishing houses, and was on friendly terms with, or at least well known to, among others, Lucien Lévy-Bruhl, Jean Paulhan, André Gide and André Malraux. The young Albert Camus was also deeply influenced by his writings. And Georges Bataille helped with the French publication of his *Tolstoy and Nietzsche*. On top of this, Shestov had two faithful followers in France, who spread his teaching and commented on it: Benjamin Fondane and Boris Schloezer.

Yet Shestov's real interest was in German philosophy.

He admired Husserl above all, and stubbornly sought to make his name known to the French public, even exposing himself to a rebuke from Malraux, who saw it as below the dignity of a thinker of Shestov's class to concern himself with such second-rate authors as Husserl or Bergson.[1] Unperturbed, however, Shestov continued to maintain that Husserl was the greatest living philosopher. He organized Husserl's visit to Paris and his lectures at the Sorbonne in 1929, which gave rise to Husserl's famous *Cartesian Meditations*. Shestov was equally fascinated with the early works of Heidegger, to which Husserl introduced him. He also made efforts to bring Martin Heidegger to France, as well as Max Scheler and Martin Buber, with both of whom Shestov was similarly on good personal terms. Quite particularly, however, Shestov committed himself to spreading the name and ideas of Søren Kierkegaard in France, where he was completely unknown at this time. He was one of the first to recognize the new actuality of Plotinus' philosophy, and the interpretations of Tolstoy's and Dostoyevsky's work that he offered in several of his essays and lectures were also of considerable importance for the philosophical reception of these two writers in Europe. We can thus say that Shestov made an essential contribution to creating an intellectual atmosphere in France that later made possible the rise of French existentialism.

And yet Shestov's own thought belongs far less to the existentialist paradigm than this might suggest. Although he felt himself close in many respects not only to Husserl but also to Kierkegaard, Nietzsche and Dostoyevsky, these authors were important to him chiefly because they most consistently embodied the underlying philosophical attitude that Shestov himself combated

---

1. *Die Memoiren von B. Fondane*. See N. Baranova-Sestova, 'Zisn' Sestova', *La Presse Libre*, Paris 1983, vol. 2, p. 132.

extremely vigorously throughout his life – it was only by arguing against these authors that he was able to articulate his own position so effectively. This position, moreover, he had developed much earlier in Russia, in the context of the Russian philosophy of the turn of the century, and it clearly bears the hallmark of the Russian intellectual situation of the time, although even in Russia Shestov was a definite loner.

Leo Shestov was born as Lew Schwartzmann, into the family of a wealthy Jewish businessman in Kiev. His father had distanced himself somewhat from the traditional Jewish faith, and supported the secularizing Zionist movement that was then in its infancy, but he still participated in the religious life of the Jewish community in Kiev. Shestov linked up with leading figures of the so-called Russian religious renaissance around the turn of the century, in particular with Berdyaev and Bulgakov, who also hailed from Kiev, and became one of the most well-known writers in this school of thought, which preached a rejection of Western philosophical positivism in all its forms, and a return to a newly interpreted Russian Orthodoxy. At the same time, however, Shestov never converted to Orthodox Christianity. He wrote only very rarely about Christ, calling him simply 'the best son of the Earth'. He never involved himself in discussions of Christian dogmatics. When Shestov spoke of God, he almost always quoted the Old Testament.

If all this never led Shestov to seriously put in question his loyalty to the Jewish religious tradition, he did not make an opposition between this tradition and Christianity. He never said anything that was not also acceptable to Christians, and never explicitly thematized the controversial relationship between Judaism and Christianity. This is all the more striking, in as much as all his Christian friends wrote in detail about their relationship to Judaism. Shestov, for his part, did not want to be seen as either a Jew or a Christian, nor even as a philosopher: all that interested him was how the personal fate of an individual was expressed in their religion and their philosophy. In relation to all the authors that he discussed in his writings, Shestov time and again raised only one single question: What was it in their life that caused them to devote themselves completely to philosophy? The content of any particular philosophical discourse, for Shestov, was interesting only insofar as it proved relevant to answering this question. At the same time, however, Shestov did not pursue any psychology: his search was for a primary event, for the real-life trigger of theoretical interest in general, including interest in psychology. This almost traumatic concentration on a specific 'primary event' forces the reader of Shestov's writings to seek such an event in Shestov's own biography. His characteristic monomania, however, does not at first sight find any explanation in the circumstances of his own life.

A relatively liberal family atmosphere, in material comfort with a large circle of friends and relatives, allowed Shestov even in his early years to pursue his inclinations in study, and to travel widely. In everyday practical life he was calm, moderate, well-behaved, and by and large successful. When his father's business ventures met with difficulty, even before the Revolution, Shestov returned to Kiev and managed to restore the family's affairs in only a short time. Everyone who knew Shestov remembered him as a loveable, pleasant and open-minded man, with a good practical sense. This picture also corresponds to the language in which Shestov's books were written: clear, cool, somewhat ironic, never straining to have a 'poetic', elevated or profound effect – let alone a 'mystical' one. At the same time, this language constantly revolved around an unnamed tragic event of his own, this being perhaps the inherent experience of such language.

In all of Shestov's writings, the same quotations are repeated time and again: from Tolstoy, Dostoyevsky, Nietzsche, Spinoza, Tertullian, Kant, Hegel, Kierkegaard and Husserl. But the overall work of these authors is never analyzed, their 'systems' are never reconstructed, described or interpreted. Only an expression, a sentence, sometimes even a word, is taken up and cited repeatedly as the key to a certain attitude or a certain problem – either in agreement or in protest. These citations seem to be wounds or sores that cut into the body of Shestov's language, and could never be cured. Shestov constantly scratches or licks these sores, but they never heal – only itching and burning the more, just as with Shestov's favourite hero, Job. The eternal recurrence of these citations often seems forced, diseased, even pathological. It is reminiscent of the fixation on traumatic events that Freud described, bound up with frustration or fulfilment of desire. These citations basically describe comparable events in the Shestovian philosophical eros – either marking an experience of despair as to the impossibility of reaching the 'best' philosophy, or remembrance of an experienced feeling of breakthrough and the brief ecstasy bound up with it. But both are painful for Shestov. Any encounter with philosophy, for Shestov, was evidently always vivid, tragic, wounding. Certain philosophical propositions traumatized his own language, making its further undamaged existence impossible, removing from it the force of the obvious that forms an indispensable precondition for the free and 'organic' development of any language. The philosophical scepticism that consequently arises makes any utterance impossible, problematic, inexpressible – even a simple, everyday one. And Shestov does not write in a philosophical language: instead he writes in the simple, ordinary language that is exposed to injury by philosophy, seeking constantly to overcome this.

This is evidently the reason why Shestov wanted to express his linguistic experiences as real and purely personal experiences. Although he describes these in tragic terms, he simultaneously domesticates them by transposing them out of the linguistic realm into the realm of life, which can seemingly be described with the means of everyday living language. Shestov's mode of procedure here essentially follows that developed by Nietzsche in his *Genealogy of Morals*: a theoretical, philosophical or scientific position is investigated not in terms of its 'objective' validity, but rather of its origin 'in life'. For Nietzsche, as we know, an 'abstract' statement, appealing simply to its own supposed knowledge-value, only ever functions as compensation for a real defeat: the person who is victorious in life does not need any 'objective principles'. On the other hand, the subjugated seek to rescue themselves symbolically from their actual unsuccessful situation with the help of such principles. Shestov takes over this strategy of Nietzsche's, but at the same time radicalizes it and uses it against Nietzsche himself. For Shestov, the 'life' that Nietzsche speaks of is a no less abstract concept than 'reason', 'science', 'freedom', and so on: basically, all these concepts are even synonymous. When Nietzsche praises victorious life, preaches *amor fati* and identifies himself with forces of nature that are bound to destroy him, he simply seeks to divert himself and others from the fact that he himself is sick, poor, weak and unhappy. The actual personal problem of Nietzsche – namely, the sickness that was steadily killing him – brings out in Nietzsche the same resentment that he denounces in all others, and forces him to adopt the pose of someone speaking in the name of life, which is a similar pose to that with which people customarily speak in the name of reason, morality or science.

Shestov diagnoses in Nietzsche the attempt to generalize his own, individual situation, and in this way force the insights that he obtained from this situation onto others as objective truth. For Shestov, this strategy is simultaneously the main strategy of philosophy. A philosopher becomes a philosopher by understanding, describing and raising to the rank of universal truth his own individual and irreducible situation. In this way, however, the philosopher commits two mistakes. First of all, he understands his situation as one that cannot be overcome in reality. Nietzsche thus does not believe in the possibility of actually healing and overcoming his sickness – and this disbelief is expressed in his *amor fati*, his readiness to subject himself to the forces of nature. And secondly, the philosopher transfers his own situation onto other people who may well be in a completely different situation. Other people are perhaps not incurably ill like Nietzsche, and therefore do not perceive any necessity for *amor fati*, instead being completely ready to struggle with fate. Why then compel these others to Nietzscheanism as a 'true doctrine'?

These two errors – the first of which he saw as by far the more important – Shestov identifies in all the philosophers with whom he concerned himself. For rationalists and moralists, such as Tolstoy, Plato or Spinoza, for example, the same critique as in the case of Nietzsche applies. But Shestov does not make any exception even for 'existentialists'. He finds the same strategy even in Kierkegaard. Kierkegaard could not marry Regina Olsen, so Shestov establishes after a brief analysis of Kierkegaard's diaries, because he was impotent. This personal problem, however, Kierkegaard generalized and made into a universal, existential, general human problem.[2] In this way he escaped his own, purely personal problem, while on the other hand he drew everyone else into sympathy with him, even though they were probably not impotent and did not necessarily have any existential problems at all.

Shestov also extends this criticism to Heidegger, whose *Being and Time* he diagnoses as simply a paraphrase of Kierkegaard's thinking by other means. Heidegger proves here to be the victim of a misunderstanding: the unhappy affair between Kierkegaard and Regina Olsen is depicted by Heidegger as a universal truth of human *Dasein*. There can be no doubt that Shestov would also have subjected French existentialism, which he made such an essential contribution towards creating, to the same criticism, for existentialists always speak just of subjectivity as such, the limit situation as such, the existential choice as such, experience as such, and so on. It is only in appearance here that the classical reason-oriented philosophical attitude is overcome: tragedy, ecstasy or despair are just as much generalized and made into abstract concepts as reason and morality were previously. Basically, here, the description of the *condition humaine* is given the same general validity as before: it is described rationalistically.

But Shestov precisely opposes a neutral, non-specific description of the *condition humaine*. For him, a personal, physically determined situation is not a concrete case of the universal condition. All that Kierkegaard really wanted was to sleep with Regina Olsen, and thereby be happy. If he had been able to do so, then according to Shestov he would immediately have forgotten his whole existentialism, and with it philosophy in general: the *condition humaine* of all other people would never have disconcerted him or led him to philosophical ideas. A cure for his impotence

---

2. Lev Shestov, *Kierkegaard i ekzistentsialnaja filosofia*, Moscow 1992, pp. 37–8.

would have been for Kierkegaard a cure from philosophy, just as for Nietzsche a cure of his sickness would have been a rescue from philosophy. And the only thing that Nietzsche or Kierkegaard wanted, according to Shestov, was precisely this cure. Their philosophy, accordingly, was only a sign of their lack of the courage to pursue their own, purely personal goal. Like Wittgenstein, Shestov saw philosophy as a disease that affects the body of language. Unlike Wittgenstein, however, Shestov did not believe in the ability of language to overcome this disease by its own powers alone, since the body of the speaker, philosopher or writer is also sick and in need of curing – something that language cannot effect.

Shestov categorically rejected all variants of sublimation or metamorphosis, of cultural or creative transformation, or of simply symbolic fulfilment. Everything that seemed to other people productive, poetic or creative, struck him as simply ridiculous. He insisted rigorously on the literal, exact, this-sided, non-symbolic realization of individual, bodily human wishes – and was fundamentally unprepared to accept a cultural substitute for this. Yet what he had in mind here was not unconscious sexual desires in the Freudian sense: the wishes that Shestov speaks of are ones of which their bearers are conscious, and they are not necessarily sexual. Above all, however, their realization is not prevented by culture, society, morality or convention, but rather by nature itself. Even if all wishes were socially redeemed, even if the unconscious and the physical were accepted, Kierkegaard would still not be able to sleep with Regina Olsen, and Nietzsche would remain sick. If these desires have any kind of general form, it is the demand to conquer nature, and above all, time – to make what has happened not happen, to reconfigure the past. For the sick Dostoyevsky, Nietzsche or Kierkegaard, therefore, it is the demand not to have been sick in the first place. Only such a demand, which is not directed against society and its institutions, but against nature itself, opened up for Shestov the space both for philosophy and for science. It was not striving for absolute knowledge or absolute morality that transcended the limits of nature: a quite basic and everyday requirement was enough to transport a person beyond the world totality and into metaphysics.

The first reaction to such a demand is quite obvious: its realization is impossible, and it is quite senseless to try to insist on it. But this spontaneously arising response is precisely what Shestov seeks to oppose. His argument here follows a consistent strategy. The difference between possible and impossible is a philosophical difference. This difference is laid down by reason. But philosophy and philosophical reason are in turn always the products of a personal catastrophe, an unrealized demand: philosophy and reason arise after this catastrophe, and not before it. But this means that the acceptance of this catastrophe and the decision to abandon the personal struggle for one's wish precede the constitution of philosophy and reason. Acceptance of actual defeat, therefore, is not the result of any reflection on the possible and the impossible, because the reason that could conduct such reflection has not yet been constituted. Reason is rather itself the product of this acceptance. For Shestov, the history of European reason begins at the moment when Plato accepted the death of Socrates (the 'best among men'), and conceived it as the expression of universal fate instead of protesting against this death.

This is where Shestov sees the essential difference between philosophy and religion, or, as he puts it, between Athens and Jerusalem. The believer does not accept the 'unchangeable laws of nature'. For him, the whole of nature is subject to the will of God, who is in a position even to change the past, to awaken the dead and heal the sick. Acceptance of the laws of nature, which show no mercy towards people, deprives the unhappy person of the force of insisting on their own personal wish, which might perhaps lead to their salvation. Instead of this, they start to philosophize – and are then irredeemably lost. Here Shestov clearly repeats in a changed form the celebrated argument of Pascal: we should believe in God, since if there is no God we are lost in any case, but if he does exist, then we have at least the chance of salvation and should not spoil this by our disbelief. Pascal, however, still appealed to reason with this argument. Shestov, on the other hand, wants to define the precise point at which reason first arises, reason that confirms sickness and makes it irredeemable, instead of striving for cure.

In this insistence on cure, against any contrary, 'natural' evidence, Shestov also situates himself in the mainstream of the Russian religious renaissance of his time. Almost all representatives of this movement had begun their philosophical career as Marxists, or at least as left socialists. Shestov himself wrote his first major work on *The Condition of the Working Class in Russia*, which was rejected by the university on account of its 'revolutionary tendency'. Besides, as a student Shestov was involved in a number of oppositional and revolutionary activities, causing him a good deal of trouble from the authorities. However, he relatively soon lost his left-wing revolutionary beliefs.

The intellectual basis for this was the same as with many other Russian thinkers of his generation. The belief in reason, science and social progress, which Russia had imported from the West and appropriated over the eighteenth and nineteenth centuries, also contained the promise of a better organization of social and private life, and hence also of growing individual happiness; it seemed as if men were more powerful after freeing themselves from the dogmas of religion.

Very quickly, however, it was understood that the very opposite was the case: the rejection of religious belief made people not more powerful but increasingly less so. Technical progress, in fact, was bound up with recognition of autonomous and objective laws of nature, which showed themselves to be both overwhelming and indifferent towards men. Political, social and technical inadequacies could perhaps be overcome – but not sickness, lunacy or death, which had their origins in nature. And if one were to believe that these evils could be overcome in future by the further advance of technology, such an advance would only relieve coming generations, and would thereby introduce an inequality in historical time that nothing justified. The evidence of logic, science and rational philosophy was thus experienced in Russia as a constraint, as a hypocritical justification of a prison controlled by natural laws, in which every man was condemned to a meaningless death. Any utopian sociopolitical project thus became an empty promise. It was not accidental that Husserl was Shestov's favourite opponent: he had like no other philosopher made the compelling power of self-evidence his theme, and glorified it.

Vladimir Solovyov, Nikolai Fyodorov, Nikolai Berdyaev and many other older and younger authors of the Russian religious renaissance accordingly turned to Russian Orthodox Christianity, in order to receive from it a guarantee, or at least a hope, of an eternal realm of universal happiness, where nature itself could be reconciled with man and society, and which even earlier generations could participate in by the resurrection of the dead. In a certain sense, the ideology of this religious renaissance represented more a radicalization of the socialist ideal than a rejection of it: nature too should obey man; natural laws should be transformed into laws of art, as Solovyov demanded. Russia in particular was seen as playing a quite exceptional, messianic role, since only Russia, in the view of these thinkers, was in a position to conceive and realize such a bold project of total transformation – not only of society, but of the whole universe, since the philosophy of the West had already lost its original powers by its acceptance of the existing order.

It is readily understandable why these ecstatic dreams of universal salvation simply failed to arouse any interest with Shestov. Privately, in his correspondence, he waxed ironic about them. He certainly did not take any position here that allowed him to debate publicly with their bearers. Under all circumstances, however, Shestov remained true to himself: he was exclusively interested in the fate of the individual. The cause of humanity, nature or history as a whole, left him completely indifferent. His protest against the evidence of reason or the laws of nature was uttered simply from a personal perspective; he could indeed imagine very well a man who had no occasion to bewail the laws of nature or the supremacy of science. The implicit presupposition of Shestov's antiphilosophy is that the majority of people do not need any kind of philosophy, since they believe, whether rightly or wrongly, that they are healthy, happy and content without it. Only a very few need philosophy: those for whom things are going particularly badly – which means that only the fate of these few is relevant in elaborating the philosophical problematic.

The reader of Shestov's writings, however, notes relatively soon that, though its author repeatedly indicated an original experience, he nowhere actually described it. Shestov constantly insists that one should speak exclusively about oneself – yet he only ever speaks about others. This observation has led some commentators to try and discover such an original experience in Shestov himself. This task, however, has proved insoluble, at least up till now.

We know that, when Shestov was twelve years old, he was kidnapped by a group of revolutionary anarchists, who attempted to blackmail his father. The father, however, refused to pay, and after a few days the son was released. Shestov never described this episode, but there are biographically plausible reasons for not seeing it as the original experience that is sought. In his Kiev period, Shestov experienced along with his family an anti-Jewish pogrom – but this again cannot be seen as the triggering experience.

From the memoirs of certain friends of Shestov, it emerges that he did in fact have an experience of absolute despair in 1895, the reason for which remains unknown. One friend wrote that something particularly dreadful had happened to him. And a woman memoirist mentioned 'a complicated and unusual responsibility that burdened his conscience'. Shestov, for his part, only expressed himself on this on one occasion, when he wrote in his diary in 1920: 'In this year it is twenty-five years since "the time was out of joint" . . . I write this down so as not to forget it: the most important experiences in life, which no one apart from you knows, are easily forgotten.'[3]

This entry is interesting in many respects. It shows that Shestov focused on not forgetting a very definite event, on staying with it and not turning away from it. The danger of forgetting, however, lies in the fact that other people did not know about this event. In his writings, accordingly, Shestov created a small society of other authors, each of whom has his own secret, and this serves as

---

3. N. Baranova-Sestova, 'Zisn' Sestova', p. 22.

metaphor, and at the same time as recollection, of
Shestov's secret. It is really no longer important here
whether the quotations from these authors to which
Shestov constantly returned serve this work of recollection, or whether this frightful original event and the
constant recollection of it were simply a pretext and a
mnemonic aid for the concentration on a single theme
that was a purely philosophical one, a theme to which
Shestov was constantly compelled to return: the wounding of language by philosophical discourse.

Shestov's texts are particularly striking because of
their extreme monotony. The same arguments are
constantly used for the same demonstration. The same
quotations are constantly cited in the same context. The
same – and sole – questioning is constantly repeated,
and its relevance indicated with the same examples. It
was not only for other people that Shestov did not admit
any development, any creativity or transformation of
the original experience by way of ideas, art or any kind
of culture. His own texts, too, show scarcely any development. There is no logic of development in Shestov, no
creative evolution, no transcending, no forward-driving
analysis, no new and more profound interpretation – in
short, no cultural producing in the customary sense of
the word. Only constant re-producing, only re-combin-
ing and re-formulating of always the same elements.

The poetics of Shestov's texts has scarcely anything to
do with the 'creative' poetics of existentialism. It is reminiscent instead of the poetics of a later time: the novels
of Robbe-Grillet, minimalist art and music, the pleasure
of repetition that was proclaimed in the 1960s and '70s.
No matter how Shestov justifies it or makes it plausible,
he was principally concerned with the possibility of a
minimalist, repetitive, re-productive writing – in other
words, not productive and philosophical.

The necessity of such writing, for Shestov, resulted

from a deep understanding of the situation of the philosophy of our time. He knew that the sciences – both
natural and human – had occupied the whole terrain of
modern thought. He also knew that philosophy had
been replaced by the history of philosophy. And he did
not believe in the success of the heroic efforts of philosophers such as Husserl, who sought to reconquer this
terrain with new philosophical methods; he saw that at
the end of the day scientific reason simply ignored such
attempts. Rich, productive, expanding philosophical
discourse had become unbelievable in the twentieth
century. If Shestov commented on this kind of discourse
from another philosopher, he always just asked: 'How
does he come to know all this?'

Shestov accordingly looked for a discourse that could
remain purely philosophical – not impinging on the
realm of the sciences, of politics, of art, or even of religion in the strict sense of the term. Philosophy no longer
methodologically subjugated other 'partial realms' of
knowledge as a super-science or total world-outlook,
but was rather a 'poor discourse' that situated itself
exclusively in the zone where neither science, nor politics, nor religion, nor even the history of philosophy
made or could make a claim. For Shestov, this zone was
the narrow limit between everyday language and the
language of reason. Scientific, reasonable discourse
always injured everyday language: not only did it deny
its desires and hopes, but it made these fundamentally
inarticulable and unexpressed. And at the same time,
everyday language constantly relativized the principles
of reason, which in it appear only as confessions of one's
own hopelessness. Hence Shestov's careful selection of
quotations, examples and questionings, which are then
only adopted in his own discourse if they cross the
boundaries between scientific and everyday language –
if they are either wounding, or else relativizing and thus

healing. Only after a careful check does Shestov start to work with these elements of discourse that he has selected – combining, positioning and considering them in different ways. In this way Shestov determines the configuration of the boundary that he had observed.

Shestov's strategy of a 'poor', reduced, limited discourse is akin to several artistic and literary strategies of the twentieth century. We need only recall the late Tolstoy, painting after Cézanne or poetry after Mallarmé. Philosophy for the most part has not gone far enough (with the great exception of Wittgenstein) to conceive and develop this strategy in a systematic fashion: the old claim of universality and comprehensiveness is too deep-seated. Academic institutionalization also offers customary philosophy additional psychological protection from the competition of other rival discourses, against which philosophy would lose if defencelessly exposed to it. For this reason, Shestov's philosophizing remains, at least initially, gripping and instructive only for the few who have already behind them the painful original experience of the limitation of all their discursive possibilities.

3

MARTIN HEIDEGGER

One of the few texts of the twentieth century that speaks about art in the highest tone is Martin Heidegger's 'The Origin of the Work of Art'. And in a certain sense, which we shall have to explain, all the high tones that can be noted in art-exegetical discourse since the start of the avant-garde strike a similar tone to this essay of Heidegger's. Modern art sought to escape the traditional criteria of judgement, classification and evaluation, by starting to present new forms that lacked any prior models against which they could be measured. In this way, not only did modern art situate itself beyond good and evil, but also beyond beautiful and ugly, masterly and amateurish, tasteful and tasteless, successful and unsuccessful, and so on. Modern art transcends or evades even the traditional distinction between art and non-art. It thereby escapes the aesthetic laws that previously made it possible to judge an individual work. The wish to escape the judgement of others, however, generally leads people to suspect a criminal intent. Where no judgement can be made, and no verdict pronounced – in other words, where law is absent – is where danger, crime and violence lurk. The question is simply what the particular nature of this danger and violence is.

An anti-avant-garde, anti-modernist criticism has believed from the start that it recognized this danger in the strategies of self-assertion and market domination that the modern artist has appropriated. And the violence that made this danger dangerous was diagnosed as the power of fashion and the manipulation of public opinion permitted by the modern media – originally meaning the press. Modern art was characterized as the work of a few sensation-hungry charlatans, who preached the new so as to avoid comparison with the old. This original assessment of the artistic avant-garde, moreover, has not been historically superseded, and despite all the seemingly established character of modern art, it crops up time and again in different variants.

The theoretical discourse that was favourable to modern art, however, has generally interpreted this avoidance of critical judgement quite differently: not as a deliberate commercial strategy, but rather as the effect of an irresistible inner compulsion, which forces the artist – even against his own conscious will – to create the Other, the new, the criminal and the dangerous. The reason for this compulsion has been sought in a number of places: personal trauma, the unconscious, or the pressure of social conditions. In all these arguments justifying modern art, the high tone in art criticism unavoidably arose, since the force that supposedly overcomes the artist in such a way that he is transported beyond all criteria of conscious judgement and into the ecstasy of the absolute new had necessarily to be described as a compelling force, almost divine and overwhelming. The figure of the artist was accordingly transformed from one of an active and criminal trickster into that of a passive and sacred object of a sacrifice that makes the inaccessible visible.

Though interpretations of this kind certainly cultivate a high tone, they are for the most part not particularly convincing. They fail to make clear why being overpowered by a supposedly irresistible inner force must necessarily generate the new. And in this way we are referred once again to the original, more modest and more sceptical explanation: market demand, the external – and not just internal – social and media pressure for innovation, a clever commercial strategy. Adorno was already able to show in his *Aesthetic Theory* that the recognition of such 'inferior' origins of the modern work of art does not necessarily lead to its moral and aesthetic condemnation: it is precisely the relative complicity of modern art with laws of the market that permits it to adopt, according to Adorno, a critical position in relation to market conditions. Because modern art has itself experienced the harshness of the market, it can obtain and demonstrate its own harshness by the ostensive irreconcilability of its innovations. With Adorno, therefore, the high tone actually experiences a certain cooling. At the same time, however, it is not completely lost: the omnipotence of the market was described by Adorno in such drastic tones that the market itself becomes an almost divine force that overpowers the artist and makes him its sacrifice – showing itself to the world by this means.

What is particularly interesting in Heidegger's essay 'The Origin of the Work of Art' consists in the way that the high tone of modern art exegesis reaches its apogee in it – though at the same time this art exegesis is itself far less differentiated from a market theory of art than one might initially believe. At first sight, Heidegger's line of argument follows a trusted strategy of modern art apologetics: an 'essential' work of art, according to

Heidegger, arises from inner compulsion, inner necessity, not from external calculation. But there is a force
that dictates an artist's work here and makes the compulsion to innovation immediately plausible to the reader
– namely, time. We expect from time, indeed, that it
should constantly bring with it changes and innovations. And so we are immediately ready to admit that
the artist, if he wants to keep up with the time, has
necessarily to produce something that has never been
seen before.

We are still always led to think, therefore, of historicism of a Hegelian stamp: every time has its own
customs and laws of taste, forming so many cultural
epochs. These epochs dissolve in the course of history,
and artistic styles accordingly follow one another in
succession. Every epoch has its own criteria of evaluation. A new epoch unavoidably demands its own
criteria of evaluation. Tradition, on the other hand,
always belongs to another, past time, and accordingly
must not determine present taste. This historicist line
of argument seems to be plausible, and has in any case
helped a great deal in the breakthrough of modern art.
With Heidegger, however, this argument is not simply
repeated but essentially modified, because Heidegger
recognized its fundamental weaknesses: the present
cannot be an historical epoch like the epochs of the
past, since the present does not have an epochal duration of its own, being simply a fleeting transition
between past and present.

Heidegger certainly writes, in the sense of a traditional historicism, that the Greek temple or the Roman
fountain represent in exemplary fashion the historical
Dasein of the peoples in question. He emphasizes that
the work of art only has its life in the epoch of its creation – being later treated in the museum merely as a
dead, archival, post-historical document that no longer

has any original relationship to truth. Thus Heidegger describes the Greek temple as follows:

> It is the temple work that first structures and simultane-
> ously gathers around itself the unity of those paths and
> relations in which birth and death, disaster and blessing,
> victory and disgrace, endurance and decline acquire for
> the human being the shape of its destiny. The all-govern-
> ing expanse of these open relations is the world of this
> historical people. From and within this expanse the
> people first returns to itself for the completion of its
> vocation.[1]

The high tone that we hear in this passage, however, diminishes when museum art is in question:

> Well, then, the works themselves are located and hang
> in collections and exhibitions. But are they themselves,
> in this context, are they the works they are, or are they,
> rather, objects of the art business? . . . Official agencies
> assume responsibility for the care and maintenance of
> the works. Art connoisseurs and critics busy themselves
> with them. The art dealer looks after the market. The
> art-historical researcher turns the works into the objects
> of a science. But in all this many-sided activity do we
> ever encounter the work itself?[2]

The answer to this question is not hard to guess: no, for 'the world of the work that stands there has disinte-grated. World-withdrawal and world-decay can never be reversed. The works are no longer what they were. The works themselves, it is true, are what we encounter; yet they themselves are what has been . . . Henceforth, they remain nothing but objects of this kind.'[3]

---

1. Martin Heidegger, *Off the Beaten Track*, Cambridge 2002, pp. 20–1.

2. Ibid., p. 19.

3. Ibid., p. 20.

Museum art is thus not essential art for our present time, and can never become so, since it always already belongs to the past and has decayed internally along with it – even if its dead, external form continues to remain worthy of preservation on both scientific and commercial grounds.

Despite this historicist, romantic, anti-classical stance, Heidegger is not just concerned to repeat the platitude that art belongs to its time and has to change with time. And in fact, the experience that modern art has had since the birth of the avant-garde shows that what we have here is an art that precisely does not correspond to the criteria of its time, one that precisely does not fit into its own time. Modern art is created against the prevailing contemporary taste – not only against the taste of the past. In this respect, modern art does not change with time but rather against time, or at least according to a different temporal logic than the prevailing ideas of art and the historical *Dasein* of the people. Modern art may well be called 'modern', but it is foreign to its own epoch. This is why it generates in the spectator the suspicion that it, too, as well as the museum-stored art of the past, is simply a matter of the art market and art scholarship – and does not show any connection to the 'living present of the people'. In order to dispel this suspicion, a decidedly high tone is required.

This is indeed the tone that Heidegger deploys, since, as quite soon becomes clear, his intention is to justify modern art. If we overlook many things and simplify others, but seek nonetheless the underlying intention of his text, we may say that Heidegger relates the modern work of art neither to the past nor to the present, but rather to the future. Heidegger's theory of art is in this sense radically futuristic. The essential artist, for him, is someone who is open to what is coming, to the advent of the future – someone who has a premonition of the future that will dissolve the present. In this context, Heidegger expects from the future – and here he was at one with most of his contemporaries (the text stems from 1935–36) – more change than constancy, more rupture than continuity, more event than inertia.

Heidegger defines art as 'the setting-itself-to-work of truth',[4] an original and genuine kind of self-disclosure of being, which can only be compared with the founding of a state, with fundamental sacrifice, and with the question of the thinker (but not for example with science, for science is concerned with what already exists); and art, like the founding of a state or the sacrifice that founds a religion, is concerned with what is coming, what is only now announced but will perhaps come about in the future. The essential artist is capable of divining the future, and of paving a way for it through his work: 'Precisely with great art (which is all we are concerned with here) the artist remains something inconsequential in comparison with the work – almost like a passageway which, in the creative process, destroys itself for the sake of the coming forth of the work.'[5] The true artist is passive. But this is a particular kind of passivity, which opens the doors to the most powerful mastery of being – or, to put it another way, with the world-historical tendency that always already prevails in secret, but is still hidden from most people. This is why art is the 'founding of truth'. Ancient Greece is again the prototype of this: 'What would, in the future, be called being was set into the work in a standard-setting way.'[6]

The self-disclosure of being, or self-revelation of truth in art, makes art prophetic. Art, in this connection, is in no way blind – or simply beyond itself. The artist may be overpowered by the force of being, but he

---

4. Ibid., p. 44.
5. Ibid., p. 19.
6. Ibid., p. 48.

lets himself be overpowered. The passivity of essential art, for its part, is strategic and thus also active. Art shows us the future, but at the same time it establishes this future. In this sense art is originating, since it stands at the beginning of the history that is still to be lived. Modern art thus belongs as little to the present as classical art does – it belongs rather to future epochs. Heidegger extended classical historicism towards the future, and justified modern art by way of this expanded concept of historicism.

The definition of art as the revelation and establishing of the truth of future being certainly bestows on art the highest praise of which the philosopher is capable, his vocation requiring him to concern himself above all with the truth. This formula gives art the highest possible praise, and as we have said, it is only 'essential' art that is spoken of in this way. It is only essential art that cannot be criticized, judged and scientifically analyzed, since it shows future truth incipiently and originally, and hence stands above the present:

> Nothing can be discovered about the thingly aspect of the work until the pure standing-in-itself of the work has clearly shown itself. But is the work ever accessible? In order for this to happen it would be necessary to remove the work from all relation to anything other than itself in order to let it stand on its own and for itself alone.[7]

Only if a work of art is freed from any connectedness to its present, and thereby from any possibilities of critically judging it, can it show itself as a prophetic image of future being. Then it is the work of art itself that judges the present by showing it its future, and simultaneously by putting this future into work. The positions of the

---

7. Ibid., p. 19.

work of art and its spectator are exchanged: it is not the spectator who now judges the work of art, but rather the work of art that judges the spectator, by showing the spectator the future in which they will maybe no longer be present.

Already in *Being and Time*, the truth of individual *Dasein* was inferred from the existential project – in other words, from the anticipated future. Later, this primarily individual project was considered as a counterpart for the reception of being – as a prophetic acceptance of the inescapable historical future, as a readiness to accept the providence of being, as what Heidegger, in his 'Letter on Humanism', called *engagement pour l'être*. At every stage in Heidegger's thinking, however, the future is unambiguously privileged. Both essential philosophy and essential art are those that might be called 'future-oriented' in contemporary management-speak – and as such they must remain immune from criticism, analysis or contradiction. No contemporary critic can decide the fate of such future-oriented thinking or creation. For no one can really know what the future will bring. Every investment in the future involves an unavoidable risk factor. Only the future itself will decide whether an intellectual and artistic investment has paid off or not. At all events, however, the person who takes such a risk is fundamentally superior to a calculating scholar, since even his failure says more about the being of beings than all scholarly analysis. At least in this sense, Heidegger's art exegesis is a management or market philosophy – as well as a philosophy of struggle and war. The issue here is one of the chances of our success in the future, which remain insuperably hidden from us, but also of our determination to reach the future despite everything, to establish it, to enable its world-historical breakthrough. In resolving these tasks, all present references and insights are of only dubious value.

But if our ability to experience the work of art 'standing on its own and for itself alone' depends on the decision that we remove it 'from all relation to anything other than itself', such a decision must therefore be in some way unfoundable, if it is to make a selection. Otherwise we can imagine that any work of art may be experienced in this way. The difference between an 'essential' and a non-essential work, which Heidegger certainly seeks to maintain, or a 'great' work and one that is not, would in this case be accidental, since by a mere operation of separating a work of art from all its external references – the museum, the art market, and so on – we can make any work of art we like into an essential one. In relation to the museumized art of the past, Heidegger tacitly follows the established tradition in his choice of works. He assumes as accepted fact that the museum, the art market and art scholarship are exclusively concerned with those works of art that have at some time in history established themselves as foundations of the historical fate of an historical people. To start with, however, a work of art must establish itself in living historical reality – then at some other time it becomes obsolete and lands in a museum. Heidegger sees this succession as the only one conceivable.

But how does one recognize a new essential work of art, when its future historical success is still only a promise? How is an unessential work distinguished from an essential one that goes beyond the horizon of the existing and all the criteria associated with it?

The answer to this question, which like many things in Heidegger's essay is more suggested than made explicit, indicates that a complete surpassing of the present by the essential work of art does not in fact take place. A key criterion is still always maintained: the criterion of formal innovation. The essential work of art shows itself to be so by dint of being innovative. Heidegger writes:

> The setting-into-work of truth thrusts up the extra-ordinary (*Ungeheuere*) while thrusting down the ordinary, and what one takes to be such. The truth that opens itself in the work can never be verified or derived from what went before. In its exclusive reality, what went before is refuted by the work. What art founds, therefore, can never be compensated and made good in terms of what is present and available for use. The founding is an overflowing, a bestowal.[8]

And at another point: 'The more essentially this thrust comes into the open, the stranger and more solitary the work becomes.'[9]

What presents itself in these passages as a mere description is evidently a normative proposition: the essential work of art is one that cannot be understood in terms of the past, one that breaks with the habits of perception. It follows from this, if also not explicitly, that only art that cannot be understood in terms of the past is essential art. And this yields the formal criterion for determining essential art: essential art is an innova-tive art, for if a particular art cannot be understood in terms of the past, it has to be understood in terms of the future. If Heidegger himself did not have any particu-larly 'progressive' artistic taste, and evidently stuck with moderate expressionism, his theory of art nonetheless privileged a radical, avant-garde, innovative art by encouraging the artist to present the decidedly 'extra-ordinary'. In this way, Heidegger's theory of art shows itself to be an apologia for artistic modernism.

The general premise of Heidegger's thinking on art

---

8. Ibid., p. 47.
9. Ibid., p. 41.

seems immediately plausible here: everything that happens
in art, happens in time. If a work of art has its references
neither in the past nor in the present, it must come from
the future. What today presents itself as new is a promise
of a future historical norm: the innovative work of art is
a prospect of a later, this-sided, historical norm. This
sounds plausible. And yet, how is it possible that what
will happen only in the future is nonetheless expressed in
a work of the present – and can be seen as art?

The answer to this question is given in Heidegger's
discourse on 'clearing'. Or rather, the possibility of
anticipating the future is described and postulated as a
clearing of being: 'In the midst of beings as a whole an
open place comes to presence. There is a clearing.
Thought from out of beings, it is more in being than is
the being. This open centre is, therefore, not surrounded
by beings. Rather, this illuminating centre itself encir-
cles all beings – like the nothing that we scarcely
know.'[10] If beings as a whole are everything that already
is – in other words, the present, which can be investigated with the means of science – clearing affords a
prospect of the coming, the future, the uncertain; which
however is more powerful and more 'being' than the
mere present, since it is capable of transforming the
present. At this point, the high tone in Heidegger
reaches its clearest expression.

The high tone, moreover, always marks a threat. And
every threat has the same general form: 'You'll soon see
what happens to you'; 'You'll soon experience something that you've never experienced before'; 'I'll show
you something so extraordinary that you'll lose your
sight', and so on. The high tone is always apocalyptic. It
promises the light within the clearing, which shows us
the extraordinary and causes everything ordinary to

---

10. Ibid., p. 30.

fade. Every prophecy conjures up danger for the unbe-
lievers, who try to measure and judge the future with the
criteria of yesterday and today. In the clearing of being,
we have an inkling of what will be valid in the future,
what will break through and be successful. To resort
once again to management-speak, the clearing of being
is a gap in the market which the future-oriented entre-
preneur has to jump into.

Heidegger's philosophy is a philosophy of historical
success – and this is most likely the very reason that it has
itself been so historically successful. It is at the same time
a philosophy of struggle. But, as distinct from Nietzsche,
who was also a philosopher of struggle but did not believe
in the otherness of the future, Heidegger promises his
reader the possibility of victory in the future – and at all
events the possibility of a change, an event, an advent of
the completely other. The hopelessness of Nietzsche's
eternal recurrence of the ever-the-same is not considered
a possibility. Formal innovation, or the extraordinariness
of the work of art, is accordingly for Heidegger the sign
of its fitness as a prospect of the future.

Any philosophy of victory, however, must equally be
a philosophy of defeat. And both defeat and victory may
await us in the clearing:

> But concealment, though of course of another sort,
> also occurs within the illuminated ... Concealment,
> here, is not simply refusal. Rather, a being indeed
> appears but presents itself as other than it is ... That,
> as appearance, the being can deceive us is the condition
> of the possibility of our deceiving ourselves rather than
> the other way round.[11]

We may note that Heidegger already had the experience of his rectorship behind him at this point. But

---

11. Ibid., 30.

only those who risk are likely to win – those who dare to engage in the 'struggle between clearing and concealment'. In the work of art, in particular, it is its materiality, its thingly character, which connects it to the 'earth' and to the being that conceals the future being behind it. Since a work of art is always only a thing, it cannot be innovative through and through. The earth holds it. Though Heidegger warns the reader that the earth is not automatically the concealing and the truth is not automatically the open, his lengthy discussions at the beginning of the essay show already that the thingliness of the work connects the world that the work of art opens to the present.

Heidegger wants to show with utmost determination that a work of art is nothing that is not material and thingly. Any work of art, no matter how high the claims made for it, is merely a thing, Heidegger says, that the cleaning woman who works in a museum knows and handles. It is only the ability of this thing to open up a world that distinguishes it from all other things. But this ability in no way changes the fact that the work of art remains a thing through and through. How the thing as work of art can make the world visible, Heidegger famously shows by the example of a painting by Van Gogh that shows a pair of boots. This example has become famous, and been discussed in detail from different points of view in many essays by other authors.[12] What interests us here, however, is a different aspect of Heidegger's text – namely, the central question as to whether the origin of the work of art does actually lie, as Heidegger maintains, in the 'struggle between clearing and concealment', which is only at first glance reminiscent of the dualism between Dionysian and Apollonian that Nietzsche wrote about. Or, to express it better,

---

12. On this question, see Jacques Derrida, *La Verité en peinture*, Paris 1978, pp. 293ff.

since for Heidegger this struggle determines our relationship to the future, to future being: Does the origin of the essential work of art really lie in the future?

First of all, it can be maintained that the formal innovativeness of a work of art does not necessarily mean that it comes to us from the future. Heidegger in fact sticks to the traditional idea that the work of art must necessarily correspond to a vision that precedes it. If the work of art does not depict reality as it is directly familiar to us, it must at least depict its future possibilities – as the extraordinary that is always already concealed in the familiar. This future vision is granted to the artist by the clearing of being; the clearing sends him a new vision – which might also be a deceptive one – and thereby permits him to go beyond the ordinary and already familiar. But this original vision, as the precondition for the origin of a work of art, is in actual fact not necessary. An artistic innovation can come about from a purely technical, material, thingly and manipulative play of formal repetitions and deviations. It is sufficient for the production of innovation that there be an overview of the art that is already in existence, and a decision to produce something formally new in comparison with this existing art. That the clearing of being is needed in order to ascribe this new form as being originated in the future, and thus having a prophetic dimension, can in fact only be understood after this new form has already been seen. It can therefore be maintained that the clearing itself can only be conceived in the light of this new form – and not the other way round. Only if one is faced with a new art form does one need the clearing of being as explanation for the origin of this form. The clearing of being, therefore, has its origin in the modern work of art, and not the other way round.

But where does the origin of the modern work of art lie, if not in the future? A response to this question is made more difficult by the prejudice holding that every work of art arises in a particular historical time, whose historical being it expresses – a prejudice that Heidegger, as we have said, completely shared. In accordance with this prejudice, the museum exclusively collects (and the art market exchanges, art scholarship discusses, and so on) art that has already asserted itself, established itself and made its breakthrough in historical reality. It would seem that an innovative work of art has likewise to assert itself first of all in future reality so that it can later take its place alongside the artworks of the past, as witness to its own epoch – to exist first in reality, and then enter the museum. But this is precisely the succession that modern art puts in question.

The modern work of art, in other words, proceeds in the opposite direction: it must first assert itself in the museum in order subsequently to enter reality. Just like all other creations of our time, it has to undergo a technical examination before it can be released for consumption. The modern principle of artistic autonomy is precisely founded on this reversal of the relationship between art institutions and historical reality. The museum, in the modern age, presents a gigantic reservoir of signs that can be used by present-day people for self-description. This is why it is not pertinent to say, as Heidegger does, that the art forms of the past have definitively lost their relevance to life, and live out their marginal museum existence exclusively as documents of historical recollection. We know, in fact, that the art forms of the past can be used in completely new ways, so as to mark a particular position within the present. In just the same way, however, a new and unfamiliar art form can be used in order to lend someone or something a futuristic appearance.

The production of new art forms, which in modern conditions immediately enter the museum if they seem interesting in comparison with the art forms already stored there, serves to expand the repertoire of signs available to society for the purpose of a differentiated self-description. This does not mean that these new art forms will determine the historical being of the future – nor again that they will be used chiefly in the future in the context of historical reality. Perhaps they will, but perhaps they will not. For this reason, it is impossible to distinguish the 'essential' work of art from the non-essential one in terms of its origin. Accordingly, moreover, the work of art in question may not be 'essential' in the Heideggerian sense – namely, indicative of the future – because the future, in the conditions of modernity, no longer faces us as a new, totalizing, historical mode of being, but rather as the opportunity to use all modes of being that are at our disposal, whether these are essential or not. The justification of the modern work of art as future-oriented and prophetic, which unavoidably triggers a high tone in the corresponding kind of critical writing, certainly means an overvaluation of the work of art – but at the same time also a possible undervaluation, should it emerge that the future looks different from what the work of art ostensibly promised.

The success of a new art form in the internal context of museums and art institutions does not mean any promise of the form's actual historical application. The absence of this promise, however, is in no way a sign of failure, defeat, deception. The discourse of art criticism has means at its disposal that allow it to offer a completely reasonable justification for a particular work of art – in comparison with other artworks – to be new. If this justification is accepted, then the work is taken into the repertoire of socially accepted signs, and is released for use. Both this justification and the museum acceptance then persist even if there is no demand for a long time and the work in question does not enjoy wide success. Modern art institutions may be market-oriented in a certain sense, but they are also relatively independent of the market. Artistic innovation in these conditions involves a certain degree of risk – if not a completely uncalculated one. The artist is not delivered entirely to struggle, to the market, to the clearing of being that conceals his fate from him, since his successes and failures may be deceptive.

The time of the museum is a different time, a heterogeneous time, compared with historical time as conceived by traditional historicism. 'Historical' time is the time in which particular art and cultural forms that have come about historically take place, forms that are available for use – or non-use. The museum in the modern age does not stand at the end of history, but at its origin – and in this way perhaps forms the real origin of the modern work of art.

4

JACQUES DERRIDA

In recent years, the apocalypse and everything apocalyptic have become fashionable subjects of intellectual publications. Today it is good form to lament scientific and technical progress, the destruction of nature, the danger of war and the decay of traditional values. The optimism of modernity has been replaced by postmodern pessimism. Not such a long time ago, the complaint about technical progress was a privilege of the 'right', whereas progress for the 'left' meant the liberation of man from the grip of nature and tradition. Nowadays, protests against progress have moved over to left publications, and it is the right who emphasize the necessity of economic growth. 'Progressivism' has become 'official', and for this reason, 'alternative' movements reject it and use lines of argument that are often classically 'reactionary' ones: Marx with his belief in the redeeming power of the 'productive forces' has been decisively replaced by Nietzsche and Heidegger.

Naturally enough, the appropriation of traditionalist arguments in the milieu of the postmodern left has not been effected without important modifications. The 'reactionaries' of the past defended tradition as long as it was alive, as long as people still believed in it. Today, this once living tradition already belongs to the past, and is revived as stylization, as retro. In a comparable manner, Léon Blois, who defined himself as a 'non-believing Catholic', simulated for the intellectuals of his time, with the latest rhetorical means, a lost harmony, which of course was not any kind of harmony in its own day, but every bit as much a struggle for survival as any other epoch of human existence, including the present. What is involved here is simulation and simulacra, whose harmlessness and aseptic character is guaranteed precisely by contemporary technological progress. Maintaining the balance of nature becomes a matter of ecology; maintaining peace an issue for a pacifism that is based on the spectre of the nuclear 'absolute weapon'.

Present-day anti-progressive apocalypticism appeals to the latest achievements of science as embodied by contemporary ecology, with the object of restoring the lost paradise by technological means. Once again, we hear arguments about paradisiacal natural life, ecological consciousness, a new sociability that will bring life back into accordance with nature. The individual project of the traditionalists and reactionaries becomes a social one, their anti-modernism is put on a scientific basis, and changed to a technological programme of environmental protection. The past is idealized as the model for a new technological utopia. The victorious scientific and technological consciousness of the modern age benevolently proclaims its readiness to realize the ideals of its deadly enemies, and in this way crown its own triumph. Left-alternative movements create new markets for industry in the sector of 'environmentally friendly products', thereby stimulating economic activity.

In the quest for a social balance, however, there is a

preference not to take individuals into account. The individual death of a person in their own bed is not a problem that deserves attention. Only death caused by war or terror – only a violent social death – draws attention. 'Natural death' is seen as a normal element in the natural ecological balance, and no pacifist rebels against it. At best, the question is raised as to how death can be made 'more humane', so that people are not treated for too long, needless outlay is avoided on unnecessary medical–technical progress, and every person given the possibility of dying in dignity and with the sense of having fulfilled their ecological duty.

In the flood of recent apocalyptic literature, Jacques Derrida's essay 'Of an Apocalpytic Tone Newly Adopted in Philosophy' stands out.[1] It is often read together with another major article by the same author, 'No Apocalypse, Not Now'.[2] Derrida is rightly considered a master-thinker, and for this reason alone his book deserves particular attention. But also considered in themselves, these two essays are distinguished by the depth of their analysis, and above all by Derrida's characteristic ability to grasp simultaneously the different and far-reaching philosophical implications of the problems he raises, and their possible solutions. This ability makes it always a pleasure to read Derrida's work. In what follows, I shall try my best to give a clear, even if unavoidably incomplete, idea of the importance of this line of argument in the context of the contemporary 'apocalyptic' discussion in general.

The title of Derrida's book refers to Kant's well-known pamphlet 'Of an Elevated Tone that has Recently Arisen in Philosophy' (1796). In this pamphlet, Kant

---

1. Translated in H. Coward and T. Fosbay (eds), *Derrida and Negative Theology*, Albany 1992.

2. 'No Apocalypse, Not Now (Full Speed Ahead, Seven Missiles, Seven Missives)', *Diacritics*, summer 1984.

takes issue with works of his contemporaries that make
a claim to immediate intuitive knowledge of the truth,
which is supposedly accessible only to initiates and can
dispense with any kind of strict philosophical method.
Kant characterizes the authors of these works as charlatans and 'mystagogues', who set out to raise the 'veil of
Isis' with a bold stroke and perceive the naked truth.
Against such claims, Kant takes the stand of an
Aufklärer, and shows that at their root lies a claim to
domination, a claim to the role of spiritual leader – in
short, an inferior interest and not a superior one. True
philosophy needs effort rather than immediate illumination, but for precisely this reason it is in principle
democratic, accessible to anyone who wants it, and
intolerant of any irrational leadership.

The strategy that Derrida adopts in his comments on
this text of Kant's, which he considers still relevant to the
present-day situation in philosophy – in view of the
growth of irrationalism and hostility to rational methods
– derives from his own 'postmodern' position in contemporary philosophical discourse. On the one hand, Derrida
presents himself as the most decisive opponent of the
rationalism – what he calls 'logocentrism' – of European
philosophy; but on the other hand, he understands his
own critique of logocentrism as continuing the tradition
of the Enlightenment. His effort thus consists in presenting himself as a successor as well as an opponent of Kant.

Derrida starts by directing attention to the etymology
of the term 'apocalpyse': the Greek αποκαλυποισ means
dis-covery – pulling away the cover or veil, exposing.
'Apocalyptic speech' in Greek also meant 'obscene
speech', which spoke about parts of the body that were
customarily concealed. What Derrida refers to in this
connection is evidently the passage in Kant on 'tearing
away the veil of Isis'. In both cases, what is involved is
the conquest of truth – of naked truth – that follows the

brave removal of the cover. In other places, Derrida speaks not only of logocentrism, but also of phallogocentrism, having in mind here the aggressive and sexually charged character of the European ideal of a 'complete possession of the truth'. Here Derrida stands in solidarity with Kant. The claim to direct perception of the uncovered truth is essentially obscene, pornographic. At the root of this claim lie motives of possession and greed, which have themselves to be 'uncovered', and about which we need to be 'enlightened'.

But this is the very place where the decisive turn in Derrida's argument is apparent: the *Aufklärer*'s striving for 'discovery' and 'light' has its origin in the same phallogocentrism. Kant is essentially led by the same impulse as his opponents; he wants to see truth just as naked, he strives in just the same way to possess it. Or to put it another way, in the struggle against 'mystagogues' and 'charlatans', philosophy repeats their fundamental movement, calling similarly for light and the unconcealed, as does unphilosophical intuitive illumination and the apocalypse that uncovers all things. Derrida particularly catches Kant out in the betraying claim that the resort to direct intuition instead of reason by the mystagogues means 'the death of all philosophy'. This means that for Kant, too, proclamation of the end, the apocalypse, serves as a means of intimidation, to enforce his own strategy. In this function that it has of intimidation and suggestion, apocalyptic discourse, according to Derrida, is a characteristic feature of the whole tradition of European thought. Derrida writes: 'Each of us is the mystagogue *and* the *Aufklärer* of an other'.[3] Noting the varied character of eschatological discourse, he continues:

> Haven't all the differences [*différends*] taken the form of a going-one-better in eschatological eloquence, each

---

3. Ibid., p. 45.

newcomer, more lucid than the other, more vigilant and more prodigal too, coming to add more to it: I tell you this in truth; this is not only the end of this here but also and first of that there, the end of history, the end of the class struggle, the end of philosophy, the death of God, the end of religions, the end of Christianity and morals (that [*ça*], that was the most serious naivety), the end of the subject, the end of man, the end of the West, the end of Oedipus, the end of the earth, 'apocalypse now', I tell you, in the cataclysm, the fire, the blood, the fundamental earthquake, the napalm descending from the sky by heli-copters, like prostitutes, and also the end of literature, the end of painting, art as a thing of the past, the end of psychoanalysis, the end of the university, the end of phal-locentrism and phallogocentrism, and I don't know what else. And whoever would come to refine, to say the finally final [*le fin du fin*], namely the end of the end [*la fin de la fin*], the end of ends, that the end has always already begun, that we must still distinguish between closure [*clôture*] and end [*fin*], that person would, whether want-ing to or not, participate in the concert.[4]

Here Derrida ironically presents a whole list of recent Paris post-Marxist, post-Freudian, post-Nietzschean and poststructuralist apocalyptic modes. This irony, however, should not lead to error: Derrida is not seek-ing so much to distance himself from the apocalyptic tone as to show on the contrary that the ironic, enlight-ening tone is itself a variant of this apocalyptic intonation. Still more, it is precisely in the apocalyptic tradition that *Aufklärung* receives for the first time its inner justification. He writes:

So we, the *Aufklärer* of modern times, we continue to denounce the impostor apostles, the 'so-called envoys' not sent [*envoyés*] by anyone, the liars and unfaithful ones, the turgidity and the pomposity of all those

---

4. Ibid., pp. 48–9.

charged with a historic mission of whom nothing has been requested and who have been charged with nothing. Shall we thus continue in the best apocalyptic tradition to denounce false apocalypses?[5]

And he immediately raises the question: 'What can be the limits of a demystification?' In other words, is it possible to distinguish between true and false apocalypse?

Derrida's answer essentially consists in saying that every claim to truth is false, but that the uncovering of all these claims possesses a genuine intention as long as it does not itself lead to the proclamation of a new and final truth. An apocalyptic text, accordingly, is not something to be exposed because some kind of truth is revealed in it in the light of which error becomes evident, but conversely, precisely because the source of light in it remains concealed. By way of example, Derrida considers the Revelation of St John on Patmos, and shows that what John wrote was not his own direct revelation (he did not appear in the role of mystagogue), but only what was dictated to him. In his summary analysis of the book of Revelation, Derrida indicates the constant change of address in the apocalyptic message that John reproduces: he hears a voice that quotes Jesus, but Jesus also speaks directly, an angel is sent who cites the words of God, and so on. All these messages and citations constantly intersect, change their addressees, but there is never an immediate revelation or direct intuition: the series of citations, messages, authors and addressees continues indefinitely. Derrida writes: 'And there is no certainty that man is the exchange [*le central*] of these telephone lines or the terminal of this endless computer. . . . No longer is one very sure who addresses what to whom.'[6]

Apocalypse thus turns out to be the model of

---

5. Ibid., p. 59.
6. Ibid., p. 57.

poststructuralist, postmodern consciousness. There is communication, and there is also a structure – but the communication has acquired an infinite number of participants, which is why the messages stray through many channels of communication, contradicting one another, changing addressees, and it is impossible to check whether they correspond to the original signal, this being lost in an undetermined past that is on principle unreachable and unreconstructable, and cannot be made present: all that remains of this past is simply a 'trace', a hiatus of its presence that cannot become present. Structuralism of the infinite structure turns out to be a mechanism for the destruction of all meaning – in contrast to classical structuralism, which strove to be a guarantee of the durability of meaning.

The apocalypse thereby becomes the absolute text, in other words the text 'without truth', without apocalypse: the elevated revelation that now maintains only its form, its style, its tone, one that anyone can in principle resort to who has caught an errant apocalyptic communication – truly a triumph of postmodern aestheticism (note that 'apocalypse without truth' serves in reality, as well as in Derrida, as discovery of truth, the truth of poststructuralism by way of a paradigmatically poststructuralist text). Derrida writes: 'Wouldn't the apocalyptic be a transcendental condition of all discourse, of all experience even, of every mark or every trace? And the genre of writings called "apocalyptic" in the strict sense, then, would only be an example, an *exemplary* revelation of this transcendental structure.'[7] And again: 'The word *sans*, *without*, I pronounce here in the so necessary syntax of Blanchot, who often says X without X'[8] – in other words X as pure form, as husk, style and intonation, as absolute citation.

But this apocalypse without apocalypse, or, more

---

7. Ibid., p. 57.
8. Ibid., p. 67.

accurately, apocalypse of apocalypse, creates at the same time the possibility of becoming an *Aufklärer*: writer and speaker equally seize this voice, this tone, that comes 'from the being beyond', from 'beyond good and evil', 'beyond being as event'. The receivers of accidental, wandering messages from nowhere – writers, philosophers, literati – reproduce this, falsifying it as they see fit. And with every right, since they constantly hear the apocalyptic 'Come',[9] which has neither sender nor addressee and is consequently addressed also to them, coming from Something that is higher than being and behind being.

In broad strokes, this is what Derrida's apocalypse looks like. And it is appropriate to note here that, de facto, he essentially repeats the classical model: the apocalypse discloses the truth – 'Speak to them of deconstruction' – and this truth sends a message to its prophet, Derrida, to proclaim it and expose those who are against it: those who believe in a visible, 'pagan' truth and do not want to know anything of a truth beyond the distinction of truth and lie, or good and evil, a truth that is the same for the just and the guilty, and shines equally on all, even though it is itself invisible and not directly perceptible. This traditional position makes it possible to turn to Derrida with the very questions that he directs at others: Who is Derrida seeking to intimidate with his prophesying, why and for what reason? What concrete aims does he set himself? The answer to these questions could be given on the basis of the essay of his we have already referred to, but the possibility is offered to a far higher degree by the article 'No Apocalypse, Not Now', which is the transcript of a talk he gave at a conference devoted to questions of 'Nuclear Criticism' held in the US. This was a conference for literati standing in the service of humanity,

---

9. Ibid., p. 65.

who reasoned about the contemporary problems of a nuclear war.

The particular question that Derrida asked in his talk was what gave literati the right to speak about nuclear strategy, of which it would seem they understood nothing. His answer was basically that they did indeed have the right to do so, given that nuclear war was exclusively a question of language, and to a still greater extent presented a literary problem. First of all, the entire strategy of the arms race was rhetorical, designed to suggest something to the adversary. Secondly, if war did break out at any time, it would consist of a series of commands, which were based on purely verbal information and whose practical verification was impossible. And thirdly – and this is the main point – nuclear war had not broken out yet, but if it should do so, there would be no one who could witness it, and there would be no sense in saying anything about it, so that nuclear war was a case of absolute fiction, a purely verbal, literary *fata morgana*.

In recent years the idea has developed that the general tendency of the present age consists in an ever-growing theoreticization of reality and a consequent fictionalizing of it, the reason for this tendency lying in the fear of apocalypse, of the destruction of the world. The secularized European consciousness, unable any longer to turn to God with a plea for mercy, has sought to convince itself that, because the world is a fiction, it cannot be destroyed by any 'actual event' such as the apocalypse would necessarily be. Derrida, it seems to me, goes still further and declares the apocalypse itself to be fiction. Yet it is precisely here that serious obstacles await him. The matter is as follows. Because Derrida fictionalizes everything, both the world and its finitude, he is compelled to materialize fiction itself. For him, any fiction has its foundation in 'literature', or, as he again

says, in the 'archive', meaning an infinite number of
texts, which all refer to one another and without which
human culture and any kind of thinking would be
completely impossible. The destruction of this archive in
the event of a nuclear war also therefore means the end
of all fictions, which are anchored in the reality of the
archive, of literature. The annihilation of literature, in
other words, is the annihilation of everything, since
everything outside of literature is literary fiction, with
no kind of reality remaining after its demise.

The apocalypse without apocalypse, which Derrida
introduced in the earlier essay by way of a textual analysis, here is given realistic and concrete shape. The
apocalypse of the apocalypse is nuclear war: this destroys
everything without uncovering any kind of truth and
without leaving behind it any kind of reality. Literature
as a whole proves to be a unique apocalyptic text, a text
about nuclear war, since literature writes about its own
mortality, about the end of its messages, about their infinite vulnerability. Derrida holds the best literature about
nuclear war to be that of Mallarmé or Kafka, who wrote
about loss and the end of literary communication, about
the end of literary fiction. As Derrida puts it: 'If, according to a structuring hypothesis, a fantasy or a phantasm,
nuclear war is equivalent to the total destruction of the
archive, if not of the human habitat, it becomes the absolute referent, the horizon and the condition of all the
others.'[10] Though he goes on to say that any war is waged
'in the name of something which is worth more than
life',[11] but that after the annihilation of all life no name
can remain, he shows that a nuclear war is waged in the
name of the *name* as such: in the last analysis, again, in
the name of literature, even for the sake of destroying
literature. The only hope that Derrida sees lies in the

10. Ibid., p. 28.
11. Ibid., p. 30.

possibility of *destinnerance*,[12] which always exists. It may well be that missiles launched against a target fail to reach it, for some chance reason, just as other literary messages fail to reach their addressees. Mistakes in addressing offer the guarantee of the maintenance and continuation of life. An understood message is just as deadly as a correctly dispatched missile that strikes its target. The hope for salvation from nuclear war is the text of the apocalypse: precisely because it is incomprehensible and infinite, discloses no truth, it is uninterpretable and in this sense exemplary literature. Postmodern literary theory presents itself in this way as a guarantee against the total annihilation that the literary theory of classically rational structuralism threatens, since according to this, all missives and missiles must reach their target. The apocalypse of the apocalypse appears as both threat and hope, designed to hold together the postmodern school or sect, as well as the authority of its leader – Derrida, in a very personal sense.

However, the break with those rationalist, modernistic opponents who bring the world total annihilation is actually not so great for Derrida as it may seem. Especially because the very idea of total annihilation of the archive is evidence of the naturalistic character of his philosophy, inscribed here in the series of other theories of the present that base themselves on materialistic assumptions. Derrida does not notice here the glaring contradiction in his line of argument: either the whole world is fiction, which means that the archive is not part of the world and cannot be annihilated by an event within the world, or else the world is reality, but in that case the annihilation of the archive as part of the world is simply one kind of modification of reality, and has no fundamental importance.

---

12. Ibid., p. 29.

Derrida – like many other naturalistically minded theorists of our time – would like to escape the paradox according to which transitory mortal man is in a position to fathom directly infinite absolute truth, to enter into it, make it his own and know it. He therefore gives an 'objective' explanation of the subjective conviction of the person speaking or writing – in terms of the apocalyptic impulse, which is captured by literature, by its infinite scope, by its incomprehensible origins, and proceeds to an indeterminable end. This explanation, it goes without saying, is more attractive than 'relations of production', 'libido', 'will to power', 'linguistic structures' and other naturalistic schemas, but is not essentially distinguished in any way from them. The difference is one that the reader himself imagines from time to time, when he reads Derrida's reflections on the text, on the inner space of subjectivity, on the silent precursor of the voice, on the book that preceded the world, comparable to the Torah in the interpretation of Jewish mysticism. And yet, in his speech on the nuclear theme, Derrida somewhat naively exposes his cards, and it emerges that by 'archi-text' he understands the diversity of literature that is present, preserved in libraries and physically destructible.

It therefore follows that this thoroughly material literature can arouse in its readers accesses of apocalyptic fantasy, itself proving to be a fiction and function of them. As fiction, fictional nuclear war, it annihilates the world; but in reality it itself succumbs. Reality annihilates fiction, fiction annihilates reality, fiction creates reality that creates fiction, and these magic transformations continue ad infinitum. The source of knowledge of the apocalypse cannot be ascribed to individual consciousness, but there is just as little occasion to ascribe it to any kind of material process, including any material process of self-reproduction and self-multiplication of literature.

Knowledge of the end and beginning of man and all

beings cannot be obtained either 'subjectively' or 'objectively', in as much as it attests to the demise of both subject and object. Individual man no more disposes of this knowledge than 'society' does. To assume that the individual has immediate, direct access to concealed truth, or can obtain such access by a process of 'discovery', is self-evidently 'idealistic', or, if you like, 'ideological'. But it is no less ideological to assume that human consciousness is drawn into the play of any material, structural, social or 'literary' forces that can be described – even in an apocalyptic fashion – and obtain its knowledge from those forces. Such an assumption does not solve the problem but doubles it: instead of answering the question of how the individual created being can understand the 'ideal', it raises the additional question of how this ideal can be produced by perishable, created – in other words material – beings.

And so, the answer to the question 'How should we conceive the apocalypse?' has to be: 'Just don't think about it!' Apocalyptic knowledge as knowledge of the limits of the world cannot be reduced to any thought processes within the world, whether an ideal process of knowledge or an actual material process of literary production, the production of signs. Thinking comes to a halt before this knowledge; it experiences its own apocalypse in it, seeing in it its absolute limit and taking this as its foundation. It is for precisely this reason that the apocalyptic always strives against being thought about as any kind of 'being'. Derrida, in his talk on the apocalypse, returns again to the question that Leibniz raised and that, according to Heidegger, was the recurring foundation of any kind of metaphysics: 'Why is there being at all, and not just nothing?' Heidegger answers this question by starting his discussion with 'being', which 'gives', 'sends', 'posits' all beings needed. This answer, which Derrida uses as the main starting-point of his theorizing on apocalyptic 'messages', offers a summary formula of present-day naturalistic thinking. The reasoning is from the beings 'given' to us to the hidden – 'subconscious' or 'unconscious' – ground of being, so that the apocalyptic, as Derrida writes, becomes not an epoch but rather *epoché* (in Husserl's terminology, the abstention from all original parts, including the existence or non-existence of the world), and for this reason reveals to us being – or in the case in question here, literature and archive.

This is why the apocalypse, for Derrida, assumes a naturalistic, social and technical character, and appears as nuclear war, even though it is obvious that any war remains an event within the world. Nuclear war only bears apocalyptic features in as much as it kills, and for this reason the apocalyptic character of war makes the assumption that each individual death is apocalyptic. Yet the difference between war and peace then ceases to be fundamental: man is mortal not just in time of war, but equally so in peace. The fear of nuclear war, in fact – and here Derrida is absolutely right – is in no way simply fear of death. It is fear of the destruction of museums, libraries, and all depositories of created works, everything written, painted, and so on, in which the intellectuals of today, not believing in any transcendence, seek social and historical immortality within the world. Nuclear war – the technological feasibility of destroying the contents of museums and libraries – is infuriating to contemporary thought, not because it destroys life, but rather because it threatens to destroy its own social immortality. The building of museums and libraries in the centres of the enlightened world's leading cities, and the creation of countless archives, national parks, architectural memorials, ecologically protected zones, and so on, are already gradually transforming the whole planet into a giant museum. And this tendency is steadily increasing: car museums, air travel museums, space travel museums, and so on, are already being established. Conservation follows on the heels of production, and almost overtakes it: artists today work 'for the museum'. The danger of nuclear war should bring intellectuals to their senses and lead them to see the illusory and artificial character of the historical immortality that makes life into a mausoleum; it should remind them that their own life is all that they have in the world. But quite the contrary: frustration finds its expression in the struggle for peace, in a 'feeling of responsibility' or the like. Intellectuals – and in the present case Derrida appears as a spokesman for their consciousness – close their eyes to the facts and prefer to see the apocalyptic revelation as having not taken place, and only war as real.

The 'man in the street' instinctively feels, faced with talk about the danger of a nuclear war, that the problematic does not affect him: he has nothing to lose, since he is not on display in the museum and his works not preserved in libraries. The problematic of the struggle for peace is essentially deeply elitist, despite presenting itself as universal and humanistic. Derrida is quite correct in this respect. He notes that man 'still always dies',[13] but he goes on to offer the following interpretation of death:

> Similarly, my own death as an individual, so to speak, can always be anticipated phantasmatically, symbolically too, as a negativity at work – a dialectic of the work, of signature, name, heritage, image, grief: all the resources of memory and tradition can mute the reality of that death, whose anticipation then is still woven out of fictionality, symbolicity, or, if you prefer, literature; . . . there is no common measure adequate to persuade me

---

13. Ibid., p. 21.

that a personal mourning is less serious than a nuclear war. But the burden of every death can be assumed symbolically by a culture and a social memory (that is even their essential function and their justification, their *raison d'être*). Culture and memory limit the 'reality' of individual death to this extent, they soften or deaden it in the realm of the 'symbolic'. The only referent that is absolutely real is thus of the scope or dimension of an absolute nuclear catastrophe that would irreversibly destroy the entire archive and all symbolic capacity, would destroy the 'movement of survival', what I call *survivance*, at the very heart of life.[14]

In the whole of world literature, there is scarcely any such touching and naive confession. Derrida thinks of his own death simply as a loss to world culture, and for this reason he already mourns it now. The only thing that consoles him is that humanity, with the help of pictures, signatures, and so on will be able somehow to symbolically reconstruct his image, and therefore world culture and world literature will not collapse on account of this loss. Only the nuclear death of all culture could put an end to this eternal mourning over his works and his presence in cultural production, which is more real than life itself and makes it possible 'to survive in life'. In other words, life poses a greater danger for symbolic mourning than death does. One can scarcely imagine any greater self-sacrifice, any greater dissolution into one's own literary production, any greater ability to see oneself through the eyes of others – and at the same time any greater vanity and lack of sympathy towards living life.

Derrida calls on us to be aware of the political motives, as it were, of apocalyptic discourse, but at the same time he avoids a political evaluation by appealing to the call of being, which says to him, 'Come!' Stressing the radical infinity of any experience, he reserves himself

14. Ibid., p. 28.

the right to receive messages from the infinite. In this respect he appears as the typical theorist: political, profane and utilitarian considerations are subordinated to theory; they receive the status of mere moves in the political game, even if with an infinite number of rules. The structure itself – the result of the game as purely theoretical understanding – dominates any concrete political step, and consequently dominates everything political. In this respect Derrida coincides with Marxism, Nietzscheanism, structuralism and the other typical modes of thinking of our time.

Derrida's theoretical politics, however, correspond to a rather traditional strategy in European philosophizing. The philosopher generally finds himself between the theorist and the crowd, and sets each side against the other. He terrifies the crowd by saying that the theorist is preparing their doom, and uses the potential for confusion that follows from this against his own colleagues, by accusing them of turning away from living experience, from the diversity of everyday life, from the irreducibility of forms of human experience, and so on, in favour of dead formulas that aim at domination over life. At the same time, however, the philosopher uses theorizing against 'sound common sense', in order to gain power himself over the crowd, to rob them of the conviction of the justification of their trivial knowledge, their 'sound common sense', and appear to them as saviour both from their own ignorance and from the pseudo-enlightening machinations of his colleagues. This whole policy of manipulation, however, depends very much on how far the philosopher is in a position, in any particular concrete case, 'to speak apocalyptically': with awareness of the unity of fate (his own and other people's) in the general event of finitude.

Undoubtedly, Derrida performs precisely this fundamental step by drawing the attention of competing theories in the human sciences to their common foundation in the single – if not palpable and generally describable – 'archive'. But by this artifice, he gives intellectuals the opportunity, as it were, to become conscious of themselves as a class. Poststructuralism, or more broadly postmodernism, is the doctrine of the class rule of the intellectuals, the ideology of broad layers of the intellectual elite. This is absolutely indifferent towards all those who 'do not reach the museum', do not enter history, are not taken onto the library's calendar of saints. For these others, it does not even recognize an apocalypse: since they have not lived in the immortality of the archive, they cannot even die. But does this not mean that precisely these others, who already dwell in apocalyptic time, would be in a better position to speak about this than the poststructuralists who are constantly mourning themselves?

POSTSCRIPT, EIGHT YEARS LATER

This text on Derrida's apocalyptic writings was written in 1986, and published the following year in the little Russian émigré periodical *Beseda*, which appeared irregularly in Paris in the 1980s. The political context of this time, which influenced both the tone of Derrida's texts and my own reaction to them, is now part of history. The underlying themes of the archive and the apocalypse, however, have continued to loom large in Derrida's work.

In his book *Spectres of Marx* (1993), Derrida insists on the necessity of defending the apocalyptic perspective of Marxism against any attempt to proclaim the present state of the world as the end of history. Derrida continues to see this apocalyptic perspective as a collective one: only the apocalyptic generates the 'we', by disclosing to 'us all' the possibility of the unforeseen, the event-full, the absolute Other. We are divided by our self-evidence, and united by our fears and hopes. Literature, for Derrida, always still refers to something that promises it a referent – beyond the paper on which it is written. This referent remains always unreachable; literature always proves to be only writing on paper, which blocks the way for it to reach the presence of the referent. This paper, however, must not become a final self-evidence: the promise of the referent must remain, like the carrot held before the donkey, so that the donkey keeps moving and the writer keeps writing, so that communication, the collective, the social, continue to function, despite the fact that only the paper creates the apocalyptic illusion that something 'Other' lies concealed below its surface.

And if the paper burns? In his book *Archive Fever* (*Mal d'Archive*, 1995), Derrida again tackles the question whether a radical, physical destruction of the archive can still be inscribed in this archive, as the texts that I discussed above assume. At the end of the book, Derrida reaches the conclusion that parts of the archive can be irrevocably destroyed, can be forever lost. This possibility of pure material loss is already familiar to us from Derrida's criticism of Lacan: it is a possibility that makes complete psychoanalysis impossible.

The private, therefore, may burn in the archive. But the archive as a whole? The collective in the archive?

There is still the original ambivalence. If the archive is completely material, if it is no more than a pile of paper, then the whole archive can also burn. It is just that this total destruction of the archive does not reveal any refer-ent that remains behind the paper. Such a referent (including a referent of the Nothing) is only an illusion, only an effect created by the archive itself. A partial destruction within the archive is then possible, but a

total destruction of the archive remains just as inconceivable as it did before.

But if on the other hand a total, collective, apocalyptic destruction of the whole archive cannot be conceived,
all that then remains is the paper – and this paper itself
becomes the end of history. The paper, however, is
always only paper, and it is divisible to the nth degree:
the archive breaks up into individual texts. And if each
piece of paper can burn, then all paper can also burn.
Poststructuralism's infinite space of signs disappears.

Derrida is caught in the contradiction between two
underlying assumptions of his thought: the materiality
of signs and the infinity of the play of signs, of *différance*,
of deconstruction. No paper is infinite in space and time.
The material, moreover, has always a certain inertia, a
certain durability. As soon as we have written a bit of
text on paper, we have withdrawn something from the
play of signs – even before any possible destruction.
When the whole text is written down on paper, everything then is quiet and becomes the passive object of
external manipulation. Only consciousness continues to
move and cannot be materially divided. The appropriate
medium for the Derridean archive could only be the infinite memory of God (which however does not include
forgetting). Paper is clearly not enough.

5

WALTER BENJAMIN

The relationship of the intellectual to politics is generally described in terms of commitment. The impression is thus given that the intellectual is relatively free in such a choice: he may commit himself, or he may not. But there are conflicts that the intellectual cannot escape, that force him into politics whether he wants this or not. One such conflict is that between religion and philosophy. In the context of European culture, this conflict is unavoidable for all intellectuals. In one way or another, every intellectual is forced to take up a position, which means either confessing themselves on one or the other side, or else reconciling the two sides, declaring the conflict itself to be illusory, transcending it, deconstructing it, and so on. All these various strategic positions are political in nature – and draw in their wake other political positions in relation to other fields of conflict. For the conflict between religion and philosophy can easily be interpreted, in the context of the European cultural tradition, as a conflict between Jerusalem and Athens – the two generally recognized sources of this tradition, despite their being extremely heterogeneous. And from this conflict it is a short step to other, still more stubborn conflicts in the field of politics 'proper'. In what follows, however, I shall confine myself to commenting on the politics of Walter Benjamin in relation to the conflict between religion and philosophy, and leave other conflicts in the background.

In place of the word 'religion', 'theology' is often used, so as to define more precisely the theological discourse that stands in a relationship of competition with philosophy. But how are philosophy and theology to be distinguished from one another? I am well aware that it is hard if not impossible to pin down such a distinction, since it touches on central questions of both philosophy and theology that are anything other than resolved, and cannot even be briefly discussed here. Despite this, however, I would like to risk this attempt, with the particular aim of formulating a hypothesis on the sense in which particular (or even most) texts by Benjamin, such as his 'Theological–Philosophical Fragment', can actually be understood as theological rather than philosophical.

Theology, as we know, is just as concerned as philosophy is with the question of truth – and indeed with the truth of the 'whole', however this is understood. The relationship of each to truth, however, is completely different. Philosophy is by definition the love of truth, which presupposes the actual absence of truth, of wisdom, of *sophia*. Philosophy strives for truth, but it does not possess it – and even cannot possess it. Philosophy always expects truth to lie in the future. From its point of view, the only truth that can be valid as truth is a radically new, future, unknown, unthought-of and perhaps even inconceivable one. The philosophical project is an open, endless project, resisting its own complete fulfilment. Philosophy lives from the impossibility of ever satisfying its yearning for truth – the impossibility of a definitive union with *sophia*. If this union were to ever come about, it would be catastrophic for philosophy, it would mean the end of philosophy. Philosophy is only possible if *sophia* never abandons her game of seduction, never surrenders to the philosopher. And since philosophy in this sense is pure desire, it is also pure activity, labour. Philosophy performs an uninterrupted labour – the labour of knowledge, of criticism, even of deconstruction. This labour is also a kind of production – namely, the production of ever new philosophical discourses, writings, systems, methods, attitudes and modes of thought.

Theology, in contrast, presupposes that the truth has always already shown itself, that union with the truth has always already taken place, that the truth is always already revealed and proclaimed. This certainly does not mean that theology imagines itself in full possession of the truth, since the proclaimed truth is constantly threatened by oblivion. The advance of time leads theologians ever further away from the truth. And so the work of theologians is not a work of production, but rather a work of reproduction. A work of remembering, of care to remember the first time – the moment when truth first showed itself to man, first spoke to him and took pity on him. And the more the theologian is concerned with the work of remembering, the more clearly he notices that he is powerless against the force of forgetting, that all reproduction only further destroys the original, that all work of remembering simply furthers forgetting. The reason for this is easy to understand: even the project of producing as exact as possible a reproduction, or recalling the original event yet more exactly, still remains a project – in other words it is infected by philosophy, by the future, by progress. And everything that is infected by progress leads one still further away from the truth that was shown, proclaimed and experienced in the past.

It is incontestable, however, that Benjamin was above all a thinker of remembrance and reproduction – and for this very reason a theologian. He avoids in a most striking fashion presenting his own discourse as a new and previously unknown philosophical teaching about truth, showing how distinct it is from other previous discourses, and why his own discourse is better, more insightful and more convincing than all others. In short: he avoids demonstrations that his discourse is closer to truth than all earlier discourses – demonstrations that are customarily seen as indispensable for a philosophical text. But Benjamin is concerned not with the production of truth, but rather with its reproduction. And the reliability of reproduction is guaranteed not by philosophical innovations, new turns and breakthroughs, but rather by regulations, decrees, restrictions and prohibitions, whose aim is to exclude a possible departure of the reproduction from the original. Instead of formulating proofs, Benjamin precisely formulates such regulations and decrees. In his 'Theological–Political Fragment', for example, he writes: 'The order of the profane should be erected on the idea of happiness.' This sounds like a command. And it indeed is a command – a command to the profane to take this place and not that one in the topography of the whole. And again: 'For nature is Messianic by reason of its eternal and total passing away. To strive after such passing, even for those stages of man that are nature, is the task of world politics, whose method must be called nihilism.' This again is an attempt to draw a topography of human existence, separating the earthly from the messianic, establishing the relationship between the profane and the idea of the divine kingdom, and so on.

Benjamin's discourse is simultaneously theological and topological. In other words, his discourse does not formulate a new truth of the whole, but rather defines places, *topoi*, at which these or those always already existing discourses and practices have to establish themselves. Philosophy is topologically undetermined – it waits for truth and does not exactly know when, where and from what direction truth will appear. Theology, on the other hand, is topologically determined – since it always already knows at what place and time truth has appeared. This is the reason why theology connects remembering the truth with a care for particular places and a commemoration of particular times. And above all, every theology that seeks to express the truth of a particular religion, to formulate and codify that truth, seeks equally to distance itself both from the profane and from places where false truths, untruths, are proclaimed and nurtured. The theologizing of truth therefore means its topologizing, its determination in place – whether in a temple, in the church, in the university or in a political party. The reproduction of truth must not lead to its abandoning its place and muddling the topology of the world – a truth without place or home, equally spread everywhere, is not truth anymore. This kind of topologically undetermined reproduction of truth, according to Benjamin, definitively loses its aura – its particular connection to truth. If a theologically established topology has experienced such a decline, despite all indications and attributions, the recollection of truth seems to be definitively lost.

This means the definitive demise of theology, and the victory of philosophy. Truth becomes topologically undetermined – all one can do then is wait for it, as it can come from any direction and at any time. Truth thereby migrates from the past into the future. This leads to the belief in progress, creativity, and a utopia here on earth. This migration of truth from past to future can actually be seen as progress in itself, even as decisive progress.

Whether one welcomes this migration and diaspora of truth and adheres to it, however, is a purely political decision. It is always tempting to join the winning side – in this case, philosophy. But the desire to join the winning side is equally evidence of bad taste: the true 'gentleman' only takes up the lost cause. Benjamin, accordingly, who undoubtedly saw himself as an aristocrat of the spirit, opted not for philosophy but for theology. This political decision did not mean that he took up a defensive or 'reactionary' attitude towards philosophy and the whole secularized culture of modernity that philosophy influenced. His strategy was rather an offensive one. He described the entire modern world as a place not of production but of reproduction, and hence not of waiting for truth but of loss of truth, since to reproduce truth meant losing it.

In order to make this description plausible, Benjamin ascribed the market – and the mass commodity culture borne by the market, which he understood as a culture of reproduction – a central importance in the diagnosis of modernity. By describing mass culture that operates not with the original but with the copy as the true culture of modernity, he was able, without directly expressing this, to see advanced science and avant-garde art, based on evidence, creativity, production, innovation – in other words, on the values of philosophy – as purely and simply irrelevant. Benjamin's diagnosis of modernity therefore presents a radically different aspect from the standard diagnosis. The latter maintains that in the modern age theology has been replaced by philosophy, orientation to the past by orientation to the future, tradition by objective evidence, fidelity to origin by innovation, and so on. Benjamin, on the other hand, does not describe modernity as the age of the decline of theology, but rather as the age of its expansion into the profane sphere, its democratization, its massification, its diaspora. Previously, ritual, repetition and reproduction were a matter for religion, practised in isolated, sacred places. In the modern age, ritual, repetition and reproduction have become the fate of the whole world, the whole culture. Everything is now reproduced and expanded – capital, commodities, art. Progress itself is specifically reproductive; it consists in the constantly repeated destruction of the old. Benjamin understands modernity as the epoch of total reproduction of culture, and hence of its total theologizing. His political strategy, in the conflict between theology and philosophy, consists in linking theology with mass culture in opposition to philosophy. Against an alliance of this kind, philosophy and the avant-garde culture that it bears can certainly not hold out – philosophy retreats into complete invisibility in the face of this alliance.

The contention that mass culture is a culture of reproduction is particularly well known from Benjamin's text on the work of art in the age of its technical reproducibility. But already in a text written much earlier, on 'Capitalism as Religion' (1921), Benjamin describes capitalism as a whole as a cult, a rite, which is ceaselessly celebrated – an eternal Sunday not followed by any working day. This description seems at first sight counterintuitive, since capitalism is generally described as a machine of labour and production. But, for Benjamin, the essence of capitalism is a reproductive practice – the practice of the constant reproduction of debt, which functions like the religious ritual that constantly reproduces our indebtedness to God. In both cases, what is involved is a permanent reproduction that is not interrupted, and cannot be interrupted, by any working day – in other words, by any production, any innovation, any new truth: by any redemption of the old debt. Capitalism is thus presented here as a reproductive cult practice, which the whole profane world and the whole of human everyday life has entered into. Against this reproductive practice of capitalism, a productive, philosophical work is powerless. And since capitalism is ever-present and can no longer be located in a church or a temple, the advent of capitalism signals the definitive end of philosophy – the end of waiting for an 'original' appearance of truth. Capitalism, moreover, is a cult without dogma or theology – a cult beyond verbal legitimization. Capitalism does not need any additional discursive legitimization, since it makes the whole of the world, including the whole of speech, the temple of its cult; but for this very reason, capitalism cannot be criticized or refuted by discursive means.

Traditional power – as well as communist or, if you like, socialist power – is founded on an ideological discourse, a historical narrative. Both the individual and power are constantly compelled to justify themselves ideologically. Language thus functions both as the medium of the state's self-assertion and repression, and also as the medium of opposition. All social conflicts have to be waged, ultimately, by means of language. Against the official theology of power, the philosophical discourse of opposition arises. The struggle against power's claim to absolute truth is waged for the right of a democratic public opinion based on free discussion to question this discourse, and accordingly also any decision and any judgement that power makes. This struggle has been to a large degree successful. Society has emancipated itself from the theology of power. But, at the same time, this means emancipation from any discourse whatsoever. Ours has become a post-discursive society. Capitalism is, as Benjamin rightly says, a cult without theology. Capitalism is a silent work of repetition and reproduction. What corresponds to capitalism, accordingly, is a theology beyond theology – a thinking of reproduction that only considers the form of reproduction, but no longer asks what is actually being reproduced. The theology of capitalism and mass culture that Benjamin develops is such a theology beyond theology – a theology of reproduction beyond any question as to the original. For this reason, it evidently constitutes the highest form of theology, immune from further philosophical criticism.

Benjamin's discourse thus presupposes the end of philosophy, insofar as he describes a culture of total reproduction in which philosophy no longer has a place. In this respect, to be sure, he is in no way alone in the context of his time. We need only indicate another author who, if in a quite different form, similarly interpreted modernity as a transition to total reproduction – namely Alexandre Kojève. In his well-known seminar on Hegel, held at the École des Hautes Études in Paris between 1933 and 1939, Kojève explained Hegel's *Phenomenology of Spirit* as a book that made it impossible to wait any longer for truth, and hence also for any further philosophizing. The only possibility of speaking or writing about truth, according to Kojève, was to repeat and reproduce the *Phenomenology*. All that was really needed was to keep on reprinting this book – without even reading it or commenting on it. The philosopher's love of truth, in other words, remains only so far unfulfilled, and drives the progress of philosophizing forward until truth, wisdom, *sophia*, repay the philosopher with love and recognition. Precisely this is what occurs at the end of Hegel's *Phenomenology*, since the advent of the Absolute Spirit signals the complete recognition of each individual by the 'whole'. Once this all-embracing recognition has taken place, however, man is then without desire – and hence also without spirit. Spirit abandons man and becomes a book, a thing. Man thus becomes the bearer of truth's reproduction instead of its production. Kojève himself, as is well known, likewise abandoned any claim to develop a new and original discourse of his own, and instead of this constantly maintained that he was only repeating Hegel's discourse without seeking in any way to develop it further. Kojève hence positioned himself as the Duchamp of philosophy: he treated the *Phenomenology of Spirit* as a readymade, and saw his own role as author simply consisting in exhibiting this readymade in a new place – namely the Paris of his time.

The phenomenon of reproduction, for Kojève, was likewise central. He asks himself, in fact, why one should begin a new philosophical discourse when it was enough to reproduce a book that already existed and give it to a new public to read, or to deliver lectures on it. In the age of traditional religions, the practice of repetition and reproduction was confined to sacral places, while the profane, for its part, was left to the undetermined flow of time. Philosophy in these circumstances functioned as the expression of the hope for a profane self-evidence, for the appearance of truth in the profane sphere – and hence also for recognition and eventual immortality beyond the sacral places of institutionally guaranteed reproduction. But the situation is fundamentally changed when the processes of reproduction embrace the whole profane sphere. What is now involved is a social, political and technical guarantee of recognition, duration and even immortality, which – at least potentially – should be valid for each and all. In this way, any philosophy that still insists on the distinction between true and false is made superfluous. Under the conditions of mass culture, texts and images are distributed and reproduced independently of whether or not they are true, whether or not they 'serve' immortality by their reproduction. Nowadays, anyone can buy a camera, a sound or video recorder, a computer – and eternalize themselves by technical reproduction. A democratized and technicized theology that prevails over the profane sphere thus proves to be a far more democratic force in comparison with philosophy, whose distinction between true and false increasingly appears elitist and obsolete.

The total occupation of the profane space by the techniques of reproduction allows philosophy, which needs a free profane space for its rise and development, no chance at all of constituting itself. If everything is reproducible, then philosophy as waiting for an individual event of self-evidence becomes impossible, and above all unnecessary. It goes without saying that the 'original truth' or original aura is damaged and falsified by these profane techniques of reproduction, which do not heed the topology of the sacral, and which transport the copies of the sacral original into the profanity of the diaspora. This damage is what Benjamin famously describes as the destruction of the aura. But if reproduction becomes total, the demand for the original aura loses any meaning. It appears that the total victory of reproduction over production means at the same time the final victory of theology – understood as theology beyond theology – over philosophy. And yet for all that, the situation remains undetermined.

A compelling question, indeed, threatens to put this victory in question. To what extent is a copy really a copy, rather than something quite different? And indeed, if, as Benjamin writes in his essay on the work of art, even exact material identity between original and copy does not guarantee a genuine identity between the two, and cannot do so because the original possesses an aura that the copy lacks, it would then seem that we are basically not justified to describe a 'copy' under the conditions of its profane, diasporic distribution as a copy at all. If a work of art is maintained in a place secured by theological topology, with the sacredness of an aura – like an icon in the church or a masterpiece of painting in the museum – the identity of this work of art is still always guaranteed by reproduction. A work of art is reproduced by its restoration; and without this restoration, such a work cannot be preserved in the long run. The appearance, the condition and the continued material existence of a restored work of art are always clearly distinct from those before the restoration. A reproduction of this kind at the aura-hallowed place, however, does not change the status of the original, since it does not threaten the theologically secured topology, which is what in the last analysis secures the originality of the original. The situation is quite different in the case of an uncontrollable, topologically undetermined, diasporic distribution of the work in the profane sphere. Even if the material continuity and the complete similarity with the original are guarantees, the change of place means a profaning of the original, a loss of aura – and so also a break with the original.

There is thus not just one process of reproduction, but rather two distinct processes – one topologically determined and guaranteeing the continuity of the original in time, the other topologically undetermined, diasporic, profane, which does not guarantee this continuity. To what extent are we then justified in saying that the second reproduction is still a reproduction, and not, as it were, a kind of production? If a copy is located in a different place from the original, and in a different context, then this state of affairs may well be sufficient to say that this copy is different from its original; and still more, that the copy may thus be so significantly different from the original that we are in no way justified to speak of this copy as a copy, but should see this as another original. This consideration, moreover, has been used in a very pragmatic fashion by art ever since Duchamp, particularly by the protagonists of pop art and appropriation art, in order to establish their works, which are 'original' copies, as originals, by giving them a new position in the museum context. The diasporic copy is thus not a copy with a secured status. The situation seems rather to be that in the profane, diasporic space we are involved in an endless play of differences, which at least at first sight deconstructs the opposition between original and copy by offering the opportunity of producing originals by way of copying. The very word 'copy', just like the word 'reproduction', presupposes an identity between an original and its copy – or at least an identity between two different copies (for example, between two different copies of the same film, which in practice can never be the same). But every copy can also be seen as a different and new original. The discourse of difference offers philosophy a new opportunity, by fundamentally putting in question the process of total reproduction, of repetition. As soon as reproduction becomes diasporic, it can be given new meaning as the production of differences.

The discourse of difference frequently presents itself as a revolutionary discourse, since it deconstructs the language of identity ostensibly spoken by the scientific knowledge that is hegemonic today. In practice, the empirical, positive sciences have long found themselves on the side of difference. In a purely scientific and positivist perspective, individual phenomena always present themselves as empirically distinguishable – their arrangement under general concepts and regularities is seen in this respect as an unavoidable evil that cannot be overcome. And non-empirical differences do not exist. Even the supposedly non-empirical difference between the presence and absence of the aura can be described, as argued above, as an empirical distinction between topologically determined and undetermined kinds of reproduction. A difference can always be demonstrated empirically. Identity, on the other hand, has to be acknowledged, since it always remains contentious.

Whether a diasporic copy is described as a copy or as an original is thus not a question of knowledge, but rather of acknowledgement – a question of political, or rather theological–political, decision. We can expect from the diasporic copy or at least hope from it, that it is different, that it departs from the original, that it shows the face of the Other, the new, the unexpected. This means that we can, if we are so minded, also preserve the philosophical attitude in conditions of total reproduction – and wait for evidence of the new, unthought-of Other. This attitude is empirically supported by the fact that a perfect copy is an impossibility, so that the possibility always exists of re-signifying the process of reproduction as a process of production. Benjamin, however, does not posit this departure from the original, but rather its faithful reproduction. For him, the diaspora in the profane world is not the place of new hope, but rather a place at which the old hope is dashed. And it is so precisely on account of the fidelity of reproduction, since fidelity in the profane sphere leads to loss of aura, loss of the sacral topology. A total reproduction, which encompasses the whole world, can only be guaranteed as a genuine reproduction from an external – messianic – source, and only in this way can it manifest itself as pure power from the beyond that equalizes everything and abolishes all differences. Even waiting on the unexpected is no help here. The Other of the diasporic copy does not present itself to the viewer here as the face of the radically Other. It instead manifests itself as a slap in the face.

6

THEODOR LESSING

The basis and foundation stone of European ethics is the famous commandment: 'Love thy neighbour as thyself.' It is often assumed in this connection that a person loves himself already without any need of instruction. Aristotle, however, in his *Nicomachean Ethics*, pointed out that only the virtuous man can love himself; and the virtuous man is someone who follows the law of his people, who is moderate and just, as custom dictates. Self-love, for Aristotle, cannot be separated from a happy life among one's own people, from the love and respect that a man experiences in his original surroundings. For a pagan such as Aristotle, it was impossible to imagine that a man who had been exiled, and lived as a pariah among other peoples, could be filled with love for himself and others, and at the same time be happy.

The Jew is undoubtedly a pariah among the nations, but this means that the Jew cannot love himself. And it also means that the Jew is dangerous, for 'loving your neighbour as yourself', the basis and foundation stone of ethics, is denied him. In the best of cases, the Jew remains indifferent to this appeal. It is not ruled out,

however, that he does follow it and begins to hate
other people as he hates himself. This is the traditional
logic of anti-Semitism. In order to become happy and
virtuous, as well as harmless to the people around him,
the Jew, by this logic, has to 'become like everyone
else'. This is also what Lessing calls for in his book:[1]
the Jews should abandon their role of being excluded
from this world, and finally all live together according
to their old Jewish traditions.

First of all, however, it is not possible to accept this
appeal to be practical and reasonable. Indeed, the
emancipated European Jewry of modern times neither
managed nor sought to do what anti-Semites traditionally blamed them for – namely, to use their newly won
social influence to ensure their own well-being, or at
least their security. The total atomization and ineffec-
tiveness of Jews as a social group became fully apparent
in the context of the Second World War, when the
scattered European Jewry that rejected any kind of
inner connection was newly united by an external
hostile power – one that aimed to annihilate them.
Paradoxically, consciousness of the unity and historical mission of the Jews was stronger at this time among
the anti-Semites that among the Jews themselves, who,
represented by their enlightened intellectual elite, had
eagerly abandoned their mission in favour of 'humanity' and 'progress', and appealed all the more eagerly to
other peoples, the easier this abandonment was for
them. These other peoples often saw this message as a
cunning ruse, with which the Jews – the 'most universally human' people, since without a state of their own
– sought to gain a superior position for themselves. Yet

---

1. Translator's note: The reference here is to Theodor Lessing's
classic essay, *Jüdischer Selbsthass* ('Jewish Self-Hatred'), published in
1930. Lessing was born in Hanover in 1872, and assassinated by the
Nazis after he moved to Czechoslovakia in 1933.

this was not the case; there was no ruse involved. It would have been helpful if there had been some kind of plan like this. First of all, though the Jews with their small number and fragmentation could not have gained world supremacy, at least a few human lives might have been saved. And secondly, any idea that is transformed into practice with hypocrisy and irony is incomparably more stimulating than an idea behind which lies only bland overvaluation of oneself.

Lessing clearly recognized the threatening danger. He rightly raged against the foolishly honest, naively self-satisfied position of the Jewish intellectuals of his time: people who were not in a position to love or stand up for themselves setting themselves up to speak in the name of humanity as a whole, and forgetting that the rest of humanity was in a far better position than they were to stand up for itself, and in tricky situations would be the last to stand up for them. Lessing accordingly sought to remind educated Jews to heed their own destiny as outsiders among the peoples of Europe – a situation to which they liked to shut their eyes.

As the alternative to dissolving into Christian Europe, a development that threatened the Jews with self-estrangement and was pointless into the bargain, since the European peoples, in Lessing's view, remained as unwilling as before to accept the Jews in their midst – as an alternative, therefore, Lessing proposed that the Jews should return to a life in the bosom of their own people, a life like that of all other peoples. Yet this project, which at first sight seemed so natural, soon revealed its contradictions; the attempts to overcome these are what give Lessing's text its emotional pathos. He saw the greatest obstacle to a national life for the Jews in their striving for universality: the Jews were not prepared to accept traditions and ideals if they did not see these as generally and universally valid. The quest for this universality, accordingly, could even lead the Jews to turn away from themselves, from their people and their traditions, if they concluded that their own historical legacy was an obstacle to their attaining the universality they sought. In his philosophical views, Lessing was above all a disciple of Nietzsche: the universal, for him, was embodied in science and rational morality, which formed as a whole the sphere of 'spirit'. Following Nietzsche, Lessing accordingly saw this 'spirit' as his main adversary. Neither science nor morality could bring people happiness and inner peace: they were lifeless abstractions that could even be damaging and life-destroying if they took away from people their native earth. Lessing therefore demanded that Jewish intellectuals should give up their one-sided fidelity to 'spirit' and return to earth, to the original traditions of the Jewish people.

The paradox in this demand is clearly apparent, if we recall how for both Nietzsche and his successors in the European philosophy of this time – including Klages, the friend of Lessing's youth, whose philosophical views Lessing shared to the end of his life – the Jewish people were precisely the bearer of this 'spirit' hostile to life, the 'priestly people' par excellence. It was precisely Judaism, which counterposed to the world a transcendent God who 'blamed' the world, that the Nietzschean tradition saw as the origin of all spiritual tendencies in Europe that were hostile to life, and to Christianity in particular. Lessing's call to return to authentic Jewish traditions thus served rather as an indication that Jewish self-hatred had deeper roots than simply as an inner reaction to centuries of persecution – this self-hatred was based in the Jewish religion, according to which a Jew is always guilty towards God by dint of his earthly life. Self-hatred is therefore the Jewish lot right from the start, from which there is no escape.

Lessing was fully aware of this difficulty, which is

why he chose the only possible way out within his own logic: he distinguished between the Jewish popular and cultural tradition, and Judaism as a religion. He actually maintained that the popular religious tradition of Judaism was essentially pagan, as proof of which he particularly cited those passages from the Old Testament where the idolatry of many Jews was condemned, but he also detected pagan themes in Jewish popular customs. Lessing pointed to the Asiatic origin of the Jews, and to how they were foreign to Christian Europe, and thereby broke with those theories that pointed to the Asiatic origin of the Aryans. In another text, Lessing described Christianity in no uncertain terms as the common enemy of Jews and Aryans alike.

In Lessing's opinion, the supremacy of 'spirit' over life is thus exclusively the work of Christianity, for which Judaism is not to blame, and this in turn allows Lessing to make Nietzsche, Aryan anti-Christianity and even anti-Semitism (in the sense of 'anti-Judaism', but this is of course only a play on words, rather like modern 'anti-Zionism') his ideological allies and even instructors.

Lessing's readers are consequently faced with an extraordinarily interesting and important intellectual problem, which thanks to Lessing's theoretical honesty and dialectical skill receives a sharp profile: the call for the Jews to separate themselves off and return to their own tradition also leads to a call to break radically both with what was always seen by the Jews themselves and by the whole world as well as the most particular legacy of the Jewish tradition – its consistent monotheism, its belief in a transcendent God. The Zionism to which Lessing appealed was and remains a religiously neutral movement. From the very start, Zionism stood in a certain opposition to Judaism, which held that Israel could only be restored by the Messiah at the end of time. Zionism, however, saw itself in the final analysis as a purely secular movement, even if it did not stand in a principled opposition to the Jewish religion. Lessing's text raises the question of the religious, metaphysical dimension of Zionism and its mystical assumptions. And in reconstructing these assumptions, Lessing reaches a radical negation of what had served for millennia as the definition and preservation of Jewish identity.

It should be noted here that the thesis with which Lessing's essay commences – that self-love is dependent on connection to one's own people, one's own soil and nature – already involves a certain departure from the Judaic world outlook. Just like the believing Christian, the believing Jew generates love for himself from God's love for man. This love of God's is not dependent on anything external, such as people, tradition and native soil. Lessing already conceives of the 'spirit' in the way of a religiously emancipated man, for whom only science and morality are universal principles, and love is certainly not something that can be expected from them. For the believer, however, God is not only the accuser, but also the loving protector and helper. One may of course object that this Judeo-Christian conception of God and divine love is itself already a result of Jewish dispersion, and a compensation for the lack of ordinary human love. First of all, though, this objection already recognizes that self-hatred is not an inseparable aspect of the fate of the Jewish people, but was successfully overcome in the Jewish religion, while, secondly, it overestimates the specificity of the Jewish situation. Not to mention the fact that poverty and expulsion are no absolute privilege of the Jews; the universality of the transcendent God represents above all a response to the universality of death.

In arguments against both Jewish and Christian religions the criticism is frequently made that human life is spoiled by reference to death. This accusation was made with particular persistence by Nietzsche and his followers.

To put it mildly, however, this is a remarkable accusation. Neither the Jewish nor the Christian religion was ever needed to put the fear of death into people; on the contrary, both religions seek to free men from this fear, by promising them the resurrection of the dead and an eternal life. Judaism connects man to a God who stands outside and above the world – the experience of this tie helps to overcome the fear of death, which would be inescapable if man, as is the case with the pagans, saw himself only as part of the world. In this respect it is extremely interesting that Lessing defined authentic religious feeling in quite the contrary manner: as the experience of being one with the world, a definition one might even call anti-Judaic.

In the twentieth century, life was often proclaimed the highest value, and the experience of life, the 'cosmic feeling', praised as the highest experience accessible to man. But everything in the world is condemned to death, and so the experience of life – something that was indeed recognized by the 'philosophers of life', if they aimed to be genuinely consistent and honest – is in its limitation an experience of death, and individual life only appears in man as a process of self-destruction, since his human ego crumbles along with the entire world of phenomena. Life as the highest value is achieved only in death, with its 'eternal recurrence'; any philosophy of life based on self-preservation, such as the 'ecological pacifism' of today, is a naive banality. Only if it is oriented towards death can philosophy of life justify itself; it is really comical that Judaism should be chided by such a philosophy for being hostile to the world and to life.

It goes without saying that philosophy of life is perfectly right if it opposes its being-unto-death to the dreams of a 'perpetual peace' nurtured by science, morality, social reformism – in short, everything that Lessing described with the word 'spirit', which actually represents for him no more than an assortment of well-meaning fatuities. If man is condemned to die, does it matter at all whether he dies under capitalism or socialism, in war or in his own bed, cultured or uncultured? Such 'transcendent values', which are indifferent to the life and death of man, only deserve that men in turn are likewise indifferent towards them. And insofar as Lessing's 'spirit' is nothing else than 'the true' and 'the good', we can entirely welcome its disarming. The question is quite different, however, when Lessing identifies this impotent 'spirit' with Judaism and Christianity – neither of which religions recognize the supremacy of death.

The objection can of course be made at this point that belief in immortality and resurrection is absurd, unworthy of an 'elevated' understanding, that man actually does form part of the world, and that the pagans had the courage to admit this and live with this consciousness, whereas Judaism and Christianity, being 'slave religions', consoled themselves with fairy stories. This assessment – the central argument when the supposed superiority of the Aryan and Graeco-Roman spirit over the Judeo-Christian is asserted – suffers however from an important shortfall: it conceives the doctrine of the unity of the world, and of man as a part of this unity, as something that goes without saying. Nietzsche in his day raised the question of the genealogy of morals, and reached the conclusion that, in life deprived of its rights, morality had erupted; impotent to restore its rights, life had turned against itself. Following Nietzsche, one could pose the question of the genealogy of 'world' and 'life': Where do these really come from? In the context of the present chapter, only a very summary answer can be given to this question, but this is still important if we are to grasp the core of the dilemma with which Lessing was faced.

Lessing was inclined, following Klages, to ascribe the 'cosmic experience' of the unity of the world, and the unity of man and the world, to pagan religion. Yet such an experience was in fact totally foreign to the pagan world. The essence of the pagan religions consisted precisely in the fact that the sacral space and the profane space were kept strictly separate and did not form any kind of unity. The religious experience of the pagans, therefore, could in no way refer to 'the world as a whole'. Mathematics and rational morality did indeed receive their importance precisely in a pagan tradition – the Socratic one – since it was assumed that they described the sacral realms of the world (the life of the stars), and therefore that the man who mastered them achieved immortality. The idea that practising mathematics, and science in general, is irrelevant for victory over death, was thus in no way a discovery of the pagan world, but rather of Judaism. Jewish and Christian religion accomplished this de-sacralizing of the sacred and its equation with the profane sphere, which led to the contemporary idea of the unity of the world and its life, along with the celebrated 'cosmic feeling'. This feeling does not in any way correspond to an original experience of reality. Quite the contrary, it represents an emotional correlate to the abstract idea of the unity of the world – in other words, to an ideological fiction that has a particular developmental history. The idea of the unity of the world, and the inclusion of man in this unity, is generally used to demonstrate the fictitious character of immortality. But if this idea turns out to be itself a fiction, the question of immortality then at least remains open. And anyone who seeks to resolve it is at all events not justified in basing himself on any kind of indubitable facts.

But if the idea of the unity of the world and life stems from the world of Judaism, it seems all the more significant that it is precisely Judaism, in Lessing's opinion, that dispenses with the 'cosmic feeling'. This example can be seen as paradigmatic for the relationship of a certain European philosophical school of thought to the Judeo-Christian tradition. Every time a generalized, universalized concept was achieved within this tradition, this tradition itself was immediately declared to be a deviation from this concept, and necessarily therefore received a negative characterization. If the unity of the world and the primacy of the 'cosmic feeling' were affirmed, it was only Judaism, out of all religions, that allegedly did without this. If the principle of the secular state was established, only Judaism was proclaimed to be its irreconcilable enemy. If social equality was raised to a principle, Judaism was declared to be the bearer of the spirit of capitalism. And so on. If particularism was generally recognized, Judaism, by dint of its striving for universality, also remained the only exception. Here we come to the final paradox that forms the cornerstone of Lessing's essay: if Jews seek to be 'like everyone else', they must separate from all others and become dissimilated – but in order to become dissimilated, they must first of all renounce precisely what makes for their originality.

This negative characterization of Judaism can be readily explained in purely logical terms. Any theory that makes a claim to universality is in a position to explain everything apart from how it itself arose, and consequently it must make its origin taboo. The question arises, however, of where this striving for a universality without presuppositions comes from. And here, different psychological presuppositions can be discovered in the case of Europeans and Jews. One such presupposition, for Europeans, would be their constant striving to identify with their own culture, and their inability to achieve this identification.

The ease with which European Jews in the age of Enlightenment turned their backs on their specific cultural tradition aroused general surprise at the time

among the Christian peoples, and to a certain extent
also contempt. Europeans saw in this turn, its radicalism and the feeling bordering on hatred that the
educated Jews of this time bore towards their past, a
confirmation of their very far-reaching anti-Semitic
prejudices. This reaction of Europe to the sudden
assimilation of the Jews, however, presupposed that a
series of truths had been concealed, in part deliberately, but now had become manifest. The most
important of these truths was that the Jews did not see
European culture as something foreign, and could not
do so. The holy scriptures of Christianity were also the
history of the Jewish people, its poetry, wisdom and
religious faith. Although Christian Europe had also
taken much from the Greeks, the Romans and other
peoples, the rupture in its consciousness caused by
accepting the Bible as its sacred book was insuperable.
The Jewish spiritual tradition became the foundation
of European culture; Europe had no other. It is not
surprising, therefore, that the Jews in the age of
Enlightenment entered into European culture as into
their own house, and sought to forget as quickly as
possible the time when admission to it was barred to
them. It could not have been otherwise. The surprise of
Europe, and especially the idea that things could have
been different, shows the extent of the confusion in
which Europe found itself at that time.

Europe was of course always aware, in the depths of
its soul, that it had received its culture second-hand, had
taken it over from another people. This is also the source
of the hysterical anti-Semitism of the Europeans, which
has little in common with that moderate irritation and
distrust which any people habitually feel towards
another. European anti-Semitism is a purely European
problem. It arises time and again from the depths of the
European soul, when this soul does not find in itself the

spiritual origin of the culture that it confesses and has to call its own, as it has no other culture.

This is also the origin of the perpetual discontent and disquiet that is so characteristic of Christian Europe. The Europeans are always nostalgic, and aggressive in their nostalgia, since they never possessed the homeland for which they yearn – this homeland belongs to another people, the Jews. If the culturally aware European turns his gaze deep within himself, he finds there an Other, the Jew. Aside from the Jew, all that exists in the soul of the European is pure Nothingness, the aggressive barrenness that is a legacy of the barren wastes of Asia, from which the Europeans came as out of Nothing, out of historical unawareness, to appropriate something foreign to them.

The spiritual history of Europe can be conceived as a constant and vain effort to expel the Jew from its soul, and finally place itself at the beginning of a culture of its own. The Jewish ghettos of medieval Europe were symbolic of this effort; the strict territorial separation of the Jews from the mass of the population created the illusion of an inner distance. Rummaging in the depths of Jewish history, European Christians perceived their own life as its unique historical continuation, and the isolated life of the Jews in the ghetto kept this comforting illusion in place. Such an illusion, however, was not sufficient to achieve inner peace as well, which is why the European knights erupted on exhausting Crusades, to take possession at least territorially of the origin of their own religion and culture in the land of the Jews, Israel. The military defeat of the Europeans only covered up their spiritual defeat – it very soon emerged that there was really nothing for the Europeans to look for in the Holy Land.

The failure of the Crusades led to the project of taking possession of the spiritual origin inwardly. Protestantism proclaimed that the Europeans stood at the origin of faith, outside of tradition and continuity, eye to eye with God. The messianism of the Protestant community was designed finally to drive out Jewish messianism – hence, too, the militant anti-Semitism of Luther. Many Protestant sects called themselves 'New Israel', children were given biblical names, and finally they set out for the promised land of America, so as finally to identify with the Jews in this definitive gesture of a breach with the Old World, and relive Jewish history anew. The whole enterprise, however, necessarily led to stylization – just like Kierkegaard's crazy project of an inner unity with Abraham, following the eternal call, of whose origin Kierkegaard, unlike Abraham, was only too well aware.

This intensive effort to stand at the start of their own history, by imitating either outwardly or inwardly the sacred history of the Jewish people, re-emerges time and again in European religion and culture. Just as frequently, we also encounter the attempt to break the connection with Jewish history. Already among the Gnostics, doctrines arose that interpreted the God of the Jews as the devil, who fought against Christ and from whose power Christ had freed the world. Many Gnostics did recognise the Jewish prophets not as precursors of Christianity, but rather as builders of the tower of Babel, the inhabitants of Sodom and Gomorrah, Cain and not Abel – in other words, all those who had opposed the Jewish God. As we know, the church condemned the Gnostic views as heretical in their time. The line of tradition from the Old to the New Testament forms the core of Christian doctrine, and simultaneously fixes the inner spiritual dependence of the European on the Jew – a painful dependence, on which many bitter and even injurious words are already said in the New Testament. We need only recall what Christ said to the woman of Canaan: 'I was sent to the lost sheep of the house of

Israel, and to them alone. It is not right to take the children's bread and throw it to the dogs' (Matthew 15: 24, 26), or the long discussions of the apostles about preaching to the pagans. There is no doubt that these words still echo in the European ear, even if Europeans act as if they do not notice them, or interpret them in such a way that they seem to lose their polemical, unambiguous meaning. Finally, the Christian finds these harsh words not in the Old Testament but in the New. It is from the mouth of Christ and the apostles that he takes this judgement about himself – and deep in his soul he is always aware that it is he who is being talked about, even though he generally acts as if this is not the case, as if 'the people of Israel' means the church – in other words, himself – and 'the others' actually means the Jews. It is only natural that the European from time to time considers finally getting rid of the Jews, and seeks other putative origins for his culture. We should note here that anti-Semitism, in all its varieties, always proves to be also a battle against the church, which maintains steadfastly and courageously that European spirituality derives from that of the Jews. The struggle against the Jews has necessarily always transformed itself in European history into a struggle against the church; and conversely, the struggle against the church has constantly led to anti-Semitism.

The European Renaissance was one such attempt finally to cast off the Jews and the church, but its very name already predicted its failure: the stylization of the Europeans as Romans or Greeks had still less chance of success than their Protestant stylization as biblical Jews. The philosophers of the European Renaissance and Enlightenment poured more than a little oil on the flames of anti-Semitism: they saw the main evil affecting Europe as the church, but they identified the church with the Jewish spirit. Yet the attempts to find a new

foundation in 'reason' – understood in the sense of
Antiquity – and to turn away from 'traditions' proved
unsuccessful. We should not forget that the legacy of
Antiquity was preserved in the monasteries. The new
European reason was not at all similar to the Greek; its
biblical origin very soon became apparent. So soon,
indeed, that already within a short time, science and
rational ethics were denounced as purely Jewish inventions, designed to cut Europe off from its traditions.
The sterility and universality of Enlightenment reason
only made the barrenness in the European soul stand
out the more strikingly. The Enlightenment laid particular stress on 'clear and explicit ideas', on the
self-evident, and it turned out, as was to be expected,
that the Europeans saw as clear, explicit and self-
evident what they had been taught to do so by their
European – in other words, Jewish – culture. It was
precisely this conclusion that pressed itself on the
Europeans at the end of the Enlightenment with the
greatest clarity and explicitness. Precisely when Europe,
intoxicated by its total break with the Judeo-Christian
tradition, felt itself strong enough for the first time to
tear down the ghetto walls and allow the Jews access to
social life, convinced that the Jews would no longer
have anything to seek there, it suddenly emerged that
the Jews were only waiting for this, and that the knowledge free of prejudice that the Europeans had
spontaneously taken over was precisely that Jewish
culture in which the Jews felt perfectly at home.

The awareness of this situation produced a real shock
in Europe. Finally, the European had taken an unpreju-
diced look into his soul, and again what he saw there
was the Jew. This shock released a new wave of anti-
Semitism, which put everything that had previously
happened in this respect into the shade. The sense that
the Jew was present in the most secret depths of the

European soul found a kind of outward counterpart in the territorial intangibility of the Jews, who had spread across all Europe after leaving the ghetto. The European now lost all confidence in himself and his own future, and in everything he had found convincing in the arguments of others. He was immediately plagued by the notion: Was it not the Jew who was leading him by the nose in these apparently convincing arguments? Was not the Jew seeking, in the context of a worldwide and intangible Jewish conspiracy, to turn his cultural superiority to advantage? As we know, this counter-reaction to Jewish–Enlightenment reason found strongest expression in German philosophy.

Tradition holds that the Germans consider themselves the most interesting people of Europe, and not without reason. If the Latin races of Europe have so far forgotten their non-European origin that they bear no memory of a different cultural legacy than the Roman, and hence can only oppose the alien Jewish–Christian culture with that of an Antiquity no less foreign to them, the Germans for their part have still preserved in their soul the memory of their distant pagan past, the memory of other images and myths. For this reason, the Germans feel themselves inwardly furthest removed from their 'official' culture, a situation that finds expression in inward insecurity and melancholy. The Germans still know that at one time they had something different, but no longer know what this actually was, no matter how much they strain their memory. The Germans still feel that Asiatic Nothingness within them, while the other Europeans have forgotten it once and for all. And German philosophy raises this Nothingness to the rank of a virtue: German Romanticism yearningly strove for vanished distances: without listening to the arguments of reason, it sought to flee, to hide itself from the Jew. It proclaimed – right through to Heidegger – that only the

'Nothingness' was creative, 'gathering' man and culture; since the entire sphere of the spoken word was occupied by the Jew, the place of the true word lay in silence. The Germans cut themselves off from culture, entering a 'cosmic unity' – no matter how this was conceived – to which, they believed, the Jew had no access.

But Lessing's essay served as a refutation of this thesis. Lessing drew a gallery of psychological portraits, whose subjects were all Jewish intellectuals whom the break with their people, as a result of the Enlightenment, had poisoned; they hated Jewishness and were hell-bent on identifying themselves with the Aryan world, albeit unsuccessfully. If possible, Lessing's Aryan-feeling Jews were still more Romantic and refinedly decadent, lived still more in Nothingness, than the Romantic Aryans – and for the attentive reader this was already a sign that not everything was right with the Aryan dream. Certainly Lessing made fun of his heroes, but his purpose was far more to console them. One possible consolation he saw, as we have already said, in the fact that, although they had adopted the Aryan notion of the superiority of 'soul' over 'spirit' (Klages), and that of people (*Volk*) and soil over cosmopolitanism and the abstract humanist ideas, they were no longer concerned with blending into the higher Aryan race, but rather with realizing the Aryan idea in the Jewish world, transforming the Jewish people into a variant of the Aryan. The fate of the Jews, in this light, once again turned out to be a universal human fate, since the Jews were far more removed from their roots than all others, and would yearn for them all the more. And so, even before the Aryans disappeared into Nothingness and blended with nature, the Jew had got there first. Lessing's essay may well itself be a more glaring example of Jewish self-hatred than anything he describes. In his rejection of a specifically Jewish cultural heritage, Lessing not only effected a break with Jewry, like the subjects of his book, he actually set out to destroy this heritage and rebuild the life of the Jewish people on a completely different foundation, ascribing to them once again a leading position in the world. It is completely understandable why European philosophy was constantly obsessed by the idea of seeking a new foundation – one could even say that this quest was the very essence of European philosophy, its definition and *raison d'être*. European philosophy expresses the need of the European soul to free itself from the Jew, from the Judeo-Christian tradition, which it has always perceived as foreign. It is equally natural that European philosophy was prepared to explain and justify everything – apart from the Jews: to justify them would have meant admitting that the attempt at explaining oneself on one's own basis was quite impossible, like pulling oneself up by one's own bootstraps – prepared to confess, therefore, that European philosophy was in fact simply a ritual of the same tradition that it only existed in order to negate. The question arises, therefore, as to why the Jews for their part were so ready to participate in this European philosophical tradition – why it was precisely the Jews who created the most radical doctrines in this respect: just think of Marx, Freud or Wittgenstein. There are also reasons for this, and ones that are rather different from the case of the Europeans.

The Jews suffer from what one might call a 'chosen people complex'. This complex also affected those European intellectuals who completely adopted the Judeo-Christian tradition. The Jews were chosen by God without the slightest merit on their part – Abraham was just an ordinary man in his town. What may be called the second choosing of the Jews, at the time of Moses, is still more characteristic; at this time the Jews were slaves, a despised breed in Egypt. And it was precisely to them, the outcast, that the Lord turned

– precisely because they were outcast, because they were
not good for anything. Throughout the Old Testament
it is repeatedly stressed that the Jews are not good for
anything, on account of not only their deficient practical
qualities, but also their moral ones, and that God did
not choose them because of what they represented, but
for quite the opposite reason. Thus, although the Jews
did not possess their chosen status, and did not receive
their religion and culture second-hand, as did the
Europeans, but rather first-hand, they still did not
possess that pride in themselves and self-certainty that
the Hellenes for example had – and how could they?
The Jews felt secure only as long as God did not abandon them; or as long as they themselves did not abandon
God. As soon as the Jews lost the feeling that a right that
was 'not of this world' stood on their side, they were
immediately overcome by the awareness of their
unhappy situation in the world and their own imperfec-
tion. The Pharisee can easily be criticized for feeling the
pride of a just man towards the tax-gatherer, but this
pride is the only refuge of the Pharisee; he has no other.
This is also why 'self-hatred' particularly affected the
European Jews of the modern age who had lost their
faith; in their own history there was nothing to be found,
once God had been eliminated, apart from misfortune
and self-reproach. They were compelled to turn towards
European culture, where they found their own spiritual
values, but spruced up and full of self-confidence.

   All the outward successes they had in European culture,
as Lessing shows convincingly in his essay, could not
console the Jews, since they had lost the sense of being
just, as well as the love of God. This gave rise to the
project of regaining the status of a chosen people, becoming once more a part of the people of God. This project,
however, could not lead a Jewish intellectual who had
lost his faith back to his people. That would have meant

returning to the faith of his forefathers, which was impossible simply on psychological grounds. In a time of confusion, however, a 'chosen people complex' necessarily took hold of the Jews with irresistible force, since they had imbibed this with their mothers' milk, and then we had such things as 'Proletarians of all countries, unite!' In other words, the Jews sought in their environment the oppressed and deprived, just as the Jews had been when God chose them, and burned with zeal to choose them and see them as the new people of God. Even their own people could be the chosen ones, but only if the Jews saw them really suffer – but in the late nineteenth and early twentieth centuries, the Jews of Western Europe were not suffering enough to appear chosen.

The model that served for this kind of choosing was of course the history of Christendom. The Christian truth had been revealed to the poor in spirit, but remained hidden from the wise – in particular from Jews learned in the law. For the Jewish apostles, their flock became their people, while their compatriots became their enemies. It is significant how two-headed the word 'Jew' has always been, from ancient times right through to its definition in Israeli legislation. On the one hand, anyone is a Jew who belongs by origin to the Jewish people, anyone who stems from 'Abraham's seed'; but on the other hand, a Jew is someone who confesses the true faith, someone whom God has chosen. Nothing is more simple than to deduce from this double meaning that those whom God has not chosen are not Jews, even if they are Jewish by blood. If the ancient apostles turned to those who were as ready to believe as they themselves were, and therefore could be chosen just as they were, the modern prophets chose their people themselves and sought to blend in with them, which naturally led them into a difficult situation.

Jews who chose a new people – such Jews, according

to Lessing, made their choice with a quite religious fanaticism. The chosen people were endowed with a messianic function; all the world's fame was promised them, while they frequently denigrated their own people, since their claim to having been chosen had to be radically denied (all other peoples were a matter of indifference). And not only did the memory of the earlier choosing have to be erased, but future attempts also had to be forestalled, since the new prophets were well aware that the process of choosing might not have reached an end with them, and that, so long as Judeo-Christian civilization endured, the danger existed that the present bearers of the messianic idea could themselves be replaced; in order to make their choice inescapable, it was necessary to destroy the foundation that made it possible. Jews who suffered from this 'chosen people complex' therefore united with bearers of the messianic idea who did not want to be chosen by anyone, but sought rather to stand at the start of their own path.

There is also a direct connection between the universality of being chosen and the original situation of being demeaned. Only those who were previously not granted human recognition could become the universal symbol of humanity – on purely logical grounds. It is well known how Marx made this connection, and also what this led to: in all countries of the 'victorious proletariat', the rights of the intelligentsia – those who proclaimed the proletariat to be the messianic class – were considerably restricted, even to the extent that children from the intelligentsia were refused entry to higher education, so that children of workers now studied in the same places from which the intelligentsia arose. After the October Revolution, posters everywhere in Russia showed the typically intellectual countenances of the founders and leaders of the Communist movement, from Marx to Lenin and Trotsky. And yet the representatives of the intelligentsia were proclaimed to be 'foreign to the class' (*klassovo chuzh-dye*), and became time and again victims of persecution, attacks and even killings – often simply on the ground of their wrong-class origin. This immediately suggests an analogy with the persecutions of Jews by Christians, which took place against the background of scenes from the Old and New Testaments depicted everywhere. (And just as the development of European philosophy can be understood as an historical succession of attempts to escape from the 'Jew within', or, as the apostle Paul put it, from the 'circumcision of the heart', so the evolution of European art – particularly in the Renaissance, its decisive epoch – can be understood as the effort to get rid of the Jewish face.)

Despite the bitter experiences we have mentioned, the Jews and the Judaized European intelligentsia did not abandon their search for the 'chosen people'. We might also note that this choosing of the 'humbled and despised' was always bound up with practical goals – the search for new outlets for their own intellectual production when the metropolitan countries were already saturated. The objects of choice have steadily become reassuringly more exotic: China, Cambodia, Cuba, Nicaragua – or the mentally ill, on the part of Freud and Foucault; the Amazonian Indians for Lévi-Strauss; and for the German 'Greens' the trees of the German forest. No less exotic in his own time, if also more risky, was the choice made by Lessing and the heroes of his book: as the representatives, 'humbled' by fate, of a universally human principle, they chose the Germans, who proclaimed the superiority of the Aryan race.

This choice, at first sight quite remarkable, actually had profound motivations, drawn especially from the history of philosophy. The Aryan theorists might well have given the particular priority over the universal – the Aryan idea over that of humanity; but on the other hand they founded this priority by appealing to something still more general than humanity and its culture: the idea of the cosmos embracing everything both living and dead; on top of which they based the prioritizing of the Aryans on their supposedly standing in a privileged relationship to this universality. And although the Aryan theorists also criticized the striving to the universal, in fact they continued the tradition of Judeo-Christian theoretical expansion. Nietzsche is a typical *Aufklärer* in this respect – not only because, as already mentioned, his conception of the cosmos is based on the Judeo-Christian tradition, but above all because he continued the unmasking tactic of the Enlightenment, exposing reason as an aberration. Lessing emphasizes this point, and suggests to the reader that the real creator of Nietzsche's doctrine – and consequently of the Aryan idea in its intellectually acceptable form – was the Jew, Paul Rée, who, as distinct from Nietzsche, lacked only superficiality, energy, self-satisfaction and Aryan blood to make a name for himself.

Lessing and his heroes, moreover, do not value the Aryan idea where it is successful and promises success: in Maximilian Harden, Lessing presents to the reader the typical Jewish careerist, for whom he feels no sympathy at all. Lessing is drawn rather to the tragic Aryanism of Nietzsche and Klages. Nietzsche's hero is lonely and helpless; he, who alone is strong, opposes the conspiracy of the weak that embraces the whole world, and is thereby weaker than the weakest. Nothing in the world remains for Nietzsche's hero other than death, which he loves and for which he strives. Lessing's Jews are all Nietzschean heroes par excellence. In their surroundings the Aryan idea looks touchingly helpless, arousing sentimental emotion; and this is indeed how it might have seemed to many in Germany after the lost war.

But there is undoubtedly a further reason why

Lessing was attracted by Nietzsche's Aryan anti-Semitism. At the time in which Lessing wrote, Jewishness had acquired a splendid and providential significance, most strongly in Nietzsche and Klages, in comparison with all other historical forces. This significance was purely negative and destructive, but this fact is not particularly important – rather the contrary, if we consider Nietzsche's call to 'live dangerously'. For Nietzsche, Jewishness became the driving force of world history, without which the Aryan peoples would ossify in a 'love of fate'; one might even say that Jewishness was the fate that it became the Aryans to love, precisely because it aimed to destroy them.

In comparison with this metaphysical and cosmic mission of the Jewish world, the Zionist call for the Jews to remain Jews, while at the same time 'becoming like all other peoples', or the liberal call to renounce Jewishness and in this way become like all other men, were certainly far more modest.

The real tragedy of the Jews of Lessing's day – and also our own – was that they were increasingly accustomed to accepting the confirmation of their historical predestination from the anti-Semites, but had lost their faith in their chosen role and sought to realize their 'chosen people complex' elsewhere. To judge from the books of the Old Testament, the Jews at that time held it as below their dignity to see themselves as outcasts and defeated. If they were defeated or oppressed, they always interpreted this as God having 'made stubborn the hearts of their enemies', 'strengthened their enemies' and 'given them power', in order to punish the Jews for their sins and apostasy. Christianity preserved this elevated pathos, explaining the persecutions of the Jews in terms of their refusal to recognize Christ. Other peoples appear in the sacred history of the Jews only as will-less tools, who do not share the profoundly intimate relationship of the Jews to their God. These peoples start wars and win them, if this is what the Jewish God wills – but if he is reconciled with his people, then these others suffer defeat and are exterminated. And they recognize neither in the hour of victory nor in that of defeat the power that raises them and then has them fall. What a contrast there is between the exalted alliance with their own God and the calls to international humanity to which Jews of today are so habituated, though as we know they remain ineffective. (The last remnants of the old, elevated faith have not totally vanished from the Jewish people. I still recall how when Stalin died, shortly before the deportation of all Jews to Siberia that was already decided, many Russian Jews said: God did not let him go through with this.) That the Jews should take on themselves the guilt for everything in the world, Lessing saw – following Nietzsche – as only weakness and a root of 'self-hatred'. That is pertinent, but only in relation to the modern, emancipated Jews, who have lost their former faith.

Lessing's book on Jewish 'self-hatred' is itself a sign that the Jews had lost the belief in their being chosen, without which they perceived themselves as a wretched and helpless people. Looked at superficially, Lessing's essay puts forward a programme that is close to Zionism, with the sole difference that he, basing himself on contemporary racial theories, recommends to Jews a still more radical rejection of Judaism than 'official' Zionism did when it countered the messianic pathos of Judaism with the political programme of building a secular state. In fact, however, his book had a far deeper significance – Lessing undoubtedly took pleasure in his self-hating heroes, as they preferred to see their Jewishness as a world-embracing demonic power that threatened to destroy them, rather than to cast off their status as chosen. It should be borne in mind, however, that this Jewish nostalgia for being chosen sought a false ally in Nietzsche's Aryanism. In European civilization, despite everything and above everything, the universal Christian principle is the preserver and heir of Jewish messianic hopes. Europe's most recent history also attests to this: tendencies that started out as anti-Semitic prove inescapably to be anti-Christian in the broadest sense – in other words, directed against everything that makes up the strength and specific value of Western civilization. And conversely, in Europe all provincial, nostalgic nationalisms with an Indian-Tibetan aftertaste unavoidably end up in the most primitive kind of Judeophobia.

7

ERNST JÜNGER'S TECHNOLOGIES OF IMMORTALITY

Ernst Jünger's 1932 treatise *Der Arbeiter* ('The Worker') has generally been treated by critics as a political text, a project aiming to contribute to the creation of a new type of totalitarian state based upon the principles of modern technology and organization. But it seems to me that the main strategy of the text is dictated, rather, by Jünger's interest in individual immortality – that is, in the potential of a single individual human being to transcend his own death after the death of the 'old God' announced by Nietzsche. This strategy becomes particularly evident when we consider Jünger's reference to the trope of technology in the course of his polemic against 'unique' personal experience. According to Jünger, the notion that such personal experience can and should exist serves as the basis not only for the kind of bourgeois individualism which would confer 'natural' human rights on each man, but also for the entire ideological trajectory of liberal democracy which reigned in the nineteenth century. Jünger engages the trope of technology essentially as evidence to corroborate two claims:

that the bourgeois and liberal notion of unique individual experience has been rendered irrelevant in the
twentieth century, and that this notion lost its former
meaning as our social world grew progressively more
organized according to the rules of modern technological rationality.

Jünger employs the term *individuelles Erlebnis* to
denote individual experience; this term recalls a general
notion of life, since *Erlebnis* stems from the word *Leben*
or 'life'. In his text, Jünger argues that traditional bourgeois ideology holds individual life to be absolutely
precious precisely because of its supposed singularity.
For this reason liberals consider the protection of individual life as the highest moral and legal obligation. And
just as Jünger tries – again and again – to demonstrate
that the notion of such experience is neither valid nor
valuable in the world of modern technology, he also
argues against the legal protection of individual life,
human rights, democracy and liberalism. He does this
quite openly in *Der Arbeiter*.

But unlike the majority of modernist authors with
totalitarian sympathies, of whom there were many in
the first part of the twentieth century, Jünger uses
rather peculiar discursive and rhetorical devices. He
does not require the individual to submit to any state,
nation, race or class. Neither does he proclaim the
values of the collective to be more important than those
of the individual. Instead Jünger strives to demonstrate
that, since individual experience can no longer be
accessed, the individual as such no longer exists in the
world of modern technology. An attempt to protect the
individual's human rights would therefore be senseless,
since there is no longer an individual to be protected.
Furthermore, the political compulsion to force individuals to submit to the collective will serves no realistic
function. According to Jünger, the subject that demands

our attention is rather the non-individualized subject of modern technology – that is, the worker. In the technological era this subject is the bearer of experiences that are impersonal, non-individual, serial and standardized. Such a subject has no use for the protection of human rights, for just as his existence is impersonal, serial and replicable, it is also immortal. Jünger does not seek to sacrifice the individual wilfully to his political and aesthetic project – he believes, rather, that the individual has already disappeared. And given that there remains nothing to sacrifice, there also remains nothing to protect.

Although Jünger certainly does not mean that we can no longer have unique experiences, he argues that the unique, non-replicable and irreplaceable character of such experiences has been devalued. In the modern world only serializable experiences – those which can be repeated and reproduced – can have value. This process of devaluation begins precisely in the eyes of the individual himself; Jünger makes this point when he reminds us that, by and large, the general public prefers the serial over and against unique objects. The typical automobile consumer, for example, opts for standard-issue, serially reproduced cars with reputable brand names; he has little interest in possessing a one-of-a-kind model designed for him alone.[1] The modern individual appreciates only that which has been standardized and serialized. Such reproducible objects can always be exchanged; in this sense they are charged with a certain indestructibility, a certain immortality. If a person

---

1. 'The man who drives a particular car, therefore, never seriously imagines himself possessing one designed for his individual need. On the contrary, he would quite rightly distrust a car that existed only in a single example. What he silently presupposes as quality is rather the model, the marque . . . Individual quality possesses for him rather the rank of a curiosity or something in a museum.' Ernst Jünger, *Der Arbeiter*, Stuttgart 1982, p. 133.

wrecks his Mercedes he always has a chance to purchase another copy of the same model. Jünger aims to prove that we have similar preferences in the field of personal experience, such that we tend to privilege the standard and the serial. The best-received films are those that are formulaic, those that lend themselves to the same experience no matter who their audience might be. Going to the cinema, unlike going to see live actors perform in the theatre, no longer offers an experience of the singular, unique event.[2] Modern technologies have something else to offer: the promise of immortality, a promise guaranteed through replicability and reproducibility, and then internalized by the modern individual when he serializes his own inner life.

The technological and serial nature of modern experience has a certain effect on human subjectivity (which is itself a sum of those experiences): it renders the human subject exchangeable and replicable. If all our experiences share in being originally reproducible, impersonal and serial, then there is, as I have already argued, no longer any convincing reason to value a specific individual or to protect a particular human life. Jünger insists that only the human type conditioned by technology has any relevance or value in our time; the term he uses to denote this type of being is 'the figure of the worker' (*Gestalt des Arbeiters*). After having survived his own military service during the First World War, Jünger can no longer subscribe to the rhetoric of human rights. In an earlier text on 'total mobilization', he described modern war as a machine that anonymously destroys human bodies. In this mode of destruction, anything that can be understood on the level of individual experience ceases to make sense.

Yet the anonymous death of an unknown soldier

---

2. Ibid., pp. 130ff.

seems not to be senseless, for, like the Mercedes, the soldier can also be replaced.[3] To this extent, then, Jünger considers both the soldier and the worker to be immortal. In order to survive in a technological civilization the individual human being must mimic the machine – even the very war machine that destroys him. Indeed it is this technique of mimicry that doubles as a technology of immortality. The machine actually exists between life and death; although it is dead, it moves and acts as if it were alive. As a result, the machine often signifies immortality. It is highly characteristic, for example, that Andy Warhol – much later than Jünger, of course – also desired to 'become a machine', that he also chose the serial and the reproducible as routes to immortality. Although the prospect of becoming a machine might seem dystopian or nightmarish to most, for Jünger, as for Warhol, this becoming-a-machine was the last and only chance to overcome individual death. Jünger's main strategy is this: to reach immortality through alienation.

In this respect, Jünger's relationship to institutions of cultural memory such as the museum and the library is especially arresting, since, in the context of modernity, these institutions are the traditional guarantors of immortality. But Jünger is prepared to destroy all museums and libraries, or at least to allow their destruction. Because of their role of preserving one-of-a-kind objects which exist beyond the limits of serial reproduction, these institutions have no value for the technological world.[4] Instead of maintaining the museum as a space of private aesthetic experience, Jünger wants the public to reorient its gaze and contemplate the entire

---

3. 'The virtue of the nameless soldier lies in the fact that he is replaceable, and that behind every one who falls there is already a relief in the reserve.' Ibid., p. 153.

4. Ibid., pp. 206ff.

technological world as an artwork. Like the Russian
Constructivists of the 1920s, Jünger understands the
new purpose of art as identical with that of technology
– namely, to aesthetically transform the whole world,
the whole planet, according to a single technical,
aesthetic and political plan. The radical Russian avant-
garde artists also required the elimination of the museum
as a privileged site of art contemplation; together with
this demand, they articulated the imperative that the
industrial be seen as the only relevant art form of the
time.[5] Jünger may well have been directly influenced by
this radical aesthetic. In his treatise, he frequently
makes affirmative references to the politics of the Soviet
workers' state; but he seems at the same time to have
been influenced by Tatlin's so-called 'machine art'
(*Maschinenkunst*), an artistic programme that was
introduced to Germany by both Berlin Dadaists and
Russian Constructivist avant-garde figures like El
Lissitzky and Ilya Ehrenburg. The difference that distinguishes Jünger's aesthetic from that of the Constructivists
is really only perceptible at one point: Jünger combines
Constructivist slogans with admiration for all archaic
and classical cultural forms, provided that they also
demonstrate a high degree of seriality and regularity. He
is fascinated not only by the world of the military
uniform, but also by the symbolic universes of medieval
Catholicism and Greek architecture, for all three of
these traditions are characterized by their commitment
to regularity and seriality.

Inherent to Jünger's line of argument is a contradiction which can also be found in the aesthetic discourse of
Russian Constructivism. On the one hand, the demise of

---

5. Boris Groys, 'The Struggle against the Museum, or the Display of
Art in Totalitarian Space', in D. Sherman and I. Rogoff, eds, *Museum
Culture: Histories, Discourses, Spectacles*, Minneapolis 1993, pp.
144–62.

traditional aesthetics and the victory of new technologies are each described as indisputable facts that demand acceptance. But on the other hand, we can also discern a shared set of normative statements, as well as a three-part programme that promises a new aesthetic, a new aesthetic sensibility and a new aesthetic–political order. But what is the necessity for such a programme if the victory of modern technology has already been established as fact? Obviously, for Jünger a mere historical victory of technology would not suffice. Technology must be *seen* in a certain way as well; it must be interpreted as a new art form, as a new generic and impersonal consciousness, as a new kind of immortality. What is of paramount importance for Jünger is not technology as such, but rather the change in perspective that it augurs and the new mode of experience and apperception that it offers the modern world. His goal is to bring the reader to regard technology in a new light. To this end, Jünger suggests that modern civilization, as well as the entire planet that supports it, be taken as a unique technological readymade, as a total artwork. Duchamp had already demonstrated this possibility when he installed everyday objects produced by modern civilization in the museum environment. So, although Jünger's strategy is perfectly understandable within the general context of modern aesthetics, such a strategy is only possible *inside* the museum, *inside* the cultural archive, or – at least – inside the field of interpretation. And such a change in perspective itself constitutes a unique aesthetic experience, a singular aesthetic operation that is neither replicable nor serializable. This happens because this aesthetic operation relates to the technical world as a whole; the world becomes a unique and self-sufficient totality, as a singular and total object of contemplation.

If Jünger claims in his treatise the impossibility of unique personal experience, *Der Arbeiter* presents itself

at the same time as a unique aesthetic experience, understood as a unique revelation of this impossibility. The
treatise promises an immortality which is interpreted by
Jünger as seriality, but at the same time it aims to function as the final, apocalyptic revelation of the end of
history as we know it. It is precisely this performative
paradox that lies at the core of Jünger's text. In the technological world Jünger evokes in *Der Arbeiter* his text
itself would be incomprehensible, superfluous even,
because such a world would have no place and no need
for any kind of personalized aesthetic message.

Clearly, Jünger's deep dissatisfaction with his position as a writer vis-à-vis the masses of both bourgeois
and proletarian readers provided the initial impulse to
write *Der Arbeiter*. Jünger did not want to restrict his
social role to that of the kind of author whose books
would function merely as market commodities, and be
evaluated according to criteria such as the psychological
impact or aesthetic pleasure produced in the soul of an
individual reader. Like many authors of his time, Jünger
did not just want to supply his reader with 'individual
experiences'; he wanted to form the consciousness and
very life of the reader. Instead of seeking the approba-
tion of literary consumers, he himself sought to judge
their life and then act upon that judgment. As Alexandre
Kojève wrote somewhat later, 'the writer can have only
success. But we want an achievement.'[6] This disdain for
the reader leads Jünger to identify with the producer
and the worker; it also contributes to his disgust for
consumers in general.

This will to suppress the consumer, who plays a
central role in the functioning of the modern liberal
economy, is the most striking aspect of Jünger's

---

6. Alexandre Kojève, 'Les philosophes ne m'intéressent pas, je
cherche des sages. Propos recueillis par Gilles Lapouge', *La Quinzaine
Littéraire* 500, 1–15 January 1988, pp. 2–3.

political vision. Although the worker labours, there is no one who could consume the products of his labour since the whole of society has thoroughly submitted itself to the ideal of unlimited production. It follows, then, that war becomes the only possible consumer of the material goods produced. In a world divided between societies organized as work units, war constantly emerges out of their competition, and victory in war remains the only available criterion of production in a world devoid of normal practices of consumption. But Jünger does not consider war to be the ultimate telos of modern industrial production; for him the paragon of technological civilization is the 'figure of the worker', the *Gestalt des Arbeiters.*

Unlike most of his colleagues, Jünger praises technological progress. But he champions it only because he believes this progress to be historically limited and finite. Throughout the period of modernity, modern writers traditionally imagined themselves to be in hostile opposition to the relentless onward march of technological progress. Such progress relativized and put in question each and every finite and individual artistic achievement. But Jünger sees these advances as moving towards a distinct historical goal: the embodiment of the 'figure of the worker' and the transformation of all human beings into perfect workers. Jünger's conception of the 'figure of the worker' recalls the Aristotelian notion of God, for he characterizes this figure as an unmoving mover of technological civilization.[7] The entire history of technological and military advancement is, in essence, a history of the self-materialization of the 'figure of the worker'. Such an absolute worker has no need for

---

7. 'But if the figure of the worker is recognized as the determining force that magnetically draws movement towards it . . . this means that these processes of technical progress are its pre-given goal.' Jünger, *Der Arbeiter*, p. 180.

anyone to consume the products of his labour; neither would he tolerate it. As a result, mankind must come to rest once it has realized the 'figure of the worker'. Technological progress reaches its end at the same moment in which it achieves complete perfection. The absolute worker finds his well-deserved eternal rest, but only after he has destroyed and eliminated all potential consumers through a long and exhausting period of terror and war.

This vision of eternal peace, of an eternal weekend marking the end of technological progress, closely resembles Malevich's dream of the future 'white mankind'.[8] This vision, of course, outdoes the Marxist vision of the advent of unlimited consumption that would follow the end of history. The 'figure of the worker' does not consume – which means that, after its grand historical victory, work becomes identical with non-work, or leisure. More importantly, by binding *Der Arbeiter* to this apocalyptic future, by prefiguring the endpoint of technological progress in his writing, Jünger immortalizes his text in the here and now. He writes his book not for the audience of future readers, but for the future without readers. The man of the future is not a potential reader of *Der Arbeiter* – rather, he must inhabit the life-world envisioned by Jünger. Yet it is strikingly clear that such an outcome cannot be brought about by technology alone. Jünger proclaims the imperative that the state must exert its power to transform his aesthetic insights into political practice, and thereby overcome the gap separating the reality of the technical world from the public's understanding of it.

This political project, however, is infected by the same paradox as the aesthetic project I discussed earlier. Jünger tries to persuade his audience that behind

---

8. Kasimir Malevich, *The Non-Objective World: The Manifesto of Suprematism*, New York 2003, p. 98.

liberal-democratic freedoms and the liberty of economic choice there lies hidden the power of the techno-bureaucratic apparatus. This hierarchically organized technocratic control is in no way liberal; it is absolutely despotic, for the very existence of each civil subject depends completely on the proper functioning of modern technology. The best example of this condition that Jünger provides is that of electricity: under democratic rule one can quit a political party without suffering any major repercussions, he argues, but one could not break one's connection to the system that supplies electricity without having to endure a whole series of uncomfortable and inconvenient changes to the rhythms of everyday life. Our dependence upon technology is so deep and intimate that we can hardly imagine ourselves to be free in any substantive way.[9]

Jünger's description of our situation may, in fact, be correct – an element of profound truth can certainly be detected within it. But, at the same time, the particular political programmes Jünger develops, as well as the perspectives of the new totalitarianism he offers, are based on the abolition of all traditional political and economic rights. And this is no simple rhetorical device: Jünger argues repeatedly that academic freedom constitutes treason against the nation-state; that freedom of the press must be abolished; that the fate of the individual should be determined ruthlessly, even cruelly; that there is no place for any sort of human compassion – and so on. However, despite the deliberate manner in which Jünger expresses these programmatic requirements and aspirations, there is something odd about his agenda: his radicalism seems superfluous to the framework of his analysis. If techno-bureaucratic control is already a reality, if bourgeois freedoms are only illusory,

---

9. Jünger, *Der Arbeiter*, pp. 129ff.

then why does Jünger have to be so vehement in his call
to liquidate these freedoms? After all, in his earlier essay
on 'total mobilization' he wrote that such mobilization
is much better implemented in a democratic country like
America than anywhere else.[10] Why, then, does he
demand the supplement of political dictatorship, if
modern technology alone is already doing the job?

The immediate answer, here and in the case of
Russian Constructivism, is this: because of the actual
limitations of the technologies in place at that time in
Germany or Russia, those in power had to resort to the
rhetoric of technological mastery in order to compensate for their nations' relative deficiencies. In lieu of
actual state-of-the-art technological systems, political
hierarchies were constructed. Here political extremism
functioned in several ways: as a simulacrum of real
technological progress, as a kind of functionalist artistic and political design instead of a real technological
supremacy, and as an artful mimicry instead of a real
threat. Indeed, it was this very strategy that the Soviet
Union used to great effect.

It strikes me nonetheless that Jünger is interested not
so much in actual efficiency as he is in the aesthetic
experience of efficiency. He knows that his passionate
affirmation of modern technology will fascinate his
audience – and he revels in this knowledge. Above all,
Der Arbeiter reminds contemporary readers of the
Hollywood science-fiction genre (already prefigured by
Fritz Lang's *Metropolis*) that is animated with robots,
medieval knights and mysterious monks, and depicts
hierarchically disciplined secret organizations that
produce things indecipherable but clearly very dangerous in their technological complexity. Such sci-fi movies

---

10. Ernst Jünger, 'Total Mobilization', in R. Wolin, ed., *The
Heidegger Controversy: A Critical Reader*, Cambridge, MA 1993, pp.
122–39.

– think of *Independence Day* or *Starship Troopers* – are very often populated by a cast of strange insects, a cast which certainly would have appealed to Jünger, given that his passion for the insect world was so intense. Each of the creatures and machines that marches across the screen in these films is equally exchangeable, reparable and replicable. And nearly every one of these cinema characters can cross the centuries with the aid of his trusty time machine. In this sense the hero is immortal.

Although in his text Jünger refers to the aesthetics of the historical avant-garde, Constructivism and Bauhaus, he does not himself belong among the most advanced artists of his time. His writing is not experimental; neither is it ironic or defamiliarizing (*verfremdend*) in the Formalist sense of the word. His vision of the perfect worker-state is much more germane to the mass culture of our own time, since in the 1930s, when Jünger was working on his text, modern mass culture as we know it was only taking its first tentative steps. Seen from this perspective, Jünger's text appears to have particular and significant historical relevance – it is one of the earliest manifestations of both the aesthetic and political imaginations of mass culture. What he envisioned as the supreme aesthetic and political project for the new Europe would indeed be eventually realized. Not in the Old World, however, but in the studios of Hollywood.

8

THREE ENDS OF HISTORY: HEGEL, SOLOVYOV, KOJÈVE

During the last few decades we have been time and again confronted with a discourse on the end of history, the end of subjectivity, the end of art, the death of Man – and especially the death of the author; on the impossibility of creativity and the new in today's culture. This discourse has its origin in the course of lectures on Hegel's *Phenomenology of Spirit* that was given by Alexandre Kojève at the École des Hautes Études in Paris between the years 1933 and 1939. This course was regularly attended by leading figures in French intellectual life at that time, including Georges Bataille, Jacques Lacan, André Breton, Maurice Merleau-Ponty and Raymond Aron. The transcripts of Kojève's lectures circulated in Parisian intellectual circles and were widely read there – including by Sartre and Camus. These courses, known under the simple title 'Séminaire', acquired a semi-mythical status at that time, which they retained almost until our own day. (Lacan later likewise called the course of lectures he started after Kojève's death 'Séminaire'.) Of course, apocalyptic discourse on the impending end of history is not new. But Kojève asserted that the end of history does not wait for us in the future, as was usually thought. Rather, the end of history has already taken place in the past – namely, in the nineteenth century, as was certified by the Hegelian philosophy. According to Kojève, we have already been living for a pretty long time after the end of history, under the posthistorical condition – now we would say the postmodern condition – but we are simply not yet fully aware of this condition.

This transfer of the end of history from the future into the past was something new at the time that Kojève tried to make it plausible to his audience. Maybe that is why he also attempted to illustrate and corroborate his theoretical discourse with the example of his own practice of writing. Kojève always maintained that he never tried to say anything new – because saying anything new had become impossible. He claimed simply to repeat and reproduce the text of Hegel's *Phenomenology of Spirit* without adding anything to it. Kojève never published his philosophical writings, and actually never finished any of them, beyond some short articles. His course on Hegel, published in 1947 under the title *Introduction à la Lecture de Hegel*,[1] is a loose patchwork of texts and notes written by Kojève, along with transcripts made by different members of the audience. This collection of heterogeneous textual fragments was produced not by Kojève himself, but by the Surrealist writer Raymond Queneau. After the war Kojève abandoned philosophy altogether – because to philosophize after the end of history made no sense to him any more. Instead, Kojève entered a diplomatic–bureaucratic career. As a representative of France in the European Commission, Kojève became one of the creators of the

---

1. Alexandre Kojève, *Introduction to the Reading of Hegel*, New York 1969.

contemporary European Union. He worked out an agreement on tariffs that remains one of the pillars of the European economic system. Kojève died from a heart attack during a meeting of the European Commission in 1968. One can say that Kojève was a kind of Arthur Rimbaud of modern bureaucracy – a philosophical writer who consciously became a martyr of the posthistorical bureaucratic order.

Today, discourse on posthistoricity or postmodernity has become ubiquitous. But we still have no single example – with the exception of Kojève's writing – of a body of theoretical writing that would proclaim its own complete unoriginality. We have several such examples in the field of literature and art, but not in the field of theory. Blanchot, Foucault or Derrida – who wrote extensively on the death of the author – never said at the same time that their own writings were completely unoriginal, that they were merely the repetition of some already existing and well-known theoretical writing. Under the postmodern condition, theoretical writing remains the last area where the claim of originality is allowed and even required from the writer. So the case of Kojève remains even today unique and exceptional. He is the only philosophical writer who can be compared to Duchamp, Warhol or Pierre Menard – the hero of the famous tale by Borges. Thus, Kojève's claim of radical philosophical unoriginality, his assertion that he simply transposed Hegelian philosophy from the context of nineteenth-century Germany to the context of twentieth-century France without any transformation, innovative interpretation or change remains extremely original even for our own time. That is why the singularity of the Kojèvian claim of unoriginality calls for explanation in the first place – to a greater extent than his philosophical ideas themselves.

Now, I would like to suggest that the clue to this

claim of unoriginality can be found in a dissertation on
the work of Vladimir Solovyov that Kojève had written
(in German) at the University of Heidelberg in 1926,
with the title 'Die religiöse Philosophie Vladimir
Solowjeffs', under his original name, Alexander
Koschewnikoff. This dissertation, supervised by Karl
Jaspers, was published in a very limited edition in
Germany in the 1930s, and was translated with some
minor changes into French in 1934.[2] I read the original
version of the dissertation in the library of the University
of Heidelberg (with handwritten remarks by Jaspers or
some of his assistants). But my topic here is neither the
textological analysis of this dissertation, nor the question of whether Kojève interpreted the philosophy of
Solovyov in an adequate way. Rather, I would like to
draw the reader's attention to some key formulations in
this dissertation that allow a better understanding of
how the specific Kojèvian conception of the end of
history emerged. In particular, I will try to show that
Kojève's discourse on the end of history can be rightly
understood only in the context of the 'historiosophical'
and 'sophiological' discussions among representatives
of post-Solovyovian Russian thinking during the first
quarter of the twentieth century – discussions about the
future of mankind, and specifically about the future of
Russia.[3] Kojève does not argue explicitly against the
views of Berdyaev, Bulgakov or Frank – he does not
even mention them – but he proposes an interpretation
of Solovyov's philosophy that is clearly directed against
the eschatological hopes and sophiological visions that
were characteristic of these authors. Instead, he proposes
what he himself calls a pessimistic reading of Solovyov's
writings. And it is in the context of this pessimistic

---

2. In the *Revue d'Histoire et de Philosophie Religieuse*.
3. On this, see Vladimir S. Solovyov, *Divine Humanity*, Herndon
1993.

reading that the main figures of his later discourse on *post-histoire* were formulated for the first time.

I would like to begin, however, with a short characterization of the standard reception and interpretation of the Kojèvian 'end of history'. This reception took place mainly in the context of political philosophy – through the mediation of authors like Raymond Aron, Leo Strauss and Francis Fukuyama, who used Kojève's conception of history primarily in the context of their polemics against Marxism. That is why the Kojèvian reading of Hegel's *Phenomenology* was and still is compared, as a rule, to the interpretation of Hegel that was given by Marx. And, in fact, there are many parallels between the Marxian and Kojèvian readings of Hegel. Kojève proclaims the 'struggle for recognition' to be a motor of universal history. This formulation is reminiscent, at first glance, of the Marxist 'class struggle'. Kojève refers also to the same section on 'the dialectics of the relationship between master and slave' in the *Phenomenology* as did Marx. Hegel describes in this section the historical moment at which self-consciousness manifests itself for the first time. This primary scene involves two men who are ready to risk their lives in a kind of 'mortal combat' to be recognized mutually as being not simply material objects in the world, but two self-consciousnesses that are in pursuit of their individual desires. There are three possible outcomes at the end of this combat: 1) one can win, 2) one can lose and die, or 3) one can lose and survive. The winner becomes a master. The loser, if he chooses to capitulate and to survive, becomes a slave. The master uses the slave to satisfy his desire. The slave renounces his own desire, becoming merely a tool for the satisfaction of his master's desire.

But Hegel does not believe in the long-term stability of the master's domination. The master gives orders – but it is the slave who interprets and fulfils them. The slave works – but his work transforms the world in which the master lives, and also transforms the master's own desires. The master becomes a prisoner in the world that is built for him by the slave. Work becomes the medium of the further development of Spirit, the motor of universal history. Hegel understands his philosophy as an intellectual reflection of the slave's work that makes history. For Marx, history must also lead not only to this kind of philosophical reflection, but to the ultimate political victory of the working class.

In any case, for Hegel and Marx the struggle for recognition remains only a transient moment in the historical development of Absolute Spirit. Universal history was seen by both Hegel and Marx from the perspective of the slave, not from the perspective of the master. Both saw themselves as losers in the historical battle – and reflected on ways to compensate for this loser's status by creative work. But for Kojève, the struggle for recognition remains the only motor of history from its beginning to its end. He does not believe in a possibility of transforming the world by work. He believes only in war and revolution – in direct violence. That is why, for Kojève, the end of history manifests itself in the paradoxical character of modern revolutions, from the French to the Russian: the revolutionary people begin the mortal combat against their masters, and win. But after having won the struggle, the people go to work again. And this is something that Kojève – his reader feels it very strongly – just cannot understand. He cannot understand how a man who has won the battle for life and death can simply go to work after that. Kojève draws from this fact the conclusion that the winner is already satisfied – he has no desires anymore that would remain unsatisfied and lead him into further battles. For Kojève, the emergence of this figure of the 'armed worker' (*chelovek s ruzhyem*) marks the end of history. The citizen of the modern post-revolutionary state is a master and a slave at the same time. The state itself has become, in Kojèvian terms, universal and homogeneous. And the emergence of this kind of state that fully satisfies its citizens makes any desire for recognition – and, therefore, any history that is driven by this desire – impossible, because this desire is now fully satisfied. The history of Man ends. The human being returns to its original prehistorical animal condition – to animal, unhistorical desires. The posthistorical condition is this return to original animality – to socially guaranteed consumption as a unique remaining goal of human existence. Of course, the influence of Nietzsche is immediately recognizable here; and Kojève was accused from time to time of being a crypto-fascist even if he himself insisted to the end of his life that he was a Stalinist. But the usual critique generally overlooks the fact that the universal and homogeneous State is for Kojève only one figure among three figures emerging at the end of history. The other two figures are the Sage and the Book.

These two other figures have usually been overlooked by interpreters of Kojève's writings, because they have no place in Hegelian or Marxian philosophy. But the Kojèvian discourse on the end of history cannot be understood without taking into consideration these two figures as well – and, first of all, without asking the question: What is the meaning of desire, as this notion is used by Kojève? I will now try to show that this notion has its origin not in Hegel but in Solovyov; specifically, in Solovyov's *The Meaning of Love*, as this text was interpreted by Kojève in his dissertation.[4] I shall begin

---

4. V. Solowjev, *Der Sinn der Liebe*, Hamburg 1985.

by treating the figure of the Sage, and turn later to the figure of the Book.

1. THE SAGE

In his *Introduction*, but also in rare interviews given after the Second World War, Kojève insists time and again that at the end of history the figure of the Philosopher is substituted by the figure of the Sage. The Philosopher is moved by desire, by his love (*philia*) of absolute knowledge, of *sophia*. But at the end of history the Philosopher acquires absolute knowledge; he unites himself with *la sagesse*, with *sophia* – and becomes a Sage, or a Man-God (*Homme-Dieu*, *čelovejobog*). This absolute knowledge means for Kojève the state of absolute self-consciousness. Kojève says that the philosopher becomes a Sage if his own actions become completely transparent and understandable for him. Or, to use Freudian language, absolute knowledge means for a philosopher the complete overcoming of his own unconscious or subconscious. The Philosopher submits to the power of desire. And his desire for absolute knowledge, the desire for *sophia*, manifests itself, at its first stage, necessarily as a specific kind of unconscious desire; in fact, of sexual desire. The Sage overcomes this desire by uniting himself with *sophia* – by being fully satisfied and in possession of absolute knowledge. Now, this understanding of the historical process as a history of gradually growing conscious control by the human being over its own unconscious has, in fact, not very much to do with the Hegelian or Marxian descriptions of the historical process. But it has everything to do with Solovyov's philosophy of love.

The vocabulary that Kojève uses to describe the Sage points already very clearly towards Solovyov's philosophy and its further development in Russian thinking at the turn of the century: *sophia*, the Man-God, and so on. But first of all it sheds a completely new light on the central figure of Kojèvian thought: the struggle for recognition. The medium of this struggle is, obviously, not economy or politics, but rather desire, or love. And it is precisely at this point that Kojève's philosophical writing reveals its deep complicity with Solovyov's philosophy, as well as with the mainstream of Russian philosophy and literary writing in the late nineteenth and early twentieth centuries in general. The starting point of Solovyov's philosophical discourse – and Kojève writes about this extensively in his dissertation – consists of the philosophical writings of Schopenhauer and his disciple Eduard von Hartmann, whose main treatise bears the title *Philosophy of the Unconscious*. The pessimistic philosophy of Schopenhauer (translated into Russian by Afanassij Fet in 1888) made a strong and in many respects decisive impression on many leading Russian authors of that time, including Leo Tolstoy, Vladimir Solovyov, Nikolai Fedorov and Nikolai Strakhov. Schopenhauer argued against the autonomy of free will and reason – above all, against the possibility of attaining any degree of self-consciousness. For Schopenhauer, reason is submitted to desire, to *Lebensdrang* – and, first of all, to erotic desire. Schopenhauer deplores this submission; later, Nietzsche celebrates it. But both of them consider reason, subjectivity and self-consciousness as secondary compared to desire – as its sublimations. So philosophical reason becomes totally dependent on desire.

Already in his first treatise (*Krisis zapadnoj filosofii. Protiv pozitivistov*, 1874) Solovyov placed the relationship between reason and desire at the centre of his interest. But he formulated a philosophical and political programme that was completely opposite to Schopenhauer's. Solovyov developed this programme further in *The Meaning of Love*, and Kojève asserts in his dissertation that this is the most important text of Solovyov's, and a key to all his other writings. In *The Meaning of Love* Solovyov describes sexuality as a secondary, derivative version of the philosophical, Platonic eros – as a necessary but transient step within the development of philosophical self-consciousness. Here reason is understood not as a sublimation of sexuality; instead sexuality is understood as a specific form of reason. The sexual act is primarily an epistemological act, the sexual drive an initial form of the drive for knowledge. For Solovyov, reason is in its origin not cold, 'rational' and mathematical, but hot, desiring and striving: reason is longing, is love for *sophia*. Sexual love is only a projection of this philosophical love onto concrete, individual objects (for example, women); but at the same time it is its highest manifestation, because through sexuality the philosopher discovers the body of the other and his own body. For Solovyov this discovery – and not the reproductive function – is the true meaning of sexuality. The meaning of sexual love is the complete recognition of the other by myself, and of myself by the other. Solovyov insists at great length on that point: the complete recognition (*utverzhdenie, opravdanie, no takzhe priznanie*) of the other can be achieved only by sexual love, by eros. The human personality (*lichnost*) is an original unity of soul and body. To love somebody means to recognize this unity (not only spirit, and not only matter) as it truly is. And this means that love is the medium of absolute knowledge – because absolute knowledge is, precisely, the knowledge of this unity.

This discovery then leads the philosopher to a second one. Absolute knowledge itself also has a body, and that body is humanity in its entirety. The individual philosopher can achieve unity with mankind as a whole only if mankind itself achieves the status of mutual recognition through mutual love, because only in this case does the body of mankind become transparent and accessible to philosophical reason. This mutual recognition is, in its turn, prefigured by the relationship of mutual recognition between Christ and the universal Church – understood as 'free theocracy', meaning a Church without any established hierarchy, or a homogeneous Church. The individual philosopher can thus unite himself with absolute knowledge – he can become a lover of *sophia* – only if he can penetrate its transparent material body: the body of the universal and homogeneous Church, or the body of a united, homogenized mankind. Otherwise, his knowledge remains only abstract and incomplete, only spiritual and non-corporeal. True and absolute knowledge is for Solovyov the only knowledge in the biblical sense of the word: the act of the real, material penetration of the other. And Kojève dedicated the greater part of his dissertation to analyzing precisely the most erotic–ecclesiastic texts of Solovyov dealing with the sexual relationship between the body of the philosopher and the body of mankind.[5] Now, it is obvious that the universal and homogeneous State, as described by Kojève, is a secularized version of the Solovyovian universal 'free theocracy' – mankind as a female body open for penetration through the philosophical *logos* – with very little to do with either Hegel's or Marx's theories of the state.

The Kojèvian reading of Hegelian philosophy follows the path of Solovyov's metaphysics, not the path of Hegelian or Marxian dialectics as these are usually interpreted. Both Hegel and Marx understood

---

5. *Istoria i budushnost teokratie. Issledovanie vsmiro istoriskogo puti k istinnio shisni* [*The History and Future of Theocracy: An Investigation of the World-Historical Path to True Life*], 1885–57, and *La Russie et L'Église universelle*, 1889.

nature as an external, objective reality that should be investigated and controlled by science and technique. But Kojève – following Solovyov – understands nature primarily as object of desire. Kojève speaks of 'desire' using hunger as his model, and stating that every desire is utterly destructive: we destroy food by using it. But on the level of self-consciousness this destructive force of desire can be compensated by mutual recognition, since on this level we want not the body of the other but its desire. The ultimate goal of my desire is the recognition of this desire by the desire of the other. This formulation – which is a reformulation of the Solovyovian definition of love – lies at the core of Kojève's philosophical discourse. At the beginning of his *Introduction*, Kojève speaks about the *désir anthro-pogène*, which is fundamentally different from the *désir animal*. This 'anthropogenic desire' produces Man as Man, constitutes *le fait humain*: 'Thus, in the relationship between man and woman, for example, Desire is human only if the one desires, not the body, but the Desire of the other . . . that is to say, if he wants to be "desired" or "loved", or, rather, "recognized" in his human value'. And again: 'human history is the history of desired Desires'.[6]

Recognition is characterized here as explicitly identical with love. At this human, anthropogenic level of desire, the desire for natural objects is also mediated by the desire of the Other. Kojève writes: 'Thus, an object perfectly useless from the biological point of view (such as a medal, or the enemy's flag)' – in fact, all the things of our civilization – 'can be desired because it is the object of other desires.'[7] That is why we are able to risk our life for things that are completely unnecessary from the standpoint of practical, economic, animal desire.

6. Kojève, *Introduction*, p. 6.
7. Ibid.

The desire for these things is dictated to us only by the desire to be recognized, loved, desired by others.

These formulations have very little to do with the Hegelian or Marxian descriptions of the struggle for recognition. Kojève's struggle for recognition is modelled on the struggle between genders – not between classes. The goal of this struggle is to obtain the love of the other – not to eliminate the other. It is no accident that the most stable core of Kojève's seminar consisted of members of the French Surrealist movement: Georges Bataille, Jaques Lacan, André Breton. And the text of the *Introduction* itself was compiled, as I have said, by Raymond Queneau – one of the leading Surrealist writers of that time. All of these authors were interested principally in developing a general theory of culture and society based on the notion of sexual desire. I cannot expand on that in the framework of this text, but it would not be very difficult to show that the notion of desire as it is used by Bataille and Lacan has, in fact, much more to do with its use by Solovyov and Kojève than with its use by Freud. This is especially obvious in the case of Lacan. But it would lead me too far away from my topic – even if it seems to me that a comparison between the Solovyovian erotization of theology and philosophy and the Surrealist erotization of economy and politics, using Kojève as a middle figure between them, could be very productive for the understanding of both these phenomena.[8]

But Kojève himself developed his discourse on love as recognition not in the context of the Surrealist movement,

8. In this context it is interesting to note that this notion itself as it is now used in the international context – *désir*, desire – was introduced by Kojève as a translation of the word *Begierde* used by Hegel. But Kojève gave this word a more general, Solovyovian meaning. It is very characteristic that it is translated back into German now not as *Begierde* but as *Begehren* – a word that did not previously exist in the German philosophical lexicon.

but in that of the traditional Russian utopian vision of a
society based on love – as opposed to one based on
economic interest. This utopia can be found in the work
of Dostoyevsky, Tolstoy and Solovyov, as well as that of
their followers in the first decades of the twentieth
century. The position of Kojève in relation to this utopia
is ambivalent, or, better to say, ironic. Kojève identifies
himself with these utopian aspirations, but at the same
time points out that the realization of desire, the realization of love, means their disappearance. Every desire
can be satisfied – and, therefore, finalized. Satisfaction
puts an end to desire. The end of history is possible and
inevitable because there is no such thing as infinite
desire. The universal and homogeneous state is for
Kojève the final truth, because it is the state of love that
satisfies in a finalizing way our desire for recognition.
Kojève carried out a radical sexualization of reason,
history and politics; the sexualization that he learned
from Solovyov. It is this total sexualization of knowledge that was so attractive to the French Surrealists. But
the difference between Kojève and the Surrealists – and
for that matter between Kojève and Solovyov – is that
Kojève is thematizing in the first place not desire itself,
but rather the philosophical state of mind after its satisfaction. Kojèvian thought is posthistorical because it is
post-coital. Kojève is interested not in the pre-coital
surge of desire but in the post-coital depression – one
might even say, in post-revolutionary, post-philosophical
depression. The perfect society of realized, recognized
love that emerges after the revolutionary paroxysm,
after the penetration of mankind's body by *logos*, is a
society without love.

   That is why Kojève proclaims himself a Stalinist:
Stalin realized the society of love by abolishing love. In
this sense, Stalinist Russia fits the general pattern of
post-revolutionary states. The moment of complete

satisfaction of philosophical desire, the moment of unification with *sophia*, with absolute knowledge, is only a
moment. After that moment, this desire – as the specifically human desire, as the desire to be desired – disappears
once and for all. Under the posthistorical condition
philosophy becomes impossible, because man loses
anthropogenic desire and becomes an animal again.
Kojève sees the United States as the best example of the
posthistorical, purely animal, economic mode of existence. But he sees also a second possibility of posthistorical
existence – the possibility of, as he says, pure snobbery
that is realized, as he believed, in Japan. This snobbery
is a struggle for recognition beyond desire, as a pure
play of signifiers. Under the posthistorical condition the
philosopher becomes a snob. To understand that means
to reject the philosophical attitude, to reject philosophy
– and to become a Sage.

According to Kojève, this dialectics of desire, of its
fulfilment meaning its disappearance, was overlooked by
Solovyov and many other authors because they postulated a theological, infinite guarantee of desire: God.
Kojève saw himself, on the contrary, as an atheist and, in
this sense, a true philosopher. In fact, Kojève's dissertation is already full of critical remarks directed against
Solovyov for being a non-philosopher. Time and again,
Kojève accuses Solovyov of not understanding this or
that famous philosopher, of being superficial and impre-
cise in his own philosophical formulations. Specifically,
Kojève states that Solovyov did not understand Hegel.
The critical stance that Kojève takes toward Solovyov is
unusually sharp and uncompromising for somebody
writing a dissertation on a chosen author. In many cases
this critical overkill sounds irritating and annoying. But
soon enough the reader recognizes that Kojève is using
this accusatory language primarily to avoid the necessity
of comparing Solovyov's philosophical discourse with

other philosophical discourses. By stating that Solovyov is in fact a non-philosopher, Kojève assumes the right to neglect everything in Solovyov's writings that looks like epistemology, ethics or aesthetics – everything tradition-ally associated with 'philosophy' as an academic discipline. Instead, Kojève asserts that there is a unique fundamental intuition that lies at the core of Solovyov's writing: the intuition of the original unity of reason and desire, corresponding to the original unity of soul and body. Kojève asserts further that at the end of his life Solovyov became deeply disillusioned and abandoned his belief that desire has a theological guarantee, that there is an original and infinite unity between Man and God that can be rediscovered by love. Instead, Solovyov began to develop a different, pessimistic ontology (as Kojève puts it) of separation between man and God. But he died before completing this task. And it is obvious that Kojève sees his own task as creating such a pessimistic ontology – and, accordingly, a new, pessimistic vision of the post-historical condition.

2. THE BOOK

At the centre of this other, pessimistic vision we find not the Sage but the Book. The Sage finds himself inside the transparent body of *sophia* – all his desires are recog-nized and he recognizes all her desires. But what is most important is that the Sage knows this. He is in full possession of his self-consciousness. According to Kojève, this self-consciousness is utterly unstable: it disappears immediately after its emergence. By losing his desire, the Sage also loses his self-consciousness, and even his knowledge of being satisfied. Posthistorical man is fully satisfied, but he does not know this anymore. He has forgotten the moment of satisfaction and cannot explain his own lack of desire. In his *Introduction*

Kojève writes that Hegel's *Phenomenology* introduces a new kind of time: not linear, but also not cyclical.[9] This Hegelian time is a circular time – human desire makes a whole circle; it frees man from his natural, animal condition, and then brings him back into this animal condition again. But this circle cannot be repeated, cannot be turned into a cyclical movement. At the end of history man is prevented from the possibility of philosophical desire arising in him anew – prevented from this precisely by Hegel's *Phenomenology of Spirit* itself, because this book already describes the whole circle of options that desire can and must realize.

This means that, instead of man, it is now the Book that functions as medium, as material bearer of philosophical desire, of Spirit. At the end of history desire changes its material body. Desire substitutes the body of the Book for the human body – Spirit becomes printed, it becomes inhuman, it dissociates itself from human history. The relationship of humanity to the truth becomes purely external. The *Phenomenology of Spirit* itself fulfils the role of an eternal reminder of the end of history, preventing the return of Spirit into the human body. Kojève proclaims the end of man, the end of the subject and the end of authorship much earlier than Foucault or Derrida. And he does this in a much more consistent way, because by doing so he also abandons his own original philosophical discourse. After Spirit has changed its body, the only possibility for man to relate to absolute knowledge is in copying, reproducing either certain earlier moments of the development of desire or the whole circle of this development. And that is indeed what Kojève is doing. The posthistorical role of man is not production but reproduction, repetition.

Solovyov started his philosophical discourse on love

9. Ibid., pp. 107ff.

by dissociating sexual desire from its reproductive function: for Solovyov the meaning of love lies in recognition, not in reproduction. But after universal recognition is achieved, mankind has no other choice than to turn back to reproduction as the only activity that still remains possible. For Kojève, the main function of post-historical mankind is to reproduce the Book: to reprint and to repeat the *Phenomenology of Spirit*. Man – humanity as a whole – becomes the reproductive mechanism, or, to use the famous formula of Marshall MacLuhan, the sexual organ of the book. Of course, this all sounds very postmodern. And, indeed, we are dealing here with a very precise description of the post-modern cultural condition, which is characterized by reproduction and appropriation of existing cultural forms. But there is also an important difference between standard postmodern discourse and the Kojèvian discourse. The standard postmodern discourse celebrates play with existing cultural forms as the manifestation of an individual freedom no longer subjected to any form of historical necessity. For Kojève, the end of history is also the end of freedom: freedom, as well as knowledge, spirit and creativity themselves, become artefacts. That is why Kojève does not describe this postmodern repetition in terms of his own, original, new and authorial philosophical discourse – as other theoreticians of the postmodern condition do. Instead, Kojève uses Hegelian dialectics as a readymade. He uses Spirit itself as a readymade – to reveal the gap between philosophical desire and the animal mode of existing that characterizes the posthistorical condition. And by doing so, Kojève explicitly positions himself inside this condition by reducing his own discourse to the same gesture of repetition. Kojève does not even claim to understand and teach Hegelian philosophy, because such a claim would mean that this philosophy has its

Spirit or meaning outside the text. Instead, Kojève insists that the *Phenomenology of Spirit* has already absorbed every Spirit, every meaning. That is why Kojève does not teach Hegelian philosophy – he merely recites it.

The notion of the Book, as Kojève uses it, is in its turn a secularized version of Solovyov's late 'pessimistic' notion of God as a 'super-consciousness' (*sverkh-soznanie*) external to human consciousness, being separated from it by an original, ontological gap. This notion of an impersonal 'super-consciousness' was developed by Solovyov primarily in his *Theoretical Philosophy* (*Teoreticheskaya filosofia*, 1897–99). In his dissertation Kojève refers extensively to this text. But he takes the central idea of his philosophical discourse from a different text of Solovyov's, *The Notion of God* (*Ponyatie o Boge*, 1897). Kojève quotes from this text: 'Our personality is not a closed and full circle of life that has its own content, its own essence . . . but only a bearer, or a pillar (hypostasis) of the Other and Higher.' The metaphysical belief in the ontological priority of the human personality and its initial participation in the truth is denounced here as an illusion: the human personality, the *Dasein* as such, being proclaimed external to the truth. The human personality discovers at the end of history that it can be only a material bearer and a reproductive mechanism of the truth, but cannot possess the truth. And for Kojève, as an atheist, the external status of the truth means its materiality, not its spirituality. The 'super-consciousness' becomes a Book – like the Bible, or like the *Phenomenology of Spirit* (according to Kojève, writing is, in general, '*le suicide médiatisé*').

Of course, The Kojèvian description of the post-historical, or rather post-revolutionary mode of existence had an obvious political edge. It was directed against the nostalgic, Slavophile utopias of the Russian emigration. In his dissertation, Kojève many times and in different contexts recapitulates the historiosophical views of Solovyov and stresses that Solovyov had never been a Slavophile in the sense of being a Russian nationalist. This means for Kojève that Solovyov never believed in something like an original Russian spirit, or the intrinsic value of Russian culture. Instead, Solovyov valued Russian culture and the Russian imperial state only as a passive material bearer – an historic medium and a reproductive mechanism for the eternal truth of Byzantine Christianity, which he believed was the final revelation of Absolute Knowledge. At the same time, according to Solovyov, Russian culture was able to transport and reproduce the Absolute Knowledge embodied by Byzantine Christianity precisely because it had remained completely external to this knowledge, confined in what could be called a purely animal, material way of life that was characteristic of the social condition of the Russian peasantry. And this means that Solovyov, as a Russian philosopher, already conceived of himself as a philosopher after the end of the history of truth – understood by him as the history of Christianity. That is also why Solovyov never claimed to reveal his own, original, new philosophical truth. Instead, he claimed only to repeat the Absolute Truth already revealed by Byzantine Christianity in philosophical terms understandable to his own modern cultural milieu. And that is why, as Kojève says, Solovyov was not a philosopher. Being a part of Russian culture, Solovyov could only repeat or reproduce, because Russian culture as a culture of reproduction and appropriation was an originally posthistorical, originally postmodern culture. One can say that Kojève himself merely repeats this gesture of Solovyov's – the gesture of abandoning the individual, personal claim of originality – transposing this gesture from the theological into the philosophical context and substituting the Bible and the writings of the Fathers of the Church with the *Phenomenology of Spirit*.

At the same time, Solovyov's insistence on the originally external position towards truth and Absolute Knowledge is described by Kojève as the end of love – the end of love for the West. Solovyov was fascinated at one time by the free and creative spirit of the West. Kojève devotes several pages of his dissertation to a description of the various hopes and illusions that Solovyov nurtured in regard to Western culture, as well as to the unusual amount of energy that Solovyov invested in attempts to unite the passive, material body of Russian culture, understood as the mute and submissive aspect of *sophia*, with the masculine, desiring, free spirit of the West. Solovyov tried to achieve this unity on the theoretical as well as on the practical level – through his project of reunification of the Eastern and the Western Christian churches. Through this unification, Solovyov hoped, the Western spirit would be able to penetrate the material body of Russian culture and produce a new culture which would be the true end of human history. But Kojève asserts in his dissertation that at the end of his life Solovyov became completely disillusioned and abandoned all these earlier political projects and hopes.

Russian culture tried time and again to emerge from its semi-animal, material condition by approaching the West, attempting to unite itself with the West – and by assimilating its cult of personality. But the historical path of Western culture itself brings it back to the animal, purely material mode of existence, since the satisfaction of philosophical desire leaves the West to purely material, animal consumption – in no need of any kind of recognition. Russia wants to become like the West. But in fact the West is becoming like Russia. Trying to escape the premodern animality of Russian life by emigrating to the West, the Russian philosopher must necessarily go the whole way to postmodern animality – following the logic of Western culture itself. He cannot escape this chain of repetitions and become historical. His travel from the prehistoric in Russia to the posthistoric West means ultimately a repetition of the same.

At several places in his *Introduction*, Kojève insists that Hegel's philosophical discourse should be understood as primarily a kind of commentary on the historical mission of Napoleon. Napoleon was a man of action who introduced the new universal and homogeneous order at the end of European history – but who did not perceive the meaning of his own action. It was Hegel who understood the historical role of Napoleon, and who functioned as the self-consciousness of Napoleon. In the same sense, Kojève understood himself as the self-consciousness of Stalin who, in his turn, repeated the historical action of Napoleon by introducing the universal and homogeneous state in Russia. In this sense, too, Kojève interpreted himself as repeating Hegel: Kojève understood his own repetition of Absolute Knowledge as an effect of the repetition of Napoleon's action by Stalin. At the same time, both of these figures repeat the figure of Christ, who initiated a universal and homogeneous Church. Of course, both rulers were often enough compared to Anti-Christ. But from the Kojèvian 'atheistic' perspective, the difference between Christ and Anti-Christ that was of such central importance for Dostoyevsky or Solovyov loses its relevance. So Kojève can himself repeat Solovyov, who presents his own philosophical discourse as the self-consciousness of Byzantine Christianity – beyond the difference between theology and philosophy, or between the Bible and the *Phenomenology of Spirit*. Every end of history repeats other ends of history. This endless sequence of repetitions is interrupted from time to time by short periods of philosophical desire, of futile longing – periods that disappear without any trace, even without any memory as soon as these desires are satisfied. The role of a Sage is to prevent the seduction of philosophical desire. His role is to testify that the animal condition is not something to be overcome, to be transcended in the form of the Hegelian *Geisterreich* or the sophiological 'God-Man' (*obozhennoe chelovechestvo*), but that this is the ontological condition of the human being as a bearer but not an owner of Absolute Knowledge.

9

NIETZSCHE'S INFLUENCE ON THE NON-OFFICIAL CULTURE OF THE 1930S

This chapter will discuss several Russian thinkers of the late 1920s and 1930s, few in number but historically significant, who remained active during the Stalinist period but kept their distance from the official ideology: Gustav Shpet (1879–1937), A. A. Meier (1875–1939), Mikhail Bakhtin (1895–1975) and the writer Mikhail Bulgakov (1891–1940). During the 1930s, these authors strove to continue the tradition of Russian non-Marxist thought and to examine the cultural situation in the Stalinist Soviet Union in terms of this tradition. While one cannot really speak of a consensus among them, all of them still, to a greater or lesser degree, based their thought on the ideological heritage of the Silver Age, which was based primarily on a combination of Nietzscheanism and the Russian sophiological tradition (the latter derived primarily from the philosophy of Vladimir Solovyov). The influence of Nietzsche in their texts was translated into the specific philosophical language of Russian religious philosophy at the beginning of the twentieth century, a language which continued, as late as the 1930s, to provide a fundamental lexicon for describing the world.

This circumstance makes the above-mentioned authors especially interesting for the history of ideas, in as much as they continue the Nietzschean tradition in the circumstances of Soviet socialism of the Stalinist period, which is radically different from the context of the bourgeois culture of the nineteenth century in which Nietzsche himself developed his discourse and critique of culture. In the West, this context subsequently underwent significantly fewer radical changes than in Russia, so that Western followers of Nietzsche could identify relatively easily with cultural positions taken by him. Russian authors in the 1930s, on the contrary, found it necessary to redefine, in terms of the Nietzschean tradition, their own cultural point of departure in a cultural situation that was entirely new for them personally, and also historically unprecedented. It is exactly to an investigation of these attempts at self-definition in the culture of Stalin's time that this chapter is dedicated.

Stalinism and the contemporary totalitarian structure of power associated with it constituted the essential reality to which all writers of the 1930s constantly had to relate, whatever their actual theme at any given moment, even if necessity demanded that they do so in a more or less veiled manner. A major determining factor in the relationship between Stalinist ideology and the heirs of the Russian religious renaissance is specifically the Nietzschean component, which contributed to both the official culture and to the non-Marxist world-view. This Nietzschean component did not allow these non-Marxist thinkers to assume a position in radical opposition to official culture; at the same time, Nietzsche's legacy prevented them from identifying with official culture. More importantly, they used the terminology of Russian Nietzscheanism to comprehend and theoretically resolve this conflict.

The 'atheistic' line of Russian Nietzscheanism, which was thus mainly absorbed into official Soviet culture, was complemented by a second, considerably more philosophically developed line. As a result of post-revolutionary repression, however, this second 'religious' reception of Nietzsche had become almost extinct by the 1930s. The very possibility of such a reception, despite the genuinely inimical attitude of Nietzsche himself towards Christianity, arose as the result of a particular philosophical situation that had taken form in Russia at the very moment when interest in Nietzsche's work first emerged.[1]

In the 1870s and 1880s the philosophical pessimism of Arthur Schopenhauer (1788–1860) made a lasting impression on a series of Russian thinkers. In his relatively early work, 'The Crisis of Western Philosophy' (1984), Vladimir Solovyov (1853–1900) interpreted the Schopenhauerian self-negation of the World Will as an extreme radicalization of the one-sided rationalism of Western European thought, with its emphasis on abstract reason to the detriment of the world and matter.[2] Following the old Slavophile tradition, Solovyov saw the sources of Western philosophic rationalism and Schopenhauer's nihilism in the abstract rationalized theology of Western Christianity (Catholicism and Protestantism). According to Solovyov, this one-sidedness corresponds to the one-sidedness of Schopenhauer's understanding of the World Will as 'unconscious' and,

1. For more detail on the religious reception of Nietzsche in Russia, see Ann Lane, 'Nietzsche Comes to Russia', and Bernice G. Rosenthal, 'Stages of Nietzscheanism: Merezhkovsky's Intellectual Evolution', both in Rosenthal, ed., *Nietzsche in Russia*, Princeton 1986, pp. 51–68 and 69–94, respectively.

2. Vladimir Solovyov, 'Krizis zapadnoi filosofii; protiv pozitivistov', *Complete Works*, Brussels 1966, vol I, pp. 27–151.

consequently, purely destructive. Solovyov saw the only way out of this situation as a return to the principles of true Christianity, preserved but insufficiently articulated philosophically in the tradition of Russian Orthodoxy. In Solovyov's reading of Orthodoxy the spirit is not opposed to matter; its aim becomes the deification of matter, the world, and mankind. Solovyov wrote elsewhere about the necessity of the union of the free human spirit (endowed in Solovyov's interpretation with a fair portion of materialism, militarism, eroticism and aestheticism) with the Church, or *sophia*, as the eternally feminine 'divine matter' – an 'enlightened' variant of the Schopenhauerian World Will, understood as the World Soul.[3]

The philosophical and aesthetic teachings of Nikolai Fyodorov (1828–1903) and Leo Tolstoy (1828–1910) also constitute an original response to Schopenhauer's philosophy. While both Fyodorov and Tolstoy saw in Schopenhauer's thought the self-negation of Western culture, Tolstoy turned for salvation to a de-individualized, elementary life, understood positively, not negatively as in Schopenhauer, while Fyodorov demanded the restoration of all individual life and its reintegration into universal life. Both Fyodorov and Tolstoy pinned their hopes on Russia.

Nietzsche's teachings came to Russia at the very moment when Russian thought had already made an optimistic 'positive' reinterpretation of Schopenhauer's World Will, which in its own unique way represents the philosophical essence of Nietzscheanism. In this context, Nietzsche's *The Birth of Tragedy from the Spirit of Music* was his first work to become especially popular in Russia. In the Russian philosophy of the Symbolist period, Nietzsche's 'Dionysian impulse' merged with

3. Vladimir Solovyov, 'Chteniia o Bogochelovechestve', *Complete Works*, vol. III, pp. 179ff.

Slavophile 'unity in love and freedom' (*sobornost'*) and Solovyovian '*sophia*-ness'; in fact, it became a codeword for an image of a Russia that carried within itself both the destruction of Western culture and the possibility of its renewal. Furthermore, although Nietzsche's Dionysian impulse met with complete acceptance in Russia, his idea of the *Übermensch* ('Superman', or, in the terminology of the Russian Religious Renaissance, the 'man–god') was basically rejected, or at the very least understood as a dangerous deviation from the path that led to the Solovyovian integrity of the 'god–man', a deviation dictated by Western rationalism and individualism, reaffirmed and perpetuated by the figure of the *Übermensch*, and thereby potentially depriving Russia of her eschatological victory.

This negative attitude towards Nietzschean 'will-to-power' does much to explain the way in which the heirs of the Russian Religious Renaissance comprehended the Russian Revolution and Stalinism. In the Revolution they welcomed the Dionysian impulse that was destroying the old world of European culture; at the same time they feared the threat of the deification of man, 'the man–god' (as opposed to Solovyov's 'god–man'), which they perceived as a new victory for Western rationalism and individualism in an even more radical form. This man–godhood, however, which was becoming more definitely established in the 1930s, could not be completely rejected by them as long as there was hope for its 'transfiguration into god–manhood'. As long as this hope continued, the force of man–godhood kept its hidden attraction even for those who more or less openly opposed it.[4]

Educated primarily on the 'Russian' Nietzsche, the heirs of Russian Silver Age thought could not speak

4. Typical in this respect is the work of Nikolai Berdiaev, *Istoki i smysl russkogo kommunizma*, Paris 1955.

out in the 1930s against the new Stalinist regime from the position of individualism, the rights of man, moralism, democracy, and so on, as would seem natural to us from today's perspective. On the contrary, they saw the source of the rationalism, utilitarianism, alienation, coldness and hierarchic tendency that characterized the new regime specifically in this Western individualistic tradition, and they strove to counteract it with an ever greater Dionysian dissolution of the individual, an ever greater loss of the boundaries, privileges and security of the individual. The protest of this group of thinkers against Stalinist culture can most accurately be described as favouring the early Nietzsche and rejecting the later Nietzsche.

Let us see how this was reflected in the writings of four major figures within Russian unofficial cultural circles on the eve of the Stalinist period, beginning with A. A. Meier, whose late philosophical essays represent a transformation in his own view of Nietzsche. A writer of the Symbolist period and an active member of the Petersburg Religious–Philosophical Society, Meier published his work in various places, including the almanac *Fakely* ('Torches', 1906–08); he played a substantial role in the formulation of the program of 'mystical anarchism'. After the Revolution Meier took part in the work of the last officially tolerated centre of non-Marxist Russian thought, *Vol'fila* (the 'Free Philosophical Association' 1919–24). Late in 1917, Meier and G. P. Fedotov organized an unofficial religious–philosophical circle in Petrograd. This circle, striving to continue the work of the Petersburg Religious–Philosophical Society under the new political conditions, played an important role in the intellectual life of the old capital in the 1920s. In 1928, Meier and other members of the circle were arrested. Meier was freed in 1935, and before his death in 1939 wrote a large number of works on philosophy and culture, in which he attempted to reflect the new historical experience he had gained.[5]

The basic tenets of Meier's world-view were delineated in his early article, 'Religion and Culture' (1909).[6] Its main thrust lies in its discussion of the conflict between relative cultural values and absolute religious claims, expressed through the rejection of culture in the name of a higher Divine impulse. This conflict in the Russian thought of that time is usually associated with the opposition between the 'Hellenistic' line in Christianity – whose major representative was considered to be Viacheslav Ivanov (1866–1949), who tried to unite Christianity and Dionysianism – and its 'Judaic' line, represented by Lev Shestov (1866–1938), who urged that God be sought beyond the limits of all rational, ethical, aesthetic and other cultural criteria. Both Ivanov and Shestov were inspired by Nietzsche: the difference between them lay only in the fact that Ivanov, rejecting rational science and ethics, preserved aesthetics and 'myth', while Shestov rejected the sphere of culture in its entirety. Although Meier's point of view is close to Ivanov's in many of his other works, in 'Religion and Culture' Meier essentially shares Shestov's position.

Meier begins his article with a reference to Nietzsche: '"It has become cold", as Nietzsche's wise man, seeking God, said. An awareness that the "murder of God" created this cold, that life is becoming an ever emptier and pettier game, is beginning to take hold.'[7] Here

---

5. For A. A. Meier's biography and a history of his circle, see N. P. Antsiferov, 'Tri glavy iz vospominanii', in *Pamiat'; istoricheskii sbornik* 4, Paris 1981. See also Foreword and Addendum in A. A. Meier, *Filosofskie sochineniia*, Paris 1982.

6. Meier, *Filosofskie sochineniia*, pp. 31–95.

7. Ibid., p. 31.

Nietzsche appears as the initiator of a new search for God and for a new religious consciousness. But this is not the only role Nietzsche plays in 'Religion and Culture'. Just as important for Meier is the Nietzschean analysis of culture as the sphere of the will-to-power; Meier uses this as a basis for the rejection of culture as a whole. For Meier, culture is fundamentally oriented towards the satisfaction of the demands of the individual, isolated man. However:

> having bowed down to himself, man bowed before the worst of gods – the man of the future – We are people, and bowing down before the man of the future, we bow before the oppressor of the future. The God of the future is the great Solitary One, standing on the corpses of millions, he is the Powerful One, loving no one, but subordinating all ... Power is not an empty word. Power is beautiful and vital, and the ideal of power can be an inspiration. The Superman is not a dead impulse, and serving him is a whole religion in itself, but it is the inverse of the religion of overcoming, the religion of freedom, the true religion.[8]

Meier thus sees the Nietzschean analysis of culture in Shestovian terms as a total critique of culture, necessitating a search for a transcendent God – in other words, as the direct opposite of the position explicitly advocated by Nietzsche himself.[9]

Meier subsequently connects this search with Communism, which he sees as a secularized version of the chiliastic, religious impulse leading to the 'Kingdom of God on Earth'. Within this religious perspective

---

8. Ibid., pp. 39–42.
9. Lev Shestov considered Nietzsche's teaching about the Superman to be the rejection of a philosophical position proper and a transition to traditional moralizing, always having as its aim the maintenance of the status quo. See Lev Shestov, *Dobro v uchenii gr. Tolstogo i F. Nietzsche*, St Petersburg 1900, pp. 200ff.

Meier criticizes the actual socialist movements of his time for their inability to achieve true collectivism and for reducing it to the demand for the collectivization of property; this leaves the individual relatively autonomous, and does not completely abolish its legal and cultural basis. Meier writes: 'The sin of the collectivists possibly lies in their acceptance of the freedom which contemporary humanists prize into their kingdom of the future.'[10] Meier contrasts this limited socialist ideal with the religious communist ideal, based on love, and the community of life as a 'wedding feast', a holiday, the beginning of all creativity. He asks: 'How could [such Communism] do otherwise than forget all about the guarantees of freedom and about the autonomy of the individual, if it was born from faith in the liberating power of love?'[11] Meier sees the basic threat to this chiliastic hope once again in culture, understood as the power of man over nature and consequently over other men. And so in our time, writes Meier, with another reference to Nietzsche as 'the last great European thinker', culture appears to be of necessity syncretic and cold – a symptom of the waning of life.[12]

The strategy behind Meier's handling of Nietzschean thought, generally representative of Russian thought of that period, becomes clear in this article. Meier seems to subject all of European culture, including all of its scientific, moral and legal values, to Nietzschean criticism. He agrees with the later Nietzschean diagnosis of culture as the expression of the will-to-power, having as its telos the birth of the Superman, but he understands this diagnosis not as a new foundation for culture, but as its final negation. He opposes to it the Dionysian ecstasy of the early Nietzsche, purified of all

---

10. Meier, *Filosofskie sochineniia*, p. 89.
11. Ibid., p. 94.
12. Ibid., p. 74.

cultural–mythological deposits – in other words from all things 'hellenic' – and in such form taking on a Judaeo-Christian chiliastic orientation.

Within the context of Meier's early chiliastic expectations, which persisted during the 1920s in the ideology of his circle (it was dedicated to 'making the Bolsheviks listen to reason'), Meier's writings of the 1930s are particularly interesting when viewed as a reaction to the development of actual cultural processes of the time.[13] In articles such as 'Revelation (On the "Revelation [of St John the Divine]")', written between 1931 and 1934, Meier re-examines the very concept of Life, which earlier, under the influence of Nietzschean *Lebensphilosophie*, stood at the centre of his philosophical interests and aspirations. Meier now views Life not as an alternative to culture, but as an abstraction which has meaning only within the framework of general cultural and, concretely, philosophical discourse; consequently, according to Meier, life cannot be a foundation of culture.[14] Further on he emphasizes the personalist source of culture, founded in the idea of a personal God. The personality receives its basis in the 'glorification' of God, in prayer, in 'personal song'.

Correspondingly, Meier also re-evaluates the choral source of Greek tragedy. He now sees Dionysian dithyrambs as 'unenlightened' and juxtaposes them to individualized psalmody.[15] Culture no longer appears to Meier exclusively as the expression of the will-to-power. He now uses this designation basically to describe the culture of the 'new age'. The religiously oriented and enlightened Dionysian ecstasy, directed towards the transcendent, is consolidated in the Word, in the

---

13. See E. N. Fedotova, 'Vospominaniia', in Meier, *Filosofskie sochineniia*, p. 454.

14. Meier, *Filosofskie sochineniia*, pp. 178ff.

15. Ibid., p. 148.

transcendently oriented culture of the Middle Ages. For Meier, the alternative to culture as a whole thus loses its Nietzschean character of unconscious vital force or unarticulated Dionysian 'other', and acquires the character of an articulated, but demonic, cultural impulse. Hence Meier directly criticizes Nietzsche on the very point on which earlier he had agreed with him.

In his extensive study, 'Thoughts on Reading *Faust*' (1935), which is basically a critique of the Faustian orientation to 'the deed' (Meier prefers the Christian orientation to 'the word'), Meier specifically writes about the 'doubling of Faust', seeing in Mephistopheles Faust's inevitable companion:

> In the antique tragedy, if you will, there were also two heroes, not one: the second and no less important character was the chorus, the carrier of consciousness, always standing beside the consciousness of the hero . . . After Nietzsche we also know that the chorus provided the hero with the opportunity to 'see himself surrounded by a crowd of spirits and feel his inner unity' with them . . . Still, in antique tragedy this second 'major' character was more closely tied to the first, being the expression of a single truth, binding for all and affirmed by all; on the other hand, this second character was somehow separate from the hero himself, stood outside him, and, on occasion, was even opposed to him. In the modern tragedy, the situation is different. On the one hand, the second person should be completely and distinctly an 'other', a separate, almost independent personality, with a different attitude towards life and with a different will (because here the hero's 'I' is doubled); on the other hand, this is not really another person, but the very same hero, his other 'I', his *Doppelgänger*, his shadow, his demon. There is no wholeness of the antique hero, but there still is no opposition of the communal choral consciousness to the individual consciousness of the hero. True, the double sometimes plays the role of the chorus – but he plays

this role weakly because the chorus and one of the two souls of Faustian man are two different things. In *Faust* choruses of good and evil spirits frequently appear instead of the traditional chorus, but they are already far removed from the people.[16]

In this passage, which is highly reminiscent of Bakhtin (Mikhail Bakhtin was connected with Meier's circle and arrested for virtually the same 'crimes' as Meier),[17] the place Nietzsche's Dionysian impulse now occupies becomes clearly visible: it loses its impersonality and authority and becomes the individualized voice of the philosopher's own alter ego, or even that of many different alter egos – the different 'good and evil spirits' no longer comprising a unity. Meier's thought develops through constant dialogue with Nietzsche, but this dialogue itself is now placed in a cultural context. The individualization of the voice of the 'other' is undoubtedly connected above all with the reification of Communism and the revolutionary impulse in Russia during the Stalinist regime. In other words, the single, ambivalent Dionysian impulse – as destructive as it is creative – becomes individualized, and as a result divides into the 'good' religious element and the 'evil' Superman element, and to unite these becomes just as impossible as it is simply to separate and juxtapose them. Just as the religious philosopher is aware of his demonic double, this double is innerly connected to the philosopher, and needs him. (The idea is that Satan needs God for his

---

16. Ibid., pp. 305–6.

17. On Bakhtin's ties to the religious–philosophical circles of the 1920s, see Katerina Clark and Michael Holquist, *Mikhail Bakhtin*, Cambridge, MA 1984, pp. 125–41. The philosopher S. A. Askol'dov, a member of Meier's circle, also wrote on the problem of 'the other' in the context of Dostoyevsky's novels. See S. A. Askol'dov, 'Psikhologiia kharakterov u Dostoevskogo', in *F. M. Dostoevskii; Stat'i i materialy*, Moscow/Leningrad 1924, Book 2.

self-definition and self-assertion). Thus Meier continued to find religious content in socialism of the Stalinist kind even in the 1930s, anticipating its internal religious transfiguration.

At the same time, probably under the influence of the rise of German fascism, Meier wrote a political critique of 'naturalism' and its claims of the superiority of the Aryan race, even though in this case, too, he found a hidden religious perspective.[18] For Meier the criticism of modern totalitarian movements, which he designates 'sociologism' and 'naturalism', does not imply a turn instead to a third force – 'humanism.' He writes: 'Indifferent humanism is in the religious sense a blank space, and, if you like, most distant from Christianity.'[19] Meier further proclaims that Buddhism, as a religion of universal indifference, is the fundamental opponent of Christianity. The acme of religious consciousness for Meier becomes the sacred sacrifice to the highest Divine 'I', in which he sees an enlightened and individualized variant of the Dionysian mystery.[20]

Here Meier's Nietzschean training becomes apparent: for him there can be no moral, legal and individualistic censure of the 'tragedy of life', including the tragedy of the Russian Revolution and the Stalinist terror, because he comprehends such censure as being based on irreligious, vile *ressentiment*, which was described by Nietzsche as being Buddhistic and nihilistic. On the contrary, he strives to give meaning to his own experience of suffering by understanding it as a sacrifice in a sacred mystery drama.[21] In such a sacrifice, everything

---

18. See Meier, 'Mysli pro sebia' (1937), in his *Filosofskie sochineniia*, pp. 445–46.
19. Meier, *Filosofskie sochineniia*, p. 444.
20. Ibid., p. 447.
21. See Meier, 'Zametki o smysle misterii (Zhertva)' (1933) in his *Filosofskie sochineniia*, pp. 105–65.

individual and separate, as well as the internal dichotomy of consciousness, becomes irrelevant; in this sense
one can speak here of the affirmation of the Nietzschean
Dionysian impulse. But Meier integrates this impulse
within ritual, so that it becomes subject to 'the word'
and is given the goal of glorifying the transcendent God
– in other words, the Dionysian impulse here loses its
'vitality' and spontaneity, and becomes rooted in culture
and tradition. In his doctrine of sacrifice Meier continues to adhere in essence to the original programme of
the Russian Religious Renaissance, trying to integrate
Nietzscheanism into the Christian perspective, but with
a corresponding correction of this perspective.

Meier is not alone in describing the cultural situation
of the 1930s as the dualism between the Stalinist state as
Apollonian (Superman) supremacy, and personal life in
that state as Dionysian sacrifice. Another example of the
same dualism can be found in Mikhail Bakhtin's theory
of carnivalization, outlined in his book on Rabelais,
written in the late 1930s and early 1940s, but published
only in 1965.[22] In this work Bakhtin interprets the
European carnival as a form of repeated levelling of all
existing social hierarchies, and the temporary abolition
of individual isolation in favour of collective ecstasy and
'people's laughter'. The carnival tradition is examined
further by Bakhtin as a source of 'carnivalized literature', or, more broadly, carnivalized culture within the
general culture of modernity. Bakhtin claims that the
'impulse toward laughter' and the use of 'low' genres
usually excluded from 'official culture' are characteristic
of carnival culture. Bakhtin's theory is arguably an
attempt to comprehend Stalinist culture;[23] we will

22. Mikhail Bakhtin, *Rabelais and His World*, Bloomington 1965.
See also Bakhtin's essay on carnival in *Problems of Dostoyevsky's
Politics*, Minneapolis 1984.
23. Clark and Holquist, *Bakhtin*, pp. 305ff.

discuss only those of its aspects that touch on the topic under discussion.[24]

Like both the theoreticians of Russian Formalism and the theoreticians of official Stalinist culture, Bakhtin derives his general theory of culture from the Nietzschean model, according to which culture is the arena of struggle between different ideologies, deeply ingrained in the very life experience of its bearers. For example, the culturally oriented Russian Formalist school, which was close to the avant-garde and still influential in the 1930s, interpreted the entire history of culture as a struggle between different tendencies, different artistic wills – a struggle in which young, new artistic movements win because of their vitality, while old movements become 'automatized', losing their vital impulse and thus their attraction. Viktor Shklovsky's work in particular, because of its excessive use of vitalist and erotic metaphors, reveals the degree to which the apparent formalism of analysis is subordinated by Russian formalists to the logic of the artistic will and force: the new artistic device is primarily understood as an instrument employed 'in order to reawaken the experience of life, to feel things', to intensify desire.[25] Drawing on Nietzsche, this teaching about the purely vital struggle of artistic

24. For more information on Bakhtin and Nietzsche, see James M. Curtis, 'Michael Bakhtin, Nietzsche and Russian Pre-Revolutionary Thought', in Rosenthal, *Nietzsche in Russia*, pp. 331–54.

25. Victor Shklovskii, 'Iskusstvo kak priem' (1917), in D. Kirai and A. Kovach, eds, *Poetika. Trudy russkikh i sovetskikh poeticheskikh shkol*, Budapest 1982, pp. 82, 84ff. For more on the role of Vitalism in the system of Stalinist culture, see V. Papernyi, *Kul'tura 2*, Ann Arbor 1985, pp. 132ff.; see also Alexandar Flaker, '"Gesunde" oder "kranke" Kunst', in *Die Axt hat geblueht . . . Europäische Konflikte der 30er jahere Erinnerung an die frühe Avantgarde*, Düsseldorf 1987 (Kunsthalle Düsseldorf exhibition catalogue), pp. 115–21, in which the author traces the genealogy of anti-Formalist criticism of the Stalinist period from Nietzsche through Gorky and Lunacharsky to the 1930s.

tendencies, in which the new and the young must be victorious, marks the point at which Russian Formalism intersects with Stalinist culture, which insists that the struggle between progressive and 'vital' ideologies and reactionary and 'decadent' ideologies is the fundamental content of the cultural process.

Bakhtin also considers the dialogue of ideologies to be the basic characteristic of culture, most completely expressed in the 'polyphonic novel'.[26] According to him, this dialogue is not the means of a theoretical search for truth (as we find in the classical Platonic model of philosophical dialogue), but a form of living conflict in which the struggling ideologies can never be really questioned by their bearers or refuted by their opponents, since those ideologies play only an instru-mental, utilitarian role in their bearers' life struggle. The Bakhtinian dialogue is oriented not towards the achievement of truth or consensus, but towards the vital victory of one side or the other. Unlike the Formalist and Stalinist critics, however, Bakhtin main-tains that the struggle of ideologies never ends with the final historical victory or defeat of one of them. The Formalists diagnosed historical defeat of an ideology as the result of the exhaustion of its vital energy (or its 'automatization') of the obsolete ideology; the idea of a victory by means of a superior argument is irrelevant here, for if the ideology preserves its vitality, then it always finds counter-arguments that will be perceived as more convincing. For Bakhtin, however, any ideol-ogy is capable in its own way of revitalization – at least in the form of eternal life – in the ideal, eschatological space beyond life and death. For this reason the dialogue between ideologies, in which, according to

---

26. Bakhtin first developed his idea of the 'polyphonic novel' in his book *Problemy tvorchestva Dostoevskogo* (1929). For the English translation see *Problems of Dostoyevsky's Politics*, Minneapolis 1984.

Bakhtin, both the living and the dead participate equally, potentially stretches into infinity.

To the extent that Bakhtin sees ideologies as vital convictions determined by the specific inner-worldly, 'corporeal' position of their bearers (Nietzschean perspectivism), different ideologies can experience a certain kind of merging beyond any rational consensus only on the level of life, or pure corporeality. This corporeal union in the form of the 'grotesque body' is the essence of Bakhtinian carnival. During the time of carnival, any particular ideology's claim to truth, and consequently to superiority, becomes the object of derision (for Bakhtin, following Nietzsche, the claims to truth and superiority coincide). Bakhtin's carnival corresponds to Nietzsche's Dionysian mystery, transgressing all that is individual; unlike Nietzsche's mystery, however, this transgression takes place within defined, culturally coded forms: carnival is the game of masks in which Dionysian frenzy does not happen in fact, but is only staged or simulated within a particular cultural framework. Thus, although bodies are mixed, a single consciousness, or a chorus (as in Nietzsche) does not result (this is reminiscent of Meier's argument, outlined above). Carnival as a new variant of Nietzsche's Dionysian impulse subsequently becomes in Bakhtin the source of the 'carnivalesque' or 'polyphonic' novel; its author is able, from within his own consciousness, to stage a carnival of ideologies. Nietzsche himself viewed the novel as an extension of the Dionysian musical impulse; he considered it a continuation of the Platonic dialogue containing within itself all aesthetic forms and subordinating poetry to its dialectic.[27] Nietzsche's arguments were later incorporated by Bakhtin into his literary analyses.

Bakhtin opposes the carnivalesque unity of the world

---

27. Friedrich Nietzsche, *The Birth of Tragedy*, New York 1967, pp. 89–93.

to another unity, which he calls 'monologic' – a unity arising from the establishment of the superiority of one particular ideology that then defines 'serious', or true reality. In Bakhtin these two unities form not a dichotomy, but a dualism similar to Nietzsche's dualism of Apollonian and Dionysian impulses, connected by an inner interdependency. In his book on Rabelais, Bakhtin describes carnival in severe enough colours: the aesthetics of carnival generate a constant alternation of 'enthronings and dethronings' accompanied by 'mirthful' tortures, murders, insults, defamation, pelting with excrement, and so on. At the centre of Bakhtin's carnival stands the cult of '"pregnant death", active during the "mirthful time", which in death gives birth; it does not allow anything old to be perpetuated, but never ceases to give birth to the new and the young'.[28]

If it is justifiable to see a metaphor for official Stalinist culture in Bakhtin's monologism, then carnival is not a 'democratic alternative' to this culture, but is its irrational, destructive side. The Bakhtinian description of carnival more than anything else is reminiscent of the atmosphere of Stalinist show trials, with their unexpected 'enthronings and dethronings'. But Bakhtin sees this irrational side of Stalinism – now from the point of view of a victim of repressive Stalinist policies; Bakhtin was himself such a victim – in a Nietzschean way as a Dionysian or sacred sacrifice, and thereby gives a higher religious meaning to his own life as well.

At the same time Bakhtin has a negative attitude towards any form of isolation of the individual and, correspondingly, to the guarantee of his rights liberally understood, insisting on the destruction of any such self-isolation during the 'Great Time' of all-encompassing participation in the carnivalistic event. The question

---

28. Bakhtin, *Rabelais and His World*.

naturally arises here of how Bakhtin combines his emphasis on individual ideology with joy on the occasion of the destruction of the individual. For Bakhtin, the individuality of ideology is not identical with the individuality of the concrete, human 'I' as its bearer. Ideology marks a particular place in the world, a place that anyone can occupy in principle; in other words, ideology is a mask that anyone can put on. From this point of view the figure of 'pregnant death' becomes comprehensible: the annihilation of one 'obsolete' bearer of ideology puts another in his place, and this sacrifice provides every concrete ideology (and, consequently, every dialogic event as a whole) with eternal youth. Bakhtin understands concrete individuality as a particular corporeality, doomed to die: only 'ideology', and not the 'I' or the soul, can achieve cultural immortality.

The impersonal, or extra-personal, status of Bakhtinian 'ideologies' as culturally encoded states of consciousness, or types of the authorial word not rooted in a particular individual consciousness, has its most likely source in a specific variant of Russian phenomenology developed earlier by Russian philosopher Gustav Shpet. Influenced by Nietzsche and Solovyov, Shpet refuses to assign different phenomenological states of consciousness to any concrete 'I', even if it be transcendental, as Shpet's teacher Edmund Husserl does. In his relatively early work, 'Consciousness and Its Proprietor',[29] Shpet, following Solovyov's 'Theoretical Philosophy',[30] affirmed the fundamental impersonality of consciousness. He considered the concept of the subject

---

29. Gustav Shpet, 'Soznanie i ego sobstvennik', in G. Shpet, *Sbornik statei po filosofii, posviashchennyi G. Chelpanovu* ('Collection of articles on philosophy, dedicated to G. Chelpanov'), Moscow 1916, pp. 156–210.

30. Vladimir Solovyov, 'Teoreticheskaia filosofiia', *Complete Works*, vol. IX, pp. 89–166.

an abstraction and a metaphysical illusion, recognizing only the corporeal dimension of subjectivity.

In his later work, *Esthetic Fragments* (1922–23), Shpet wrote a commentary on Tiutchev's famous poem, 'Silentium':

> Truly, truly, 'Stay Silent' is the subject of final consideration, supra-intellectual and ungraspable, completely genuine, *ens realissimum*. 'Stay Silent' is the highest limit of perception, of existence. The conclusion is not the metaphysical plaything of the identity (with German influence) of being and consciousness, no mystery and no obvious Christian puzzle, but simply a radiant beauty, a triumph of light, a 'divine folly' (*vseblagaia smert*), divine because it knows no mercy for all that must die, without hope of resurrection, it is the blessed conflagration of pan-human vulgarity, a mystery revealed in the azure and gold of heaven.[31]

Shpet may be alluding to Tiutchev's poem 'Cicero', which is usually published near 'Silentium' in collections of his poetry because it was written the same year, and in particular to the famous lines:

> Blessed is he who visits this life
> at its fateful moments of strife,
> the all-wise sent him an invitation
> to speak with them at their celebrations.
> He's the witness of high affairs,
> knows their councils, sits on them,
> and a living god while there,
> has drunk immortality with them.

31. Gustav Shpet, *Esteticheskie fragmenty* II, trans. F. Jude, Petrograd 1923, pp. 76–77.

This poem was very popular at the time. Its allusion to Plato's 'Feast' (Symposium) might have been important to Shpet.

In this passage Shpet cleverly unites the Nietzschean polemic with Christianity and German Idealism and a reference to Nietzschean themes in Russian poetry (Viacheslav Ivanov's 'Ens Realissimum'[32] and Andrei Bely's *Gold in Azure*[33]) with an apologia for death phrased in such a way that death is deprived of its 'nihilistic' or 'pessimistic' pathos. This is because consciousness is impersonal in principle, and so the disintegration of concrete individual consciousness does not mean, for Shpet, its negation by the forces of the unconscious, as is the case, for example, in Schopenhauer. In this way death loses its 'sting': it coincides with a philosophical reflection that reveals that the subject is fundamentally non-subjective. Using the vocabulary of Hesserlian phenomenology, Shpet repeats the basic figure of Russian religious philosophy. In this way he prepares the way for Bakhtinian neo-Christian and neo-Nietzschean syncretism, and even for some Bakhtinian images: Shpet's 'divine death' is reminiscent of Bakhtin's 'pregnant death'. On the other hand, Shpet, referring to the Nietzschean proximity of the impersonal and the musical, emphasizes the priority of the poetic word – a position Bakhtin would oppose due to his understanding of 'the other' as 'the other ideology', the alter ego.[34]

Mikhail Bulgakov's novel, *The Master and Margarita*,

---

32. See also Viacheslav Ivanov, 'Dve stikhii v sovremennom simvolizme', *Complete Works*, Brussels 1974, vol. II, pp. 537–61, in which Ivanov likewise makes the correlation between the Dionysian mystery and individual creativity.

33. Andrei Belyi, *Zoloto v lazure*, Moscow 1904.

34. Mikhail Bakhtin, *Voprosy literatury i estetiki*, Moscow 1975, p. 81. Translator's note: *vseblagaia smert'* echoes *Blagaia vest'* – a reference to the Gospels (commonly translated as 'Good News' or 'Glad Tidings'). Shpet may also be implying a death that is good, or

can be regarded as a highly original literary illustration of Bakhtin's theory of the carnivalesque novel. There is no explicit evidence that Bulgakov was acquainted with Bakhtin's theories, but he could have read Bakhtin's book on Dostoevsky, which appeared in 1929. Written in the 1930s but not published until much later, *The Master and Margarita* develops further many of the themes of the Russian Religious Renaissance in novel form. The immediate source for Bulgakov's novel is Goethe's *Faust*. The action takes place in two 'spaces': in the Moscow of the 1930s, where Mephistopheles-Woland and his retinue stage a series of provocations, saturated with the symbolism of carnival; and in scriptural Jerusalem, where Christ and Pilate engage in a potentially eternal dialogue. The appearance of Woland in Moscow and the subsequent immersion of the Soviet capital in 'mirthful time and space' evoke death, injury, madness and destruction on a scale unknown in Goethe, but these events are meant to be perceived comically, since the victims, as Shpet would have said, are the representatives of human banality and vulgarity. In *The Master and Margarita* this terror of carnival surpasses and paralyzes the usual and 'monologic' terror of the NKVD (security police), which in the novel is treated ironically and thus aestheticized. Instead of issuing a moral judgment from the point of view of the victim of this terror (which Bulgakov certainly did during his lifetime), the novel generates a purely Nietzschean sense of superiority, abetted by the moral support of super-human forces over which the NKVD has no power – and which provide not only metaphysical consolation but also very real revenge in this world, not the next.

Even more distinctly Nietzschean motives appear in

---

positive, in that it is natural, useful, meaningful, proper, and in the natural and *right* order of things; in this respect, the concept is akin to Nietzsche's dictum: 'Die at the right time!'

Bulgakov's interpretation of Christ in the Jerusalem chapters of *The Master and Margarita*. If, in the literary–aesthetic treatment of these scenes, there is reference to Ernest Renan's *Life of Christ*, then in their philosophical–ideological content they turn out to be in exclusive proximity to the interpretation of the Scriptures and the image of Christ suggested by Nietzsche in *The Antichrist* (there can be little doubt that Bulgakov read this book, since it was rather well known in Russia at that time). Nietzsche contrasts his own conception of Christ with Renan's, maintaining that concepts like 'genius' and 'hero', used by Renan, are not applicable to Christ.[35] Nietzsche himself characterizes Christ, according to his 'psychological type', as an 'idiot'. This description undoubtedly refers to the image of Prince Myshkin ('the Russian Christ') in Fyodor Dostoyevsky's novel, *The Idiot*, especially since this description is surrounded in *The Antichrist* with numerous allusions to Dostoyevsky. Nietzsche mentions epilepsy, and Siberia, and finally writes:

> That queer and sick world into which the Gospels introduce us – as in a Russian novel, a world in which the scum of society, nervous disorders, and 'childlike' idiocy seem to be having a rendezvous . . . It is regrettable that a Dostoyevsky did not live near this most interesting of all decadents – I mean someone who would have known how to sense the very stirring charm of such a mixture of the sublime, the sickly and the childlike.[36]

Bulgakov – or rather Bulgakov's fictional alter ego, the Master – realizes Nietzsche's desire and writes the 'Russian Gospel', following Nietzsche's recipe given in *The Antichrist*, almost literally. He frees the scriptural

35. Friedrich Nietzsche, *The Antichrist*, Harmondworth and Baltimore 1969. p. 141.
36. Ibid., p. 142.

Christ from all elements of *ressentiment*, discipleship, protest, morality, and all other disturbing characteristics of the prophet, and avoids making Christ a hero. Bulgakov's 'evangelist' type (in the novel he appears under the name of Levi Matthew) is ignorant, vengeful, lower-class and infinitely distant from any understanding of Christ's actual intentions; he is inclined to attribute a fictional 'teaching' and fictional acts to Christ. Bulgakov's Levi Matthew corresponds fully to Nietzsche's understanding of the 'psychological type of the evangelist'. Through the text of the Gospel, Bulgakov's Master 'guesses' (both Nietzsche and Bulgakov use the same term here) the 'psychological type' of Christ; according to Nietzsche, one must be a combination of a doctor and a philologist to do this (Bulgakov, by the way, was trained as a doctor; his father was a theologian[37]). Nietzsche understood the 'psychological type of the Redeemer' as the result of a decadent weakening of life at the peak of its refinement and aristocratism: the Christian 'passive resistance to evil' and the 'search for the Kingdom of God within you' are presented here not as the external demands of morality, but as an internal necessity of life for nature is too over-refined, vulnerable and morbid to be capable of active, vital struggle.[38]

Bulgakov describes just such an over-refined nature in his novel, where his Christ appears under the emphatically Judaicized name of Yeshua Ha-Notsri (which possibly also refers to Nietzsche's idea of the inner unity of Judaism and Christianity). In *The Master and Margarita* Yeshua-Christ is shown basically through his 'fictional' (non-scriptural) dialogues with Pilate, whom Nietzsche characterized in *The Antichrist* as the

37. Marietta Chudakova, *Zhizneopisanie Mikhaila Bulgakova*, Moscow 1988, pp. 12–13, 50.
38. Nietszche, *Antichrist*, pp. 117–29, 126–28, 141, 159–60.

worthiest figure in the Gospels.[39] In other words, Bulgakov's Christ is first and foremost the interlocutor of authority, infinitely distant from the people and from their false, 'base' consciousness. Bulgakov's Christ does not speak in parables and does not instruct; he appears, rather, as a doctor and a psychologist.

Pilate also corresponds completely to the Nietzschean description of the refined and decadent nature of the ruler: he suffers from nervous headaches and wants only peace and quiet. To Pilate's famous question, 'What is truth?' Bulgakov's Christ gives a fully Nietzschean, 'physiological' answer: 'The truth is, first of all, that your head aches.'[40] Thus Christ appears in the novel as a character in collusion with authority and in eternal dialogue with it; he is internally bound to authority by the general experience of elitism and suffering. But since authority in the person of Pilate is subject to a false 'scriptural' interpretation of Christianity as directed against earthly power, Christ perishes. Pilate in *The Master and Margarita* is Christ's double, although he is incapable of admitting it to himself.

The Jerusalem chapters of *The Master and Margarita* appear as the fragments of a novel within a novel, written by the Master, and at the same time as Dionysian visions, or carnivalesque mysteries, evoked by the carnival atmosphere of Moscow staged by Woland. Again there is an obvious parallel to Bakhtin: the carnivalesque, Dionysian mystery turns out to be 'guessed' by the lonely author, who in Bulgakov's novel is the nameless, impersonal – or more accurately supra-personal – Master. The Master forms a new pairing with Woland, and Woland is, among other things, analogous to

---

39. Ibid., p. 162.

40. Mikhail Bulgakov, *The Master and Margarita*, London 1966, p. 33.

Stalin.[41] At the same time, Woland acts essentially 'as one' with Christ. At the same time, Woland embodies the will-to-power of which Christ is deprived. Thus Christ and Woland jointly arrange the fate of the Master, while Margarita (the Master's ideal helpmate) is transformed into a witch in Woland's service. In Bulgakov's novel there exists a unique circle of the chosen, entry to which is given 'beyond good and evil', and to which belong both political rulers, like Stalin, and rulers of the imagination, like the Master; this elite circle is opposed to the moralistic proletarian 'class consciousness'. The theme of the intimate dialogue of the artist with authority (concretely Bulgakov's dialogue with Stalin) is characteristic not only of Bulgakov's work, but also of the work of other Russian authors of that period.

All of the authors discussed above, irrespective of the degree of their personal acquaintance, belonged essentially to one and the same circle of the Russian intelligentsia, and were all formed by the influence of the religious–Nietzschean theme of the struggle against rationalism, rational morality, nihilism, pessimism, and Schopenhauerian 'Buddhism'. By the 1930s these writers could no longer support the appeal of the Russian Religious Renaissance to dissolve the individual in the impersonal Dionysian element to combine Christianity and socialism into a single chiliastic utopia. They perceived the Stalinist regime rather as the triumph of the will-to-power, the coming of the Superman, the one-sided victory of the Apollonian impulse. Nevertheless,

41. Marietta Chudakova, 'Soblazn klassiki', in E. Bazzarelli and J. Kresalkova, eds, *Atti del convegno 'Michail Bulgakov'*, Milan 1986. There is another reference to Stalin in the scene at Woland's ball in *The Master and Margarita*. A nameless villain who has sprayed his enemy's office walls with poison in order to kill him is a new guest at the ball; the author may have had in mind the ex-head of the NKVD Genrikh Yagoda (1891–1938), who was accused of just this crime during the Stalinist show trials of the 1930s.

they still positioned themselves on the side of the Dionysian impulse, which was understood by them now as the ecstasy of self-sacrifice. As early as the 1920s, many Russian writers manifested this Apollonian–Dionysian dualism as division between two characters, one a representative of the Communist 'iron will' and the other a representative of the musical–poetic impulse; these characters frequently appeared as brothers, or even twins.[42] We can say that, if the dichotomy of conscious and unconscious components in official Soviet literature identified by Katerina Clark can be understood as a variant of Apollonian–Dionysian dualism, then that dualism, taken from the Dionysian and not the Apollonian side, also determines the thought of the non-official cultural opposition of that period.

This common Nietzschean background is an explanation of the ambivalence that characterizes the position of these authors in regard to Stalinist culture: they perceive it as the one-sided manifestation of the Apollonian principle of the will-to-power that is suppressing the Dionysian, poetic and dialogic–polyphonic dimension of culture. But this one-sidedness does not provoke in them a morally motivated protest, that 'accusation to the world' against which Nietzsche warned and which he considered to be an indicator of a base frame of mind. On the contrary, they saw their own creativity either as being in a dualistic relationship with Stalinist authority (as the Dionysian impulse is to the Apollonian, or as the focus on the god-man is to the focus on the Superman, and so on), so that authority appeared to them as their own alter ego, and/or as a form of the sacred Dionysian sacrifice. Especially characteristic in this respect is the extraordinary commonality of the cultural references with which the official and

---

42. Typical examples include Iurii Olesha's *Zavist'* (1927) and Boris Pilniak's 'Dvoiniki' (1933).

alternative cultures of the 1930s operated: characteristic of both is the typically Nietzschean interest first of all in antiquity, in the European Renaissance, in early German Romanticism (especially in Goethe), and in the particular problems, arising in this context, of the heroic, the mythological, the popular, and so on. Although Aleksandr Meier, Mikhail Bakhtin, Gustav Shpet and Mikhail Bulgakov were edged out and suppressed by the official Stalinist culture, it would be a mistake to view them in terms of any moral–political opposition to that culture. It is more productive to view the Stalinist culture as a case of actual Nietzschean dualism, in which cultural–political repression practised by Apollonian power appears to its victims as an unavoidable component of a general tragic, Dionysian vision of culture and the world as a whole.

10

A GENEALOGY OF
PARTICIPATORY ART

A tendency towards collaborative, participatory practice is undeniably one of the main characteristics of contemporary art. Emerging throughout the world are numerous artists' groups that pointedly stipulate collective, even anonymous, authorship of their artistic production. What I am concerned with here are events, projects, political interventions, social analysis or independent educational institutions that are initiated, it is true, by individual artists, but that can ultimately be realized only by the involvement of many. Moreover, collaborative practices of this type are geared towards the goal of motivating the public to join in, to activate the social milieu in which these practices unfold.[1] In short, we are dealing with numerous attempts to question and transform the fundamental condition of how modern art functions – namely, the radical separation between artists and their public.

---

1. See Claire Bishop (ed.), *Participation*, London and Cambridge, MA 2006; and Nina Möntmann, *Kunst als sozialer Raum*, Cologne 2002.

Admittedly, these attempts are nothing new, and have their own well-established genealogy. One might contend that it reaches as far back as modern art itself. In the early Romantic era, in the late eighteenth and early nineteenth centuries, poets and artists started to form groups that bemoaned the separation of art from its audience. At first glance such complaints may seem a bit surprising, for the separation of the artist from his audience was a result of the secularization of art – its liberation from clerical paternalism and censorship. However, the period in which art was able to enjoy its newfound freedom lasted only a short time. Many artists did not consider the modern division of labour, which had conferred a new social status upon art, to be particularly advantageous.

The modern state of affairs can be described easily enough: the artist produces and exhibits art, and the public views and evaluates what is exhibited. This arrangement would seem primarily to benefit the artist, who shows himself to be an active individual in opposition to a passive, anonymous mass audience. The artist has the power to popularize his name, whereas the identities of the viewers remain unknown despite the fact that it is their validation that has facilitated the artist's success. Modern art can thus easily be misconstrued as an apparatus for manufacturing artistic celebrity at the expense of the public. However, what is often overlooked is the fact that, under the aegis of modernity, the artist is but an impotent agent at the mercy of the public's good opinion. If an artwork does not find favour with the public, then it is de facto devoid of value. This is modern art's main pitfall: the artwork has no 'inner' value of its own. It has no merit other than the recognition the viewing public bestows upon it, for unlike science or technology it has no compelling function independent of the whims and preferences of its audience.

The statues in ancient temples were regarded as

embodiments of the gods: they were revered, people kneeled down before them in prayer and supplication, they expected help from them and feared their wrath and the concomitant threat of punishment. Similarly, the veneration of icons also exists as a tradition within Christianity – even if God is still deemed to be an invisible deity. The artwork has a completely different significance here than it does in secularized modernity. Of course, it was always possible to differentiate between good and bad art. Aesthetic disapproval, however, was insufficient reason to reject an artwork. Poorly made idols and badly painted icons were nevertheless part of the sacred order. Throwing them out would have been sacrilegious. In the context of religious ritual, artworks considered aesthetically pleasing and those considered aesthetically displeasing can be used with equal legitimacy and to similar effect. Within a specific religious tradition, artworks can have their own individual, 'inner' value, which is autonomous because it is independent of the public's aesthetic judgment. This value derives from the participation of the artist and his public in communal religious practice, in their mutual membership in the same religious community – an affiliation that relativizes the gulf between the artist and his public.

By contrast, the secularization of art entails its radical devaluation. That is why Hegel asserted early on that art was a thing of the past for the modern world.[2] No modern artist could expect anyone to kneel before his work in prayer, expect practical assistance from it, or use it to avert danger. The most one is prepared to do nowadays is find an artwork interesting – and, of course, ask how much it costs. Price immunizes the artwork from public taste to a certain degree. A good deal of the art held in museums today would have ended up in the

2. G. W. F. Hegel, *Introductory Lectures on Aesthetics*, London 2004, pp. 12–13.

200 INTRODUCTION TO ANTIPHILOSOPHY

dustbin a long time ago had the immediate effect of public taste not been limited by economic considerations. Communal economic participation weakens the radical separation between the artist and his audience, and concomitantly forces the public to respect an artwork because of its elevated price, even if it is not particularly liked. But there is a big difference between the religious and the financial value of an artwork. The price of an artwork is nothing other than the quantifiable result of aesthetic value that others have discerned in it. But public taste is not binding for the individual, any more than is the prevailing religion. The respect paid to an artwork because of its price is by no means automatically translatable into appreciation per se. The binding value of art can thus be sought only in non-commercial – if not directly anti-commercial and simultaneously collaborative – practice.

For this reason, many modern artists have tried to regain common ground with their audiences by enticing viewers out of their passive roles, bridging the comfortable aesthetic distance that allows uninvolved viewers to judge an artwork impartially from a secure, external perspective. The majority of these attempts have involved political or ideological engagement of one sort or another. Religious community is thus replaced by a political movement in which artists and their audiences both participate. That said, the practices that are relevant to the genealogy of participatory art are chiefly those that have not only subscribed thematically to a sociopolitical goal, but also collectivized their core structures and means of production. When the viewer is involved in artistic practice from the outset, every piece of criticism he utters is self-criticism. The decision on the part of the artist to relinquish his exclusive authorship would seem primarily to empower the viewer. This sacrifice ultimately benefits the artist, however, for it

frees him from the power that the cold eye of the uninvolved viewer exerts over the resulting artwork.

THE *GESAMTKUNSTWERK*: THE SELF-SACRIFICE
OF THE ARTIST

The strategy Richard Wagner set forth in his seminal
essay 'The Art-work of the Future' (1849–50) is still
central to any discourse on participatory art, and it is
thus worth recapitulating the main points of his text.
Wagner wrote this essay shortly after the failure of
the 1848 revolution; it represents an attempt to
achieve the political aims of the 1848 uprising through
aesthetic means. At the beginning of the treatise
Wagner states that the typical artist of his time is an
egoist who is completely isolated from the life of the
people, and practises his art for the luxury of the rich;
in so doing he exclusively follows the dictates of fashion. By contrast, the artwork of the future must
realize the need for 'the passing over of Egoism into
Communism'.[3] In order to reach this goal, all artists
should abandon their social isolation in two regards.
First, they must overcome the distinctions between
various creative genres – or, as we might call them
today, different artistic media. Overcoming boundaries between the various media would require artists
to form fellowships, in which creative individuals
with expertise in different media would participate.
Second, these artists' fellowships must forgo the incli-
nation to adopt themes or positions that are merely
arbitrary or subjective; their talents should be used to
express the artistic desire (*Kunstwollen*) of the people.
Artists must recognize that the people, as an entity,
are the only true artist:

---

3. Richard Wagner, *The Art-work of the Future*, Lincoln, NE 1993,
p. 78.

Not ye wise men, therefore, are the true inventors, but
the Folk; for Want it was, that drove it to invention. All
great inventions are the People's deed; whereas the
devisings of the intellect are but the exploitations, the
derivatives, nay, the splinterings and disfigurements of
the great inventions of the Folk.[4]

Wagner views himself as a consistent materialist; he
sees not the spirit but rather matter – substance, life,
nature – as the source of truth. Wagner understands
the people to be the substance of social life, and that is
why he calls upon the artist to forgo his subjective,
active, wilful spirit and become one with the stuff, the
very material, of life.

The unification of all creative genres to create the
Gesamtkunstwerk, or total artwork, demanded by
Wagner (and put into practice in his own work) is by no
means to be understood in purely formal terms. It is not
a multimedia spectacle designed to captivate the imagination of the viewer. The synthesis of artistic genres is
for Wagner more a means to an end: the unity of individual human beings, the unity of artists among
themselves, and the unity of artists and the people.
Wagner's understanding of the people is thoroughly
materialistic – he views them primarily as bodies. In his
estimation, individual artistic genres are merely formalized, technicized, mechanized bodily functions separated
from the whole of the human body. People sing, dance,
write poetry or paint because these practices derive from
the natural constitution of their bodies. The isolation
and professionalization of these activities represent a
kind of theft perpetrated by the wealthy classes upon the
people. This theft must be redressed and the individual
reunited in order to re-create the inner unity of each
person, as well as the unity of the people. For Wagner

---

4. Ibid., p. 80.

the *Gesamtkunstwerk* is primarily a social, even political project:

> The great United Art-work, which must gather up each branch of art to use it as a mean, and in some sense to undo it for the common aim of *all*, for the unconditioned, absolute portrayal of perfected human nature – this great United Art-work [the artist] cannot picture depending on the arbitrary purpose of some human unit, but can only conceive it as the instinctive and associate product of the Manhood of the Future.[5]

Wagner's reference to the future is by no means accidental. He does not want to create his *Gesamtkunstwerk* for his contemporaries, a people divided – in unholy fashion, as he describes it – between an elite and the hoi polloi. By contrast, the identity of the people of the future will derive from the realization of the *Gesamtkunstwerk*, a dramatic synthesis that will unite every person participating in it. This drama represents nothing other than the staged demise of the individual, for only such a staging can symbolically overcome the isolation of the artist and establish the unity of the people. Wagner notes:

> The last, completest renunciation [*Entäusserung*] of his personal egoism, the demonstration of his full ascent into universalism, a man can only show us by his *Death*; and that not by his accidental, but by his *necessary* death, the logical sequel to his actions, the last fulfilment of his being. *The celebration of such a death is the noblest thing that men can enter on.*[6]

The individual must die in order to promote the establishment of a participatory – or, as Wagner puts it, a

---

5. Ibid., p. 88.
6. Ibid., p. 199.

communist – society. Admittedly, there remains a difference between the hero who sacrifices himself and the
performer who makes this sacrifice onstage. Nonetheless,
Wagner insists that this difference is suspended within
the *Gesamtkunstwerk*, for the performer 'not merely
represents in the art-work the action of the fêted hero,
but *repeats* its moral lesson; insomuch as he proves by
this surrender of his personality that he also, in his artistic action, is obeying a dictate of Necessity which
consumes the whole individuality of his being.'[7] The
performer must surrender his own specific purpose in
order to be able to represent the hero's sacrifice or, as
Wagner puts it, 'to use up, to destroy the means of art'.
In this way he is on an even footing with the hero. For
Wagner, the performer is not just an actor but also a
poet and an artist – the author of the *Gesamtkunstwerk*,
who has become a performer insofar as he is publicly
enacting the surrender of his artistic egoism, his isolation, his supposed authorial autonomy.[8]

This passage is undoubtedly of central importance
for Wagner's essay. The author of the *Gesamtkunstwerk*
forgoes his subjective authorial power by reducing his
own creative role, re-enacting the sacrificial rituals of
ancient religions, the sacred feasts of antiquity, the
hero's death in the name of the common good. As far
as Wagner is concerned, the author is not dead, as was
to be argued by French poststructuralist theoreticians
such as Roland Barthes, Michel Foucault and Jacques
Derrida. Were the author truly dead, it would be
impossible to differentiate between participatory and
non-participatory art, because the former can only
occur through the celebrated surrender of authorship
by the artist. The general delight surrounding the idea
of the death of the author should not belie the fact that

7. Ibid., p. 201.
8. Ibid., pp. 196ff.

the author must always pre-ordain this demise. One might also claim that the enactment of this self-abdication, this dissolution of the self into the masses, grants the author the possibility of controlling the audience – whereby the viewer forfeits his secure external position, his aesthetic distance from the artwork, and thus becomes not just a participant but also an integral part of the artwork. In this way participatory art can be understood, not only as a reduction, but also as an extension of authorial power.

Wagner is fully aware of this dialectic within the participatory *Gesamtkunstwerk*. Thus he speaks of the necessary dictatorship of the poet-performer, even if he emphasizes that this authority should be predicated on the basis of common enthusiasm – through the readiness of the other artists to participate. Wagner states: 'The *might of individuality* will never assert itself more positively than in the free artistic fellowship.'[9] This fellowship forms with the express goal of setting the stage for the poet-performer so that he can ceremonially forgo his status as author and be absorbed into the people. All other members of the group achieve their own artistic significance solely through participation in this ritual of surrender and self-sacrifice. Wagner's analysis of comedy is especially interesting in this regard, for only the main performer is granted the right to fall ceremoniously and tragically. Any attempt by other participants to stage their own authorship results in the demise of this authorship. In this case, however, the demise of authorship does not look tragic, but instead comical. Wagner comments in a footnote:

> The hero of the Comedy will be the obverse of the hero of the Tragedy. Just as the one instinctively directed all his actions to his surroundings and his foils – as a

9. Ibid., p. 200; emphasis in original.

Communist, i.e. as a unit who of his inner, free
Necessity, and by his force of character, ascends into
the Generality – so the other in his rôle of Egoist, of foe
to the principle of Generality . . . will be withstood . . .
hard pressed by it, and finally subdued. The Egoist will
be *compelled* to ascend into *Community* . . . and, without further breathing-space for his self-seeking, he sees
at last his only rescue in the unconditional acknowl-
edgment of its necessity. The artistic Fellowship, as the
representative of Generality, will therefore have in
Comedy an even directer share in the framing of the
poem itself, than in Tragedy.[10]

For Wagner, the artist's renunciation of his authorial
status with the express aim of establishing a communal
artistic fellowship thus remains ambivalent. The merging of the artist with the people is problematic – it takes
place on a contextual level, so the public can only identify with the demise of the hero symbolically. Moreover,
Wagner's artistic language remains alien to the broad
mass of the people. In his essay 'What Is Art?' Leo
Tolstoy describes in brilliantly ironic fashion the discon-
certing impression that Wagner's operas have on a
'normal' member of the audience, who is neither able
nor willing to penetrate its coded, symbolic meanings.[11]
Furthermore, modern art has attempted both to
de-professionalize itself and to involve the audience
more radically and immediately than Wagnerian opera
was ever able to do.

EXCESS, SCANDAL, CARNIVAL

Many radical avant-garde movements at the beginning
of the twentieth century did indeed choose the path
designed by Wagner in his 'Art-work of the Future'. The

---

10. Ibid., p. 201.
11. See Leo Tolstoy, *What Is Art?*, London 1995.

Italian Futurists and Zurich Dadaists were representative of artistic groups that pursued the dissolution of artistic individuality, authority and authorship on many levels of their respective creative practices. At the same time, they were more direct when it came to activating their audiences, deliberately scandalizing the public or attacking audience members physically. The Italian Futurists grouped around Filippo Tommaso Marinetti repeatedly provoked public scandals – often resulting in common brawls – in order to wrest the audience out of its purely contemplative, passive attitude. In this way the Futurists created a new synthesis between politics and art: they understood both as a kind of event design – as strategies of conquering public space by means of provocation, which served as a catalyst to activate and expose the concealed energies of the masses. In her book on Margherita Sarfatti, who played an important role as a mediator between the Futurists and Fascism, Karin Wieland states that the Futurists' motto was 'War on a nightly basis':

> Marinetti introduced a new tone into politics. He exposed a new socio-psychological dimension with his rebellion against tradition and the law, which neither the liberals nor the socialists had anticipated. He incorporated the methods of a political electoral campaign into art: newspapers, manifestos, public appearances, and scandals.[12]

The Futurists' strategy, aimed less at creating individual art objects and more towards events and collective experiences, was duly borrowed by the Zurich Dadaists (though the Dadaists did not subscribe to Futurism's bellicose nationalistic ideology). The majority of Dada

12. Karin Wieland, *Die Geliebte des Duce. Das Leben der Margherita Sarfatti und die Erfindung des Faschismus*, Munich 2004, pp. 93–94.

artists, who had gathered in Switzerland during the First World War on account of its neutrality, were pacifists and internationalists – a fact that is made all the more interesting when one realizes that their artistic practice owes a lot to Italian Futurism. Participants in Dada events at the Cabaret Voltaire in Zurich, which were chiefly inspired and arranged by Hugo Ball, provoked the audience and allowed the spectacle to result in general tumult. Incidentally, Ball conceived the Cabaret Voltaire as a kind of *Gesamtkunstwerk* from the outset.[13] One might contend that his cabaret was a parodic as well as absolutely serious-minded renaissance of the Wagnerian project. In public performances of 'simultaneous poetry', during which multiple speakers concurrently recited poems in different languages onstage, the meaning of any individual text and the sound of any individual voice were drowned within the indecipherable, anonymous tonal material. The disappearance of the individual voice amid the collective, resonant whole was the actual aim of the event. Ball writes that 'the *poème simultané* deals with the value of the *vox humana*. The human organ loses the soul, the individuality . . . The poem exemplifies how man is swallowed up by the mechanical process.'[14] In his most well-known performance, on 25 June 1917, Ball appeared wearing quasi-episcopal robes and reciting a poem that consisted of sound combinations having no meaning in any known language (so-called *Lautpoesie*). This 'sound poem' provoked a tumultuous response from the audience. Ball recalls that, in order to psychologically withstand the abuse from the audience, he modelled his vocal delivery on a church sermon, even if the words remained meaningless combinations of

---

13. According to Hans Richter, this was due to Kandinsky's influence. See Richter, *Dada, Art and Anti-Art*, London 1997, p. 38.

14. Ibid., p. 28.

sounds manifesting only the sonic material of language. A new paradoxical religion of materialism was being celebrated here – a transvaluation of nonsense into the highest degree of sense.[15] The same strategy may be observed in the later activities of the Surrealists surrounding André Breton, who collectively forsook conscious control over the production of art in favour of the spontaneous effect of the subconscious, but at the same time were politically engaged, and continually provoked public scandal. Various Russian avant-garde groups during the second and third decades of the twentieth century also tried to instigate the demise of the solitary creative artist in order to include the broader masses within artistic practice – and thus transform an entire nation still vibrant from the victory of communism into a *Gesamtkunstwerk* in which all things individual were absorbed into and by the collective.

The argument against such practices has often been that they are repetitive and, with the passage of time, lose their power to shock or provoke. The repetition of authorial surrender seems to diminish the value of this sacrifice, if not to nullify it entirely. However, we know from literature on the subject that the efficacy of sacrificial ritual is primarily a result of its repetitive character. Thus Georges Bataille describes Aztec sacrificial rituals as those practices that renewed the vital strength of Aztec society precisely through their constant repetition.[16] In his book *Man and the Sacred*, Roger Caillois describes the collapse of public order that wrests the people from their customary passivity and unites them whenever a monarch dies or such a death is ritually enacted.[17] It is important not to forget at this juncture

---

15. Ibid., pp. 40ff.
16. See Georges Bataille, *The Accursed Share*, vol. 1, New York 1991, pp. 46ff.
17. See Roger Caillois, *Man and the Sacred*, Urbana 2001.

that religious sacrificial rituals always featured a central protagonist who represented a king or a god, and who was publicly venerated and subsequently sacrificed. Admittedly the modern artist is allowed to live, but he does not escape completely unscathed. The artist's actual sacrifice consists in his self-subjugation to the repetition of the sacrificial ritual and his renunciation of the uniqueness of his artistic individuality – a kind of second-degree sacrifice, so to speak. And this second-degree sacrifice is unique each time it occurs; although the ritual remains the same, the artistic individuality being sacrificed is invariably different.

In this connection it is also interesting to note that if Bataille and Caillois, both of whom were close to Surrealism, described sacrificial ritual in a tragic tone, Mikhail Bakhtin places the same ritual in the context of carnival – as the entertainment and merriment of the people:

> In such a system the king is the clown. He is elected by all the people and is mocked by all the people . . . Abuse is death, it is the former youth transformed into old age, body turned into a corpse. It is the 'mirror of comedy' reflecting that which must die a historic death.[18]

Bakhtin developed his theory of the carnival during the 1930s and 1940s in the Soviet Union, which perceived itself to be an actual communist society. In such a society, individualism – to use the Wagnerian expression – was short of breath: an egoist was automatically an enemy of the people. It is not by chance that Bakhtin describes the demise of the individual, his dissolution into generality, in terms of comedy, not tragedy. This demise elicits only laughter from the people – a happy, carnivalesque laughter that, according to Bakhtin,

---

18. See Bakhtin, *Rabelais and His World*, pp. 197–98.

constitutes and supports the festival in which the entire populace can participate. Accordingly, Bakhtin sees carnival, rather than tragedy, as a model for a participatory – or, as he calls it, a carnivalized – artwork of the future. Far removed from Wagnerian tragedy or gloom, such artwork propagates an exuberant atmosphere of *joie de vivre* by staging and celebrating the victory of the collective body over individual spirit.

During the 1960s artists' collectives, as well as happenings, performances and similar events, were famously reborn on a worldwide scale. Among their number, to name only a few examples, were Fluxus, Guy Debord's Situationist International, and Andy Warhol's Factory. In all of these cases the twofold aim was both the collaboration of different artists and the synthesis of all artistic media. However, central to these activities was the readiness of artists to forgo their isolated, elevated, privileged position in relation to the audience. Fluxus practitioners played at being entertainers and event managers; Warhol propagated art as business and business as art. Whether the respective artists presented themselves as propagandists, provocateurs or businessmen is less important than the fact that they tried in equal measure to devalue the symbolic value of art and to surrender their personal individuality and authorship to commonality. All of this was conducted in an atmosphere that was more humorous or carnivalesque than tragic. The Wagnerian ideal of the tragic fall was only realized in a few, and thus notable, exceptions. Thus, Guy Debord's attempt to dissolve his artistic individuality in the collective art practice of the Situationist International collapsed, resulting in Debord's growing (self-)isolation. Debord's suicide is almost paradigmatic of the kind of problems confronting anyone wanting to stage and control his authorial demise. The insoluble nature of such problems is nevertheless no argument against the *Gesamtkunstwerk* project, but rather the reverse: the formal, logical guarantee of its realization. For it is the paradox of the consciously staged, self-orchestrated fall that causes the author of the *Gesamtkunstwerk* to fail – thus simultaneously realizing the very *Gesamtkunstwerk* itself, which is nothing other than the public performance of artistic failure.

Despite the aforementioned groups' historical, ideological, aesthetic and other differences, there is something that unites their attempts to stage the *Gesamtkunstwerk*: they all presuppose the material, corporeal presence of the artist and the audience in the same (real) room. Be it a Wagnerian opera, a futurist scandal, a Fluxus happening or a Situationist event, each has the same goal: to unite the artist and the audience at a particular location. What, then, of the virtual spaces and interactions that increasingly determine cultural practice, particularly in our own time? One is often inclined to think of contemporary digital media as interactive or participatory per se. And so it seems less imperative today to gather people together physically in one place in order to promote a sense of participation in a social event. It seems possible to create this feeling equally well using virtual means – for example, through participation in interactive digital mass media via the internet.

IS THE INTERNET COOL?

The relationship between 'actual' bodily participation and virtual participation seems particularly relevant to discussions of net art exhibitions and other practices that try to usher internet users into exhibition spaces, making the act of using computers a public event rather than one performed by the user in the privacy of his or her own home. The socialization and display of computer usage may at first appear to be superfluous, if one presupposes that it was already public, interactive and participatory (albeit virtual). In the case of virtual communication and participation, the body of the person using the computer is of no consequence – apart, say, from the physical manifestations of fatigue that are inevitable after a few hours in front of the screen. The experience of bodily presence, for which modern art has continually striven, is absent in virtual communication. As a computer user, one is engrossed in solitary communication with the medium; one falls into a state of self-oblivion, of unawareness of one's own body, that is analogous to the experience of reading a book.

Indeed, the virtual space of the internet is not as different from the traditional space of literature as one might imagine. The internet does not replace printing; it merely makes it more quickly and cheaply accessible – but also requires greater discernment and is more demanding for the user. The user is obliged to print out her texts herself, to illustrate and design them, instead of simply handing them over to a printer. Thus, when one asks oneself whether the internet is participatory, the answer is yes – but typically in the same way as literary space. Everything that ends up in virtual literary spaces is acknowledged by other participants and provokes a reaction, which in turn provokes further reactions. Literary space is fragmentary, but its protagonists do indeed participate in the competition for recognition. The internet is also a medium for competition – tallies are kept of how many hits a particular site receives, how many mentions there are of this or that user, and so forth. This kind of participation would appear to have little to do with Wagner's vision of the individual seamlessly merging with the masses. The goal of participatory art within the tradition of the Wagnerian *Gesamtkunstwerk* does not lie in waiting for technical and social progress (which, as is generally known, can never be concluded), but rather in creating universally accessible art events, here and now, beyond education, professionalization and specialization. Nevertheless, an effective use of the internet requires a good deal of specialized knowledge. The technology is subject to constant modification and updates, differentiating users from one another intellectually as well as economically.

The analogy between traditional literary space and the internet is often overlooked, for we generally perceive electronic media such as the web to be fundamentally different from the older analogue media. This view is doubtless rooted in Marshall McLuhan's 1964 book *Understanding Media*, which elucidates the difference between so-called hot mechanical media – the best example being print – and cool electric media such as television. In McLuhan's view, hot media lead to the fragmentation of society. Conversely, cool media create global, participatory, interactive spaces and practices that overcome the isolation of the individual author, and so 'it is no longer possible to adopt the aloof and dissociated role of the literate Westerner'.[19] McLuhan continues: 'Electric speed mingles the cultures of prehistory with the dregs of industrial marketeers, the nonliterate with the semiliterate and the postliterate.'[20] Under these new media conditions, the Wagnerian programme of the *Gesamtkunstwerk*, which is intent upon uniting the entire populace irrespective of varying levels of education, can be realized automatically through technical progress.

Indeed, McLuhan's understanding of the media shares many similarities with Wagner's vision. Both interpret the individual media as extensions of the corresponding

---

19. Marshall McLuhan, *Understanding Media: The Extensions of Man*, New York 2001, p. 5.
20. Ibid., p. 17.

capabilities of the human body. For both, the human being is the original medium; all other media are derived from this source. It is not by chance that McLuhan's book bears the subtitle 'The Extensions of Man'. However, unlike Wagner, McLuhan does not call for a return to the source medium (to mankind, the people) in order to overcome the isolation of the individual (codetermined by the separation of the media) and bring about the participation of all. McLuhan attributes the modern isolation of the individual – and, above all, that of the intellectual and the artist – not only to the differentiation of the respective media, but also to the specific constitution of the traditional hot mechanical media that dominated the modern period. McLuhan hopes, therefore, that the new cool electric media will enable transition to a new era of collectivity, simultaneity and openness.

Nonetheless, McLuhan does not view this transition as a return to the source medium, the human body, but as a complete anaesthetization – a 'numbing' of man, as he calls it.[21] He believes that every extension of the human body entails its simultaneous 'auto-amputation'; the human organism that has received a media extension is anesthetized, as it were. According to McLuhan, because electronic media effectuate the extension of the human nervous system, which in turn defines the human being as a whole, their generation entails the ultimate numbing of humanity. Writing is a hot medium because it mobilizes people's attention by demanding a high degree of concentration. By contrast, electric media are cold because they create a passive communicative situation that demands less attention. 'There is a basic principle that distinguishes a hot medium like radio from a cool one like the telephone, or a hot medium like the movie from a cool one like TV', states McLuhan. 'A

---

21. Ibid., pp. 46ff.

hot medium is one that extends one single sense in "high definition". High definition is the state of being well filled with data.'[22] One can reformulate this as follows: a cool medium does not differentiate between non-specialists and specialists, the trained or the untrained – it does not demand the faculty of concentration and specialized knowledge. According to McLuhan, it is precisely this removal of concentrated observation that allows the viewer to extend his or her field of concentration, to improve his or her perception of the environment and of other viewers who might enter this environment. In this sense, television is indeed participatory: turning on the TV does not require specialized knowledge. The television medium is in fact cool; it transmits information in a relatively nonsequential manner so that the viewer can relax, eschewing the need for concentration. On the other hand, work on the computer – particularly the internet – demands a degree of concentration that quite possibly even exceeds the focus required to read a book. The internet is thus a hot medium in comparison to TV.

The purpose served by an exhibition that offers visitors an opportunity to use computers and the internet publicly now becomes apparent – namely, the cooling down of the internet medium. Such an exhibition extends the attention and focus of the viewer. One no longer concentrates upon a solitary screen, but wanders from one screen to the next, from one computer installation to another. The itinerary performed by the viewer within the exhibition space undermines the traditional isolation of the internet user. At the same time, an exhibition utilizing the web and other digital media renders visible the material, physical side of these media – their hardware, the stuff from which they are made. All of the

22. Ibid., p. 24.

machinery that enters the visitor's field of vision thus destroys the illusion that everything of any importance in the digital realm only takes place onscreen. More importantly, however, other visitors will stray into the viewer's field of reference, and they will often seem more interesting than the exhibits themselves. In this way the visitor becomes one of the exhibits, for he is aware that he is being observed by the others; he is aware of his physical position in space. A computer-based installation thus prompts the viewer's conscious experience of his own body, an experience normally marginalized by solitary labour at the computer.

A computer installation stages a social event and is bestowed in turn with a political dimension. Even if it does not provoke a brawl in the Futurist manner, it facilitates an encounter between diverse individuals who become aware of the communal presence of their bodies in space. In other words, it is concerned with rendering visible the multitude flowing through the rooms and spaces of modern art museums, which have long since lost their supposed elitist character. The relative spatial separation of art exhibitions does not at all signify an aversion to the world, but rather a delocalization or deterritorialization of the viewer, which in turn serves to widen the perspective of the larger communal space. It is here, in the real space of social communication, that the cooling of the virtual can take place – a process that, if you will, counteracts the dissolution of real space into virtuality, which McLuhan once demanded of art by defining it as 'exact information of how to rearrange one's psyche in order to anticipate the next blow from our own extended faculties'.[23]

---

23. Ibid., p. 72.

LESSING, GREENBERG, McLUHAN

The rivalry between word and image is well known to have a long history. Here I shall only discuss a relatively recent phase of this history – a phase that is still underway. This involves the appearance of words in the image, which took place in the context of the art of the 1960s: in conceptual art – in the form of declarations and theoretical reflections on the limits and role of art, which were presented in written form and integrated into the work of art, but also as recordings of spoken words, as can be heard in contemporary installations, and finally as poetic lines that appear inside the image, as for example in the pictures of Anselm Kiefer. But how do these texts come into the picture? How does the spoken word appear in an artistic installation? We might believe that language is essentially foreign to the picture, that language happens outside the picture. There is accordingly a widespread demand, in contemplating such pictures, to focus on the picture itself, and let it have its effect on the spectator – despite all declarations and explanations that are ultimately external to the picture. The text or the voice operate in this case as readymades, taken from external reality and integrated into the work of art, just like any other readymade. Taken literally, readymade procedures of this kind also involve abandoning the self-reflection of the work of art, as this was practised by art of the modern age in the twentieth century. In fact, the use of this term generally applies to the opening of the work of art to the world around it, the return of art to realism, to a strategy of depicting the outside world – even if in a new form. I would like to show, however, that the picture as such is in no way foreign to speech, but rather that it always suggests a silent message, a particular intention to say something. Speech is thus not located outside the picture, but rather behind its surface, so that it should not particularly surprise us if it appears on the picture surface and the picture starts to speak.

As the starting point of this discussion, I would like to take Lessing's famous essay *Laocoon*, which aims at defining a hard-and-fast boundary between language and picture – or, more precisely, between the arts of poetry and visual depiction. Lessing defines this boundary as follows:

> If it be true that painting employs wholly different signs of means of imitation from poetry – the one using forms and colours in space, the other articulate sounds in time . . . then signs arranged side by side can represent only objects existing side by side, or whose parts so exist . . . Consequently bodies with their visible properties are the peculiar subjects of painting. Objects which succeed each other, or whose parts succeed each other in time, are actions. Consequently actions are the peculiar subjects of poetry.[1]

---

1. G. E. Lessing, *Laocoon: An Essay Upon the Limits of Painting and Poetry*, trans. E. C. Beasley, Hamlin Press 2008, p. 91.

This rather laborious formulation suggests a certain parity between painting and poetry or, more precisely, between picture and narrative. Both administer their own areas of being, clearly separated from one another. The picture handles space, while poetic narrative deals with time, history, the event. The apparent correctness of this separation of powers is still further emphasized by Lessing's concession that painting can depict not only bodies but also actions, though only, as he puts it, 'through means of bodies'. Poetry, for its part, is deficient in a similar way, since it can only depict bodies 'through means of actions'.

If we consider the overall strategy of Lessing's *Laocoon*, however, it is noticeable that this appearance of equity is deceptive. The whole text is actually directed above all against the assumption that painting not only is beautiful but also can be true, that painting is able to portray the world faithfully and true to life. The critique of this claim to truth on the part of art – and of the art of painting in particular – is certainly not new. From Plato to Hegel, philosophers have always maintained that pictures lie, or at least that they are inadequate for grasping the truth. Their various formulations are familiar: Plato blamed the artists for depicting only appearances, instead of reaching for their concealed prototypes, and Hegel, right at the start of his *Aesthetics*, maintained that in the age of the absolute spirit, art would be essentially a thing of the past. Today it can easily be said that the hostility to pictures on the part of these philosophers derived from their belief that they could establish themselves in the sphere beyond the visible world of the senses. It is just as easy to disqualify them as metaphysicians whose time is over, as today we no longer believe in the transcendent, invisible and absolute. We prefer to use our own eyes, and do not want any theories and tales of what escapes our view. We want to see; we want evidence. We want a witness who has not only heard, but seen with their own eyes. And this is why we live in a world in which the visual media have triumphed over speech. Of course, these media are constantly criticized for a distorted and falsified view of the world, but this very criticism proves our expectation that the visual media should show things as they truly are. In this sense, it seems justifiable to say that the age of metaphysics is indeed at an end, and metaphysically inspired iconoclasm no longer relevant.

What is interesting about Lessing's essay, however, is that his criticism of the truth claim of painting is free of any metaphysical argument. Lessing does not appeal to an invisible truth. And he does not reject pictorial, poetic speech for the sake of replacing it by a language of abstraction and reason. The sole reason why the picture is deficient, in Lessing's view, is that it cannot depict actions or any human practice. The reason for this is simple: in order to depict human actions, language must also be reproduced, or more precisely the live speech that people use to accompany their actions. Literature and poetry can do this, but painting cannot. People's visual images remain mute, and in this way are removed from the actual practice of life, which is inconceivable without speech. If painting attempts to depict speaking people, it simply confronts us with unpleasantly distorted faces or disfigured bodies. Lessing devotes several pages of his essay to describing his impressions of pictures that try to present people in the act of speaking. All these depictions strike him as awkward, even ugly. If a Greek or Roman poet describes how the heroes of his tale cry, curse, bewail or accuse, in Lessing's opinion this always sounds immensely more poetic and artistically convincing. If, on the other hand, a painter attempts to depict the same subject visually, by painting faces with wide-open mouths or bodies disfigured by excessive gesture, the result can only arouse a feeling of disgust on the part of the viewer. The unrealized, mute act of speech, simply indicated in a painting, degenerates into a grimace – and looks obscene. In painting, therefore, though we are not confronted with speech itself, we are time and again confronted with the silent *vouloir-dire* – with an unfulfilled, frustrated, suppressed desire to speak. Precisely this spectacle of the suppressed desire to speak makes the picture that sets this spectacle in motion obscene – fully comparable with an obscene picture of suppressed sexual desire. It is no accident that Lessing chooses the picture of the old men who silently admire the beauty of Helen, and thus comment equally silently, as a particularly telling example of painting that seeks to be realistic but has only a revolting effect.

Lessing's arguments, moreover, apply not just to still pictures, but also to the moving pictures that came later. The present-day reader of Lessing's descriptions of paintings is inevitably reminded of silent films that need the supplement of inter-titles to make clear precisely what kind of passion has distorted the faces of the actors. But despite these verbal supplements, such films seem awkward and comical to the contemporary viewer – indeed, even obscene. This impression only disappears with the introduction of a soundtrack. And it is interesting to note in this connection that Lessing's characterization of the picture as scene of a frustrated desire to speak is shared by those artists who have sought to give their pictures a wider public effect. In comic strips, the characters' desire to speak suddenly breaks through in the form of shapeless bubbles flowing from their mouths, in which individual words and phrases, as well as mere shouts such as 'Vroom!' or 'Crash!', are swimming around. Some artists, such as Lichtenstein or Erró, have used this technique in their paintings, but the great majority of modern artists have taken another path, so as not to destroy the aesthetic integrity of their picture by the obscenity of the desire to speak.

This path, which allows the artist to create an aesthetically complete, artistically integral work, was already proposed by Lessing. The depicted figures' desire to speak has to be so radically suppressed, their renunciation of speech so consistently practised, that no distortions by this suppressed *vouloir-dire* can disfigure the picture. Only in this way, Lessing maintained, can a beautiful painting be produced, its beauty guaranteed by the fact that it depicts an isolated body, reposing in itself, defined only by the position of its elements in space. As an example, Lessing again evokes a picture of Helen – but this time the painting that tradition holds was made of her by Zeuxis: standing alone, naked, completely detached from the world, and not marked by any grimace of *vouloir-dire*. And yet this explicit 'not wanting to speak' on the part of Helen can again be understood as a statement – and indeed, a statement that is expressed by her whole figure. This figure accordingly does indeed depict a grimace of 'not wanting to speak', but to understand this statement, it is not enough to contemplate the picture. We need also to read and understand Lessing's discussion of it. And it can then be said: the suppression of *vouloir-dire* in the depiction of a figure only leads to this whole figure being perceived as a grimace of the frustrated *vouloir-dire*.

The same thing applies to the modern artwork, which emerged as we know as the result of a radical struggle against narrative, recounting, 'wanting to speak'. In the course of this struggle, all depiction of bodies and things was removed from the picture surface, so as radically to suppress the grimaces of 'wanting to speak'. On top of this, it was repeatedly maintained in the modernist tradition not only that figures that might still be depicted in the picture should no longer convey any message, but that this should especially be true of the picture itself, which should not try to say anything, not suggest any desire to speak. The modernist, autonomous artwork seems to embody this completely ascetic stance towards speech. All it presents is its physical, thingly, material presence in the world – as a body alongside other bodies, which completely corresponds to Lessing's definition of pictorial art. Here we no longer have the human desire to speak, to be pictorially depicted or suppressed. What we have is rather the latent desire to speak on the part of the picture itself – if you like, the linguistic unconscious of the picture, its ability to convey through the picture surface messages that can also be grasped in words. It is precisely this desire to speak on the part of the picture, and the artwork in general, that is systematically suppressed in the modern age. The great ideal of 'not wanting to speak' dominates the whole history of classical modernity, and culminates in the works of Donald Judd, which do not even want to say that they are artworks but present themselves only as 'specific objects', which have no depth, nothing within, no content, nothing concealed or hidden, and are by nature just as they show themselves: 'You see what you see.' There is nothing more in the artwork that is hidden from view and presses outward from inside. The suppression of the desire to speak seems here to be completely successful – and Lessing's dream of the perfect artwork definitively fulfilled.

We know today, however, that this is not how such artworks actually function. Clement Greenberg had already put forward in the 1930s the thesis that the modern picture showed not only its perceptible surface, but also and above all the concealed material properties of its medium. As far as painting was concerned, Greenberg described this property as 'flatness', and he accordingly demanded that modern painting display its two-dimensional character as consistently as possible.[2] This led to Greenberg often being characterized and criticized as dogmatic. In connection with my present discussion, however, the aims that Greenberg prescribed for painting are not so important. I would rather seek to show that, de facto, by his demand for painting to thematize its own material medium, Greenberg bore in mind the picture's desire to speak. Modern painting suddenly began once more to convey messages – perhaps not the messages of the world outside, but in any case the messages of its own material medium. Here the medium became the message, and the picture once again began to speak. Or rather: the picture transformed itself once again into a grimace of the suppressed desire to speak. For the picture itself remained silent. It is only those who have read Greenberg who know that it is trying to convey the message of the medium. Otherwise, though the viewer detects that the modernistic painting is trying to tell him something, he cannot know what the content of this something actually is. Arnold Gehlen, after the Second World War, wrote about modern art's 'need for commentary', and saw in this need its particular weakness. The word 'commentary' is somewhat misleading, however, as it suggests that the artwork is originally silent and has to be explained and anchored in a language that comes from outside. But this is not the case. Any modern artwork has arisen as an action, a gesture in the history of modern art – and speech forms part of such actions and gestures, as Lessing rightly said. Modern artworks arise from a discussion, even a struggle, between competing, often antagonistic, artistic programmes – a struggle that is highly polemical, and often accompanied by insults, complaints, accusations

---

2. Clement Greenberg, 'Modernist Painting' (1960), in *Forum Lectures*, Washington 1960; F. Frascina and C. Harrison (eds), *Modern Art and Modernism*, Thousand Oaks, CA 1982, p. 6.

and outbreaks of rage. Even art that sees itself as autonomous has arisen from a struggle of this kind. The
outward appearance of the images in question, however,
only hints that they want to say something, that they
have arisen as arguments in a discussion. The halls of
today's museums of modern art therefore often convey
an atmosphere of embarrassment and even obscenity,
which is not dissimilar to the impression that Lessing
describes in his essay. People are faced with images that
seek to say something, but fail to do so. Some 'naive'
viewers react to these grimaces of 'wanting to speak'
with the confession that they do not understand modern
art. Such statements are often ridiculed by those in the
know, who believe they know that modern art is only
incomprehensible because it does not try to say anything.
Words are absent, but the grimace of the desire to speak
remains – a desire that is repressed into the picture's
unconscious, its inside, the medium that supports it.

Contemporary media theory tends to understand and
describe media in a purely scientistic and technicist fashion. This is true for the media of art, but also for the
media in the broader sense, including the mass media.
This tendency has its origin in the work of Marshall
McLuhan, who owed his understanding of the media
property of the mass media precisely to the above-
mentioned theory of modern painting. The magic
formula, 'the medium is the message', emerged first of all
in McLuhan's writing in an aside – and indeed in the
context of a discussion of Cubism. In his *Understanding
Media* (1964), McLuhan wrote about Cubism that it
destroyed the three-dimensional illusion and revealed the
media procedure with which the picture 'drives home the
message'.[3] Cubism thereby made it possible 'to grasp the
medium as a whole'. And McLuhan continued: 'Cubism,

---

3. McLuhan, *Understanding Media*, p. 13.

by seizing on instant total awareness, suddenly announced that *the medium is the message*.'[4] It was not McLuhan, therefore, who proclaimed the glad tidings about the message of the medium, but rather Cubism. But what led McLuhan to realize that Cubism proclaimed precisely this message, and not another one? McLuhan refers at this point to Ernst Gombrich as an indubitable academic authority. But this doctrine is actually proclaimed by Gombrich far less clearly than it was by Clement Greenberg, for example – who at that time, however, did not possess such unchallengeable academic authority as Gombrich. In his essay 'Modernistic Painting', much discussed on its appearance in 1960 – only shortly before McLuhan – Greenberg wrote, in connection with French Cubism: 'It quickly emerged that the unique and proper area of competence of each art coincided with all that was unique in the nature of its medium.' And further:

> The limitations that constitute the medium of paint-ing – the flat surface, the shape of the support, the properties of pigment – were treated by the Old Masters as negative factors that could be acknowl-edged only implicitly or indirectly. Modernism has come to regard these same limitations as positive factors that are to be acknowledged openly. Manet's paintings became the first Modernist ones by virtue of the frankness with which they declared the surfaces on which they were painted.[5]

Greenberg thus ascribes the discovery of the media char-acter of the medium, the explicit thematizing of the medium – in short, the proclamation of the message of the medium – quite decidedly to Cubism. The interpre-tation of the classical avant-garde as an artistic strategy that aimed above all to reveal the medium was thus

---

4. Ibid., p. 13, emphasis in original.
5. Greenberg, 'Modernist Painting', p. 6.

generally accepted at the time that McLuhan wrote his book, at least within advanced art theory.

The Cubist pictures in which McLuhan found this revelation of the medium, however, are not particularly numerous – one cannot even say that they are representative for the medium of painting. The majority of paintings we are familiar with from art history – not to mention all the other images that circulate in the mass media – do not look like the Cubist images. It seems quite implausible at first sight, therefore, that it should be precisely the pictures of Cubism that reveal the medium of painting. One might rather expect that it is a typical, average picture that gives information about this medium, rather than the highly unusual and idiosyncratic pictures of Cubism, which moreover met with a relatively poor reception from the public. The Cubist image is an exceptional image, whose characteristics cannot be generalized. To maintain that it is the Cubist image that reveals the medium of painting is rather like saying that war reveals the hidden character of man because it places man in an exceptional situation, in which it suddenly becomes visible what this man has within him, what makes the medium of man a message. We can say, therefore, that modern art places the artwork in an exceptional situation, just as war places man in an exceptional state; we can trust the modern picture in just the same way as we can trust war. In this fantasy of a serious case that offers insight into the inside that customarily – in time of peace – remains hidden by dishonest conventions, a deep connection is proclaimed between aesthetics, the search for the revelation of the concealed, and the violence that plays a key role in artistic modernism. The world must be compelled to show its inside – the artist must start by forcibly reducing the external aspect of the picture, destroying and defamiliarizing it so that the inside is revealed. This figure of insight into the inside as the effect of a forcible dismantling of the outside produces in the same fashion the exceptional cases of war, art and philosophy, which seek to reveal their own truths that are radically distinct from the truth of the 'peaceful' and 'superficial' regular case.

The Cubist painting is thus an image in the exceptional state – flattened, cut up, made unreadable. Malevich and Mondrian proceeded in a still more radical fashion, as later did Barnett Newman and Ad Reinhardt, who demonstrated the truth of the painted surface – the truth of the medium – by the radical dismantling of everything external, mimetic and thematic. They thereby completed the work of destroying the conventional picture surface that the Cubists had already begun. It is Malevich's 'Black Square' (1915), above all, that presents itself as the result of a radical extinction, alienation and reduction of all customary signs of the pictorial. What remains is the original form of any painted image as such – the picture-support after it has been cleared of all images that it customarily bears. The effect of this honesty to the medium is staged perfectly here: the 'Black Square' shows itself to be not simply an image among many other images, but rather a sudden revelation of the concealed image-support, which manifests itself with overwhelming evidence in the midst of the customary, superficial world of images as the consequence of the artist's use of force. And, we should particularly note, the fact that this is a staging in no way means that the revelation of the medium here is in any sense 'simulated'. Even a 'genuine' revelation needs a stage, a context for its manifestation, so that it can be perceived. The strategy of honesty to the medium, moreover, was not practised only by artists of geometric abstraction such as Malevich or Mondrian. For Kandinsky, likewise, every picture was a combination of pure colours and forms, as he wrote in *Concerning the Spiritual in Art* (1910–11). This combination of form and colours, however, remains invisible for the ordinary viewer, who focuses his attention on the subject of the picture. Despite this, it is precisely this combination – the basic elements that remain unconscious for the viewer – that determines the effect any picture exerts on the viewer. The true artist, for Kandinsky, is an analyst of media, who systematically investigates these unconscious effects and deploys them deliberately in his work. The artist–analyst, who operates with abstract forms and colours, is in a position then to formulate and reveal the concealed vocabulary of these forms and colours – which other artists use merely in an unreflected, unsystematic and hidden fashion – to arouse particular feelings in the viewer from one case to another. The exceptional case of an insight into the inside thereby also becomes the starting-point of a new power claim. The artist of the avant-garde, who has seen the inside of any possible picture and experienced the truth of the medium that supports all other pictures, thereby necessarily also receives an absolute power over the whole visual world – and can shape it deliberately and consistently. The exceptional case of a unique image that demonstrates the truth of the medium accordingly empowers the artist to administer the gaze of humanity as a whole – of the whole general mass of viewers. As is well known, the artists of the radical avant-garde did indeed insist on their right to shape the whole visual world of their present (Kandinsky himself, likewise the Russian Constructivists, the Bauhaus, and so on). If this claim was no longer directly taken up by a later media theorist such as McLuhan, it was not completely abandoned. The media theorist at least raised the claim to administer the gaze of the viewer to the whole of the medium – no longer by transforming the visual world, perhaps, but still by reinterpreting it.

This claim shows clearly enough how – despite all his enthusiasm for science and technology – McLuhan was far from seeing in the media only material supports and apparatuses. Rather, he took the media to be a concealed 'wanting to speak', whose gestures and grimaces it represents. McLuhan's very project, expressed in the title of his most important book, *Understanding Media*, signals that, behind the surface medium of the picture, in its sub-medium space, language, information and communication are assumed, whose message the media analyst can and must correctly interpret. The analogy with psychoanalysis suggests itself here. McLuhan thus interprets the relationship of the viewer to the medium as a hermeneutic relationship of reading and under-standing. He even heightens the emotionality of the media by dividing them into 'hot' and 'cold', raising them to partners in dialogue that can be criticized for being inappropriately cold, as one might in relations of friendship or love. By the picture receiving a hot or a cold medium of support, it is endowed with an invisible, quasi-living body, which radiates and speaks through the surface of the image, sending its own messages that are distinct from those of the image.

But how is understanding of (sub-)medium messages supposed to function? McLuhan's answer to this ques-tion is relatively simple: by comparison between different media. A deliberately intentional communication, which the speaker formulates in a medium, is abstracted from its medium of expression, so to speak, and compared with other possible formulations of this communication in other media. Since the receiver of the communication knows what the whole media paradigm – the range of options that are possible for the speaker – looks like, he can deduce whether the communication in question would be cooler or warmer in different mediums. In this way, the receiver of the medium's message can calculate by means of a relatively simple formula: the message transmitted via the medium less the intended message equals the message of the medium. McLuhan himself practises his own hermeneutic investigations of various media by way of an inter-media comparison of this kind, in a very ingenious and inspiring fashion. The basic assumption of this comparative analysis, however, is the belief that the subjectively intended message of an individual speaker can be analytically separated from the message of the medium – so that it can subsequently be shown how one message modifies or even undermines another. This belief, however, is highly questionable.

McLuhan inherited this belief in the message of the medium from Cubism, without posing the question as to the conditions under which Cubism arrived at this belief, and the methods it used to do so. Cubism, however, did not interpret the image simply as the message of the medium, but compelled it to admit its medium character by applying rigorous methods that were fully reminiscent of traditional methods of torture – reduction, fragmentation, cutting up and collage. McLuhan, on the other hand, transformed at a stroke the basic avant-garde figure of revealing the medium into a kind of explosion, by transferring it to the visual world of the mass media, which operate usually with normal, conventional pictures, and avoid any kind of exceptionalism. The models of explanation that had originally been discovered and used to legitimize the radical strategies of a particular advanced art were transposed by McLuhan to the whole visual world of the modern media – and without subjecting this world to the same procedure of reduction, the deliberate destruction of the conventional visual surface, the compulsion to honesty. Of course, McLuhan wrote his texts around the time that the pop artists were at least starting to perform a similar work of honesty to the medium in connection with the picture world of the mass media, and with advertising in particular. Reading his texts, however, produces the impression that such work is completely superfluous, and that the media have always proclaimed their message right from the start – without being brought to do so by particular artistic strategies. The active and offensive artistic practice of the avant-garde is applied by McLuhan as a purely interpretative practice, which apparently suffices for him to perceive the anonymous messages of the mass media that are concealed behind the 'subjective' intentions of the communicators and the messages they consciously send.

The impression arises from this that the messages of the medium distort and undermine the subjective authorial intention of the communicator. Thus media theory loves to speak of the death of the author, whose subjective, authorial intention is obliterated by the message of the medium. In this context, however, the possibility of an authorial intention that would consist precisely in revealing the medium and bringing it to speak – something like the intention of the Cubist painters – is remarkably ignored. Or rather, any such intention is ascribed only to the media theorist himself, who claims a meta-position in relation to speech – all other messages apart from that of media theory being classified here as merely 'authorial', individual and subjective. The dichotomy of 'authorial intention versus the anonymous message of the medium' almost completely determines the contemporary discourse of media theory – and it is obvious which has the upper hand in this unequal pairing.

The message that the medium is the message has almost completely drowned out in public consciousness any individual speech. If media theory seeks to be self-critical, it then merely turns the suspicion of anonymity, of media-dependence, of the failure of any subjective message, against itself. Thus we are reminded time and again that the media theorist also has to use the media that he analyzes and criticizes in order to formulate and distribute his message – and that this leads to his own message being undermined by the media. A media auto-critique of this kind, however, by its unavoidable tautological character, simply increases the intended credibility of media theory discourse. The actual problem of contemporary media theory does not consist in its own dependence on the media, but rather in the fact that it constantly runs the risk of overlooking that the majority of authorial messages that were formulated in the modern age – and this still applies today – are always understood as messages of the medium. The media theorist, therefore, has no exclusive right to a meta-position; many other speakers, painters or film-makers are also in a position to convey the message of the medium. And besides, media theory is itself, as we have already seen, dependent on such artificially created meta-positions, in order for it to be able to analyze and 'understand' the medium from these positions. The general image of unlimited distortion, dissolution and flux of all messages is deceptive, since countless messages – the messages of the medium itself – cannot be so easily dissolved and made fluid.

The frankness effect is involved right from the start in complicated strategies of attack and defence, through which signs of this frankness are constantly exchanged between the artist and his medium. In the context of post-avant-garde media theory, of course, the same exchange of signs takes place, even if in a somewhat concealed form. Thus, if McLuhan suggests to his readers the triumph of the medium message over the

individual, authorial message, what he means is also
the triumph of his own message over all other messages.
For the media theorist, all individual messages succumb
in the general intoxication produced by the media –
apart of course from his own message, which proclaims
this intoxication. And this means that all other messages
are distorted, dissolved, so that they fade and die, but
the message of media theory never fades or dies, since
it is the message of death – and death, as opposed to
life, does not die. To put it another way: the medium is
death, which is why the medium does not die. Someone
who speaks not in his own name but in the name of the
medium does not want to die, but rather to endure
eternally – or at least as long as the medium lasts whose
message he proclaims. If the medium becomes a sign,
this sign has the whole time of the medium at its
disposal. The avant-garde artist, and also the contemporary media theorist, want to endure, which is why
they want to become media of media. They thereby
hope to achieve a duration that is denied to all other
merely 'subjective' spirits. The question naturally arises
here as to the extent to which such an exceptional case
of media durability is possible in the context of the
media economy.

Avant-garde art is often interpreted as expressing a
radically individualistic strategy of 'self-realization' of
the particular artist, who seeks to speak his own
language and send his own message. Such a figure of
self-realization, however, unambiguously contradicts
the self-understanding of the radical avant-garde. The
intention of the classical avant-garde artist was rather,
as we said, not to proclaim his own message, but to
allow the message of the concealed medium to ring
out. The highest honesty of an avant-garde artist
consisted in giving the sub-medium space of the picture
a voice. The artist in this way made himself the medium

of the medium – and made the message of the medium his own message.

It was only in this way that the gaze of the contemporary viewer was taught to look through the picture surface at the concealed, sub-medium space. Any picture surface presents itself to this gaze as the grimace of a 'desire to speak', indicating and awaiting messages of the medium's support. It is interesting in this connection that the contemporary cinema industry and other mass media, which are exposed to the same gaze, are starting to present exceptional cases that did not yet exist in this form at the time when McLuhan was writing – exceptional cases that allow a look into the sub-medium space. We need only refer here to films such as *The Truman Show* or *The Matrix*. In both, this look into the sub-medium space is achieved in the exceptional situation by means of a struggle. *The Matrix* is particularly interesting in this context, as this film shows the digital code that customarily lies hidden behind the pictures. (The character Neo perceives the world picture itself as a grimace of the 'desire to speak' – a completely theological idea.) The digital code is actually invisible (although this film shows it as an image); only the pictures that are created with its aid are visible. What is involved here is the invisible scripting of pictures, treating pictures for the first time like language. The relationship of digitally created pictures to digital code can be most closely compared with the relationship of icons to the invisible God they represent: they are copies without the original. Any understanding thus becomes in the last analysis quite illusory – even if it gives the hero something like a new and virtual immortality.

But if the main task of modern art consists in bringing the medium to speak, it can surely not rest content with thematizing various material media supports, whether these are canvas, stone or different apparatuses that make possible the capture and presentation of photo-graphs, films or videos. The concern to thematize the materiality of the media supports is certainly very useful and even necessary, but all such supports are simultane-ously involved in sub-medium practice, by way of which they are conceived, produced, installed and deployed. Art is software. The media supports that permit the operation of software are hardware. But the hardware comes into being as a result of economic and political, and even poetical practice, since the conception of new supports is a matter of imagination and passion. Sub-medium practice, accordingly, just like any other practice, does not operate without speech. Thus the message of the medium actually remains silent, if it is sought simply at the level of the material supports. If it is only the material property of the image that is shown in the image itself, all that we see there is a grimace of the 'desire to speak'. Once again, therefore, it is not a matter of representing the human unconscious in the image, but rather the unconscious of the image itself, the poetics of its creation, the sub-medium practice of its display, and so on – in other words, the language that describes the fate of this artwork, its coming-into-the-world, and that connects this simultaneously with general social practice.

In light of the foregoing, the boundary between speech and image can be drawn more precisely. The analysis of Lessing's *Laocoon* showed that this boundary does not correspond to that separating painting as an art operat-ing with space from poetry as an art operating with time. It can instead be said that what is involved is the boundary between the medium of the image and its sub-medium space. Language is the repressed unconscious of the image – the desire to speak whose visible grimace the image presents. The appearance of language on the image's surface, which began in the art of the 1960s and has continued ever since, in no way signifies an abandonment of the modernist art strategy that aimed to thematize the inside, the concealed medium of the picture. Quite the contrary, what we have here is the attempt to penetrate still further into the sub-medium space of the image and discover the suppressed speech there – in all its political and poetic dimensions. In the conceptual art of the English group 'Art and Language', for example, the language of art theory appears in the artwork – a language that alone makes it possible for the work to come into existence. Marcel Broodthaers likewise integrates into his work the language that governs the strategies of art conservation and transmission. And Anselm Kiefer uses poetic quotations to reveal the sources that inspire his images. The examples of direct use of language in images and installations of the last decade are too numerous not only to be discussed, but even to be mentioned here. Whereas, in the examples discussed above, the use of language in the image involves mainly the language of art theory and philosophy (or, referred to) with the aim of thematizing the status of the artwork, the language used today is usually more passionate, psychological and political – but in many cases also more puzzling, poetic, even hermetic. Each of these modes of use of language deserves individual analysis. All that it is important for me to show here is that the massive use of language in present-day art is not a practice of mere quotation – not the use of text in the sense of the readymade – but rather the further result of the search for the media truth of art that has always already been practised in modernity.

But does this appearance of language in the image mean that images today have begun to speak, so that the boundary between image and language that Lessing wrote about has been definitively abolished? It seems to me that any such conclusion would be misleading. Language emerges on the surface of the artwork generally as text – and we know that the analogy between text and image is a very old one. Text makes living speech fall silent and vanish in just the same way as picture does – this has been well known at least since Plato. But even if living speech is recorded and used in an artistic installation, it is thereby removed from its living context, and can accordingly no longer be seen as genuine speech, but only as an image of speech. It is only for the first moment that language emerges in the image as revelation of its inside, its sub-medium space. Shortly after, we get accustomed to the presence of the texts in the image: they then become for us an integral part of the image, a decoration or arabesque. This effect is further strengthened by the fact that texts that are used in an artwork are not translated when this artwork is exhibited, so as not to destroy the authenticity of the image. (I mean, not translated on the visible surface of the artwork. A translation is usually made, but placed in the catalogue or on the wall next to the image, so that the text is perceived as something external to the image.) How is it then with conceptual art, and generally with contemporary art, that uses Russian, Arabic or Chinese script? Such art is then not even seen by many as speaking when it is viewed for the first time. The language used in contemporary art, in fact, is almost invariably English – the assumption being made that English is perceived and understood everywhere directly as language. This assumption, however, is false even for our own time, since there are fewer people who speak good English than is generally believed. But even if it were otherwise, what about its role in future times when English might well be as forgotten as Latin is today? Then the conceptual art and post-conceptual art of our day would be definitively perceived as an arabesque, and interpreted only as decoration – the way that many book designers, in my experience, already proceed with catalogue texts. Thus, it is impossible to maintain that the boundary between image and language can be stabilized, since it is constantly crossed in both directions; and neither can this boundary be abolished or deconstructed. The boundary is instead constantly negotiated, with words and images being transposed, imported and exported. And the economics of this trade is in many respects the actual motor of artistic development in recent decades. Indeed, this economy is far more important for art today than the economy of the art market, which has recently been both admired and bewailed in exaggerated terms. Artworks are in the last analysis not commodities, but grimaces of 'the desire to speak', which have an obscene effect until they are endowed with speech.

Index

Adorno, Theodor, xxi, 15, 16n4
  Aesthetic Theory, 53
Aesthetics (Hegel), 221
Aesthetic Theory (Adorno), 53
anti-art, vii
  and antiphilosophy, viii, xiv, xix
  See also art
The Antichrist (Nietzsche), 191–92
antiphilosophy, vii, xi
  and anti-art, viii, xiv, xix
  and art, xiii
  importance of, xi–xii
  Shestov, 45
  vs truth commodity, xix–xx
  See also philosophy
apocalypse, 69–89
  Derrida on, 71–89
    absolute text, 76
    contradiction of, 80, 89
    etymology, 72
    fiction, 78
    ideological assumptions of, 82
    Kant, 71–73
    knowledge, 81–82
    literature, 79–80, 83–85, 87–89
    literature annihilated, 80, 85, 87–89
    literature as promised referent, 88
    literature as world, 83–84
    logocentrism, 72
    museum, 83–84, 87
    nuclear war, 78–80, 83–85
    nuclear war fear, 83
    nuclear war's elitist danger, 84
    paper creates, 88
    phallogocentrism, 73
    Revelation, 75
    truth, 72–73, 75–77, 80–82
    typical theory, 86
Der Arbeiter (Jünger), 131–32, 137–38, 140, 142
  for future without readers, 140
  impulse for, 138
archive *See* literature
Archive Fever (Derrida), 88
Aristotle, *Nichomachean Ethics*, 105
Aron, Raymond, 145, 149

art
  and antiphilosophy, xiii
  desire to speak, 241
  European, vs Jews, 126
  Heidegger on, 51–68
    against time, 56
    beyond measure, 51–53
    clearing vs concealment, 64–65
    context, 54–55
    definition, 57–58
    essential vs non-essential, 60–61, 67
    futurist theory, 56–63, 65, 67
    high tone, 62
    historicist evaluation, 54, 58
    inner compulsion, 53–54
    management-speak, 59, 63
    market domination, 52–53
    origin, 65
    spectator, 59
    truth, 57–58
  Jünger on, 136–37
  Lessing on, 225
  and modernity, 198, 225–26
  original vs copy, 101–2, 237
  participatory, 197–214
    actual vs virtual, 212
    artist vs viewer, 197–200, 212, 217
    authorship relinquished, 200, 204–7, 209
    carnival, 210–11
    collectives, 211
    computer installations, 212–13, 216–17
    contemporary, 197, 240
    Dada, 207–8
    Futurism, 207–8
    goal of, 213–14
    internet, 213–16
    isolation abandoned, 201–3, 209, 211
    sacrificial ritual, 209–10
    total artwork, 202–4, 212
    value of, 198–200
    viewer attacked, 207
    viewer involvement, 200–201, 205–6
    viewer provoked, 208–9
    Wagner on, 201–6

and philosophy, ix–xii
readymade, viii, xi–xii, 220
and technology, 136–37
See also anti-art; Cubism; image and
    word; museum, art
author
    artist relinquishes, 200
    death of, 147, 161, 234
    demise of, 204–7, 209
    and hero, 27–28, 31
    medium vs intention of, 234–36
authority vs creativity, 195

Badiou, Alain, *Wittgenstein's
    Antiphilosophy*, vii
Bakhtin, Mikhail, 180, 189, 193
    on author and hero, 27
    carnival, 210–11
    Nietzsche's influence, 182–87
        carnival, 182, 185–86
        ideology defined, 187
        struggling ideologies, 183–85
    Rabelais and His World, 182n23,
        186n29, 210n18
Ball, Hugo, 208
Barthes, Roland, 204
Bataille, Georges, 23, 33, 145, 157, 209–10
Baudrillard, Jean, 29
being
    concealment of, 27–29
    vs nothing, 82
Being and Time (Heidegger), 19, 40, 59
Benjamin, Walter, 11, 92–104
    on capitalism, 97–99
    'Capitalism as Religion', 97
    mass culture, 96–97, 99–100
    modernity, 96–97
    original vs copy, 101–4
    philosophy's end, 98–99
        discourse of difference vs, 103
    'Theological–Philosophical Fragment',
        92
    'Theological–Political Fragment', 94
    theology of power, 98
    theology vs philosophy, 92–97, 99–101
        theology more so, 92, 94, 96
    on truth, 92–95
    topology, 94–95, 101–4
    truth's end, 98–99
Berdyaev, Nikolai, 35, 44, 148
Bergson, Henri, 34
The Birth of Tragedy (Nietzsche), 172
Bishop, Claire, *Participation*, 197n1
Blanchot, Maurice, 76, 147
Blois, Léon, 70
Breton, André, 145, 157, 209
Broodthaers, Marcel, 239
Buber, Martin, 34
Bulgakov, Mikhail, 35, 148
    The Master and Margarita, 189–94
        Christ, 191–94
        Faust inspires, 190
        Nietzsche's influence, 189–94
        psychological type, 191–92

Caillois, Roger, *Man and the Sacred*,
    209–10
Camus, Albert, 33, 145
capitalism, Benjamin on, 97–99
Cartesian Meditations (Husserl), 34
Clark, Katerina, 195
commonplace, 8–13, 20, 24–25
    escapes self-evidence, 10
    Kierkegaard lived, 16, 23
    medium of the new, 10
The Concept of Dread (Kierkegaard), 19
Concerning the Spiritual in Art
    (Kandinsky), 231
*The Condition of the Working Class in
    Russia* (Shestov), 43
copy vs original, 101–4, 237
Counterfeit Money (Derrida), 29
creativity vs authority, 195
criminal, 21, 23
Cubism, 227–29, 233

Dada: Art and Anti-Art (Richter), vii,
    208n13
Dada, 207–8
Danto, Arthur, 11
death and life, 110–12, 135, 150, 178
Debord, Guy, 211
Derrida, Jacques, 64n12, 147, 204
    apocalypse, 71–89
        absolute text, 76
        contradiction of, 80, 89
        etymology, 72
        fiction, 78
        ideological assumptions of, 82
        Kant, 71–73
        knowledge, 81–82
        literature, 79
        literature annihilated, 80, 85,
            87–89
        literature as promised referent, 88
        literature as world, 83–84
        logocentrism, 72
        museum, 83–84, 87
        nuclear war, 78–80, 83, 85
        nuclear war danger, 84
        nuclear war fear, 83
        paper creates, 88
        phallogocentrism, 73
        Revelation, 75
        truth, 72–73, 75–77, 80–82
        typical theory, 86
    Archive Fever, 88
    Counterfeit Money, 29
    'No Apocalypse, Not Now', 71, 77
    'Of An Apocalyptic Tone Newly
        Adopted in Philosophy', 71
    Spectres of Marx, 87
Descartes, and doubt, 3, 5
desire, 151–53, 156–58, 161
    See also image and word, painting,
        desire to speak
Dostoyevsky, Fyodor, 34, 158, 166
    on author and hero, 27
    The Idiot, 191
    and Kierkegaard, 25

Jünger, Ernst, 131–43
  Der Arbeiter, 131–32, 137–38, 140, 142
    for future without readers, 140
    impulse to write, 138
    on art, 136–37
    consumer disdained, 138–40
    contradiction of, 136–38
    individual irrelevant by technology, 132
    individuals mimic machinery, 135
    mass culture, 143
    museum destruction, 135–36
    perspective is paramount, 137
    reader disdained, 138, 140
    readymade planet, 137
    and Russian Constructivists, 136, 142–43
    serial preferences
      cars, 133
      movies, 134, 142–43
    subjectivity replicable, 134
    technology dependence, 141
    techno-rhetoric, 142
    totalitarianism, 141
      easier in US, 142
    war, 134–35, 139
    and Warhol, 135
    worker, 133
      figure of, 134, 139–40

Kandinsky, 230–31
  Concerning the Spiritual in Art, 231
Kant, Immanuel, 71–73
  'Of An Elevated Tone that has Recently Arisen in Philosophy', 71
Kiefer, Anselm, 219, 239
Kierkegaard, Søren, 1–32, 34
  on Abraham, 21–23
  attitudes to life, 24
    aesthete, 11–13, 21, 24
    ethicist, 13–15, 20–24
    religious, 24
  on author and hero, 27, 31
  choice of oneself, 13–20 passim
  on Christ, xii, 8–9, 18, 20
  on Christianity, xiii, 8–9, 18, 20, 31
  commonplace, 8–13, 16, 20, 23–25
  The Concept of Dread, 19
  'Concluding Unscientific Postscript', 18, 32
  criminal, 21, 23
  'Diapsalmata', 12
  and Dostoyevsky, 25
  doubt
    existential leap manifests, 11
    intro to, 32
    vs self-evidence, 4–7, 10
  Either/Or, 11, 14–15, 20, 23
  existential leap, 2–4, 15, 18
    manifests doubt, 11
  Fear and Trembling, 21–23, 25
  Hegel mocked, 18
  Heidegger influenced by, 19–20, 27
  historical place of, 5, 30
  historicization, struggle against, 31

  inner time, 19
  introductory manner, 1–2, 32
  isolated, 24
  the new, 7–10, 19
    philosophy excludes, 8
  Philosophical Fragments, 18, 32
  pseudonyms, 23, 26, 31–32
  radicalism of, 17
  and Regina Olsen, 14–16, 24–25, 39–40
  self-evidence vs doubt, 4–7, 10
  The Sickness Unto Death, 32
  on truth, 1–2
  'The Unhappiest One', 12
Klages, Ludwig, Lessing influenced by, 108, 112, 121, 127–28
Kojève, Alexandre, 145–67
  on Book, 151, 160, 162–63
  death, 147
  desire, 151–53, 156–58, 161
    to be desired, 157
  diplomatic career, 146–47
  dissertation on Solovyov, 148, 154, 163
    critical remarks in, 159–60
  as Duchamp, 100
  end of everything, 161
  end of history, 146, 148–49, 152, 161–63, 166
    armed worker, 151
    US instantiates, 159
  end of love, 165
  Introduction to the Reading of Hegel, 146, 156–57, 160–61, 166
    on Napoleon, 166
  on nature, 156
  Nietzsche's influence, 151
  on Phenomenology, 99–100, 145–46, 149, 155–56, 161–63, 165–66
    lectures, 145, 157
  vs postmodernism, 162
  readymade, 162
  reproduction, 161
  on the Sage, 151, 167
  sexualization, 158
  Solovyov's influence, 151, 153, 155, 158, 164, 166
  and Stalinism, 158, 166
  struggle for recognition, 149–50, 153, 157
  truth, 161–63
  unoriginality claim, 99–100, 146–48, 162–64
    exceptionality of, 147
  on writers, 138
  on writing, 163
Kunst als sozialer Raum (Möntmann), 197n1

Lacan, Jacques, vii, 88, 145, 157
Lang, Fritz, Metropolis, 142
Laocoon (Lessing), 220–21
Lessing, Gotthold Ephraim, 226
  Laocoon, 220–25, 238–39
    art defined, 225
    painting vs poetry, 220–22
    truth and painting, 221–22